FREE
business banking
for 12 months

Thinking of starting a business? HSBC can help you now.

▸ access to a Business Support Helpline

▸ fee free Business Card for the first 12 months

▸ awarded Best Clearing Bank for Small Business in 2004 by the Forum of Private Business

Open an HSBC business account today

▶ Call 08000 321 322 quoting ref ST1

▶ Visit hsbc.co.uk/startup ▶ Come into branch

HSBC

The world's local bank

Alternatively, to apply for your Starting a Business Pack send this coupon to HSBC Bank plc, Business Information Service, FREEPOST NWW 1502, Manchester M45 9AZ.

Title _____ Surname _____ First Name _____

Address _____

_____ Postcode _____

Daytime Tel no. (inc std) _____ Evening Tel no. (inc std) _____

SunTim1

Give yourself a better chance of success

Own your own business with Specsavers Opticians

Our joint venture partners are used to winning; and with Group sales exceeding £1/2billion, Specsavers Opticians provides attractive joint venture opportunities for commercially-minded retail managers. Our average turnover per store is over £1million, thanks to a combination of our partners' professional expertise and the Group's huge marketing and finance resources.

If you're as ambitious as we are, we'd like to talk to you. To arrange a confidential appointment, please call Chris Howarth on 01695 554 200.

THE SUNDAY TIMES

STARTING A SUCCESSFUL BUSINESS

5TH EDITION

MICHAEL MORRIS

RECOMMENDED BY
INSTITUTE OF DIRECTORS

KOGAN
PAGE

London and Sterling, VA

First published by Kogan Page in 1985 as *Starting a Successful Small Business*
Second edition 1989
Third edition 1996
Fourth edition 2001 as *Starting a Successful Business*
Fifth edition 2005

Kogan Page Limited
120 Pentonville Road
London N1 9JN

22883 Quicksilver Drive
Sterling VA 20166-2012
USA

ISBN 0 7494 4413 4

British Library Cataloguing in Publication Data

A CIP record for this book is available from the British Library.

Library of Congress Cataloging-in-Publication Data

Morris, M. J. (Michael John)
    Starting a successful business / Michael Morris.—5th ed.
      p. cm.
    ISBN 0-7494-4413-4
    1. New business enterprises. 2. Entrepreneurship. I. Title.
HD62.5 M677 2005
658.1′1—dc22
                                            2005009393

Typeset by JS Typesetting Ltd, Porthcawl, Mid Glamorgan
Printed and bound in Great Britain by Cambridge University Press

Contents

do you have the
ambition?

Specialising in extensions for larger houses and repairs to unique architecture, David Weeks Builders is one of over 500,000 UK companies who use Sage software to help run their business.

Starting your own business?

You have an ambition, an idea; a dream. But other areas can take your attention, and day-to-day operations, like accounts, can get in the way of that dream.

Sage software can help take care of the operational areas. Sage software ranges are easy to use and cover all accounting, payroll and other business needs.

Whether you're a start-up, self-employed or owner-manager of a small business, Sage software helps you get the job done in the easiest and most efficient way.

Sage software - giving you the freedom to enjoy your business

contact us now on:

0800 44 77 77

or visit

www.sage.co.uk

ARE YOU HUNGRY ENOUGH?

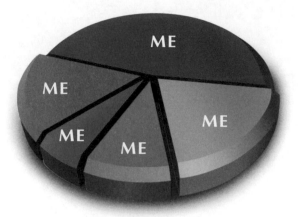

- Can you sell ice to an Eskimo?
- Can you build and retain relationships with clients?
- Can you develop a winning team?
- Do you want to call the shots and enjoy the spoils?

If the answer is yes, then a Prontaprint business franchise is ideal for you.

You can start your own franchise for as little as £30,000.

Having a sales background is more important than having a print background. We will provide you with all the training, print knowledge and ongoing support that you need.

Existing businesses are available throughout the UK and Prontaprint is planning to open new centres in:

- Bedford
- Cambridge
- Glasgow
- Guildford
- Huddersfield
- Leeds
- Liverpool
- Maidstone
- Manchester
- Oxford
- Reading
- Sheffield

To find out more call **0845 762 6748,** email franchisesales@prontaprint.com or apply online at **www.prontaprint.com** for an information pack.

Preface to the fifth edition

WHAT THIS BOOK IS ABOUT

When this book first came out in 1985, its aims were to:

- help you get into business;
- help you survive in business;
- explain it all, simply and clearly.

In the years since then, a lot of new material has been added; much updating has taken place; it has been translated into several languages – yet those ideas remain firmly at its heart.

Regrettably, four out of five new firms fail before they are five years old. That shocking statistic is bad enough, but behind it lies an appalling toll of shattered hopes and broken dreams. Despite that, every day of the week, year in year out, perfectly ordinary people set up firms that go on to succeed. What makes it work for them but not for others?

Business is a complex matter, but following a few, simple rules can make all the difference. If one rule stands out above all the others, it is this:

Look before you leap!

Consequently you will find an emphasis on researching your ideas, planning ahead and thinking things through before you act. You don't need a lot of sophisticated equipment: my favourite planning tools have saved me from many expensive mistakes, and consist of an old envelope and a stub of pencil.

WHO THIS BOOK IS FOR

The book has been written mainly for people thinking of setting up their own enterprise, though much of it can also be useful to managers in big firms who have to establish a new unit from scratch. It is meant for those who:

- provide a service;
- make or build something;
- repair, maintain or dismantle things.

The only group it is not aimed at are pure retailers. Whilst shopkeeping follows the same principles as any other business, it is a specialised field for which specific books have been written. So, whether you write software or make hard hats, this book is for you.

THE CENTRAL MESSAGE

It *can* be done; most intelligent people can do it; and proper preparation eliminates most of the risk. This book aims to show you how, step by step.

The country needs its entrepreneurs. You are the wealth-creators. You shake things up. You create jobs. You do things better, faster and with better value. Governments agree, and are quite possibly sincere, but somehow they do manage to hamper business. Don't let that alone put you off; just take it into account in your planning, deal with it as just another chore and build into your pricing the costs of dealing with the rules. All those businesspeople who are doing rather nicely do it like that.

My very best wishes for *your* success.

Michael Morris
May 2005

Acknowledgements

I must thank my colleagues who gave freely of their time to offer candid, constructive criticism.

Thanks are due to Carole and Eleanor for their considerable help and patience.

In fairness to all it should be said that responsibility for any errors of omission or commission falls entirely on me.

Consult GEE Essential HR

Consult GEE Essential HR is a comprehensive and practical service for employers. It is designed to solve staff related problems and protect your business from costly employment disputes. This service has been created specifically for companies seeking an easy to implement solution to employment problems – at a fixed cost. Consult GEE Essential HR can be supplied on a modular basis or a complete package, which comprises:

- **A 24/7 telephone advice line**

The answer to all your HR queries is just a phone call away. Experienced HR specialists and Lawyers are available when you need them – and there is no limit to how many times you can call.

- **Insurance Cover***

Your insurance cover will pay up to £100,000 per claim and up to £1m per year, covering legal fees, expenses and compensation awards for any disputes with prospective, current and ex-employees concerning employment contracts and alleged breaches of employment legislation.

- **Employment Document Review**

Our consultants will visit you and examine the procedures and documents you currently have in place. You will also receive guidance on how to ensure that your paperwork is up to date and complies with the law.

- **Online Information Support**

Our online information support is an easy and convenient way to access the HR guidance, polices and procedures you need in your business. The online information includes a practical and easy to access reference guide, which is entirely free from legal jargon. Model documents and checklists can be quickly tailored to your own requirements. It's the ideal reference tool for non-HR experts or anyone seeking a rapid yet authoritative guide to this complex area.

- **Regular Updates**

A quarterly newsletter packed with practical tips and advice will keep you up-to-date with the most recent changes to UK employment law and how it will affect your business.

*Please note that the supply of insurance cover is subject to individual company circumstances, and provided in accordance with policy terms and conditions. Insurance may vary where company circumstances change. Consult GEE is a trading style of Thomson Legal & Regulatory Europe Limited. Thomson Legal & Regulatory Europe Limited is authorised and regulated by the Financial Services Authority.

Consult GEE
100 Avenue Road
London
NW3 3PG
Web: www.consultgee.essential-hr.co.uk
Email: consultgee.essential-hr@gee.co.uk
Telephone: 0800 376 1763

Chem-Dry is the world's largest carpet and upholstery cleaning company. It was established in the USA in 1977 and now has over 4,000 franchise licences in operation, in 46 countries.

With 18 years' experience in the UK, BFA full member Chem-Dry is one of the leading carpet and upholstery cleaning franchises serving both domestic and commercial premises. Its UK network of over 630 franchisees, backed by its national service centre with over 200 staff, also provides a market-leading fire and water disaster restoration service to the major insurance companies.

Chem-Dry, with its unique, patented hot-carbonating cleaning process and 96% success rate is a proven business solution. Dedicated to success, Chem-Dry invests heavily in updating products and equipment to ensure all franchisees are fully equipped with cutting-edge technology. Chem-Dry franchisees also enjoy a first-class technical and business development support service and Continuous Professional Development through the Chem-Dry Centre of Excellence, a purpose built training complex at our UK head office in East Yorkshire.

If you have the drive, energy and commitment to make our system work for you, contact us on 01482 888195 or visit www.chemdry.co.uk for more information.

David Hunt, Castle Chem-Dry, Edinburgh – bought an existing Chem-Dry business in April 2002 after serving as a Police Officer for 14 years. Like most franchisees he started from a home base and his 100% commitment to building a balanced business was justly rewarded in only his second year, when he achieved a £100k turnover. He now works from business premises and employs three technicians and an administrator.

Darren & Sharon Barker, Chem-Dry Solutions, Burstow, Surrey – joined Chem-Dry in April 2003, Darren coming from a career in Sales Management. They really have worked the system and applied their business skills, which resulted in them achieving a first year turnover in excess of £100k. They have achieved phenomenal growth ever since, taking on business premises, adding an additional franchise licence and their first technician in November 2003, their third franchise licence in April 2004, a second technician in September 2004 and a fourth franchise licence in October 2004.

ChemDry®

The Carpet & Upholstery Cleaning Specialists

Don't cry over spilt milk...

make money out of it!

A first class business opportunity
TO BE YOUR OWN BOSS

- A complete business package with no hidden costs
- A unique, patented cleaning system
- Domestic, commercial and insurance markets
- Full technical training and ongoing assistance
- Marketing and business development support

Call now on **01482 888195** or visit us at

www.chemdry.co.uk and *determine your success*

Sunbelt Business Advisors is the world leader in the relatively new profession of business brokerage that lists and sells small to medium businesses for a fee. They help both the buyer and the seller achieve the best deals possible. When a business owner decides to sell, concerns about price, negotiations and confidentiality are paramount. The use of a Sunbelt Business Advisor eliminates those concerns for the seller and enables the owner to market the business to the widest possible audience in a professional and confidential manner.

Business brokerage is an executive franchise with unlimited potential aimed at experienced energetic professionals looking to be part of a world-wide team offering name recognition, quality of service and honest professionalism. There are more than 4 million privately owned businesses in the UK & Ireland, and approximately 20% of these are for sale at any one time due to reasons such as owner retirement, relocation, poor health, burnout, partner dispute or divorce.

As more and more big businesses make people redundant through 'restructuring', 'downsizing' or 're-engineering', thousands of potential buyers are entering the market. It is estimated that at any point in time in the UK & Ireland there are approximately 600,000 qualified buyers looking to acquire their own business. Principally, these buyers are from the ranks of 'middle management' – those who make £30,000 a year and up.

These include people who are currently unemployed or under-employed but who possess strong work ethics, motivation and education. For many of these people, jobs are scarce and the future is uncertain. They have two basic options – start a new business, or buy an existing business or franchise. New business start-ups have historically high failure rate, making purchase of an existing business a much safer way to secure their future. A Sunbelt Business Advisor has access to a large inventory of businesses for sale and can work with the buyer to find just the right opportunity. The commission to Sunbelt on a sale is generally 8% to 10% with a minimum commission of £7,000.

For more information please contact:
Stuart D. Montgomery
Sunbelt Business Advisors UK/IRE Plc
11 Henrietta Street
Covent Garden
London WC2E 8PY
Tel: 020 7836 4900
Fax: 020 7836 4904
ukinfo@sunbeltnetwork.com
http://www.sunbeltnetwork.com/uk

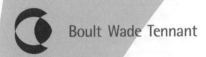

Section 1: Introduction and first steps

1.1 AIMS OF THIS SECTION

Before you actually decide to start a business you might give some thought to the demands it will make on you and those around you. Running a business calls for certain personal qualities. Your financial position will be different from that of an employee. These topics are explored, and this section aims to give a picture of what is involved in working for yourself. It also takes a look at franchising, then considers the impact of the information age. It finishes by discussing the ins and outs of starting a web-based company.

1.2 WHAT'S RUNNING A SMALL FIRM LIKE?

The first and most obvious differences are having no boss to tell you what to do, and no pay-packet at the end of the week. That excites some people and frightens others. Either way, self-employed people often say that being solely responsible for their income clears their minds wonderfully. As the owner of the business, only you know what absolutely must be done, and what can be left for another day. Only you know that you have to push ahead relentlessly with the job in hand. And only you will deserve the credit for your firm's successes, and the odium for the mistakes. So far, nice and simple. The trouble starts when you realise just how many interruptions a boss gets.

Part of the art of management – and a vital part – is cutting out the trivial, freeing time to give proper attention to the small proportion of matters that is really important. But even that small proportion is a large number, and takes up a lot of time. To see just how little time people do spend on important things, try keeping a *time log*: over a period of a week you note down on a pad every single thing that you do and for how long. At the end of the week divide them into three categories:

- items that directly work towards your aims;
- other things that really must be done, but don't mean progress;
- matters that were not really necessary.

Now add up the total time spent on each category. Most people simply do not believe their own figures!

In your business you will be a bit like a middle-distance runner who plans and programmes the race only to find that obstacles keep on cropping up. In a small firm there is only one person who makes things happen or holds things up – the boss. If you are bogged down in dealing with some official, your one-person firm just stops work. The official has all the time in the world to get absolutely everything right. And he or she likes getting out of the office, meeting people and learning about their work. You, by contrast, cannot wait to get rid of him or her and know you must not let the meeting drag on. Then, when you have escaped and got back to work, the phone rings four times in 15 minutes with other matters needing your urgent attention. Before you realise it, the clock says 5.45 and it is too late to make those pressing calls to people you have to ring back. Now tomorrow morning will be a mess because you will have to chase around town picking up the parts you meant to order this afternoon . . . and so it goes on.

It is that kind of don't-know-which-way-to-turn pressure that you need to learn how to cope with. There are always more things clamouring to be done than you can possibly do. When things are quiet it is not much better, for then you get the help-me-I-am-going-broke feeling. This is where planning and foresight come in. They are the basic principles underlying this book. They say that you can and should be in strict control of what you spend time on, concentrating on the vital and ruthlessly rejecting the trivial. When things go well and your plans work out it can be the most rewarding feeling in the world. But you can pay a high price for those rewards, and some people pay the price but are never rewarded.

Look closely at Figure 1.1. It carries one of the most powerful messages that someone in business needs to hear: **just one-fifth of everything you do produces four-fifths of your results**.

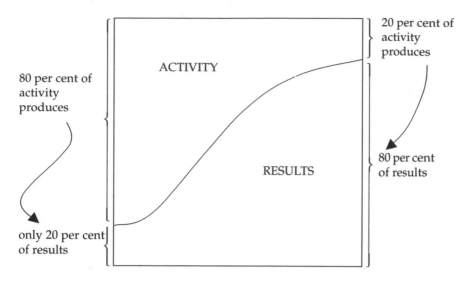

Figure 1.1 The Pareto Principle

1.3 THE DEMANDS ON YOU AND YOURS

If you have the sort of job that involves hard work, long hours, and lots of uncertainty, you begin to get some idea of what being the boss is like. As an employee you might not have had to understand the jobs done by people in other departments of firms you have worked for. As your own boss you will need to understand them well enough to do most of those jobs yourself. You probably could bumble along for some time without broadening your horizons, but sooner or later you will hit a snag that will be expensive to overcome or even fatal. In any case, this book is not about that way of doing things.

Just as ignorance of the law is no excuse, so it is inexcusable in a businessperson not to understand the basic tools of business – accounts, for example. Thus you need to have the sort of mind that can pick up new knowledge reasonably quickly, and be able to make yourself understood clearly. Being able to get your own way pleasantly is a big help. Not being taken in by appearances is an essential characteristic.

And what of your family? Apart from the strain of living with such a superhero, they will also have to get used to seeing very little of you, to having their few outings and treats cancelled at short notice, and, in the early years at least, to a permanent shortage of cash. However keen your partner or spouse is to see you make a go of the business, he or she will have to be superhuman too not to feel jealous at times. You spend all your free time at work, you cancel holidays, you plough all the spare cash back, you talk of nothing else – the business always comes first, and the family last. It is only fair to your family and yourself to warn them about the monster you are bringing into all your lives. The monster may even put the family home at risk (see Section 4 on borrowing money), so everyone has a stake in your decision. If the whole family feels the risks are worth taking for the sort of opportunity you have, or if they compare well with the awful alternative, so be it. Family backing is important, for if you do not have it and you mess things up, the effects on your most precious relationships could be dire. Indeed, these extra stresses have been the last straw in many a tottering marriage. If the family is inclined to see only the dark side of things, one or two facts might help them to be more positive. For instance, some of the most successful businesspeople in any country are immigrants who often do not even speak the local language at first. Despite this handicap, they build businesses, sometimes on an international scale. Many self-made men and women never passed an exam in their lives. Their driving force was a simple but original idea, determination to succeed, and the ability to bounce back when things go wrong. Some even failed completely before hitting the jackpot. The late Lord Thomson of Fleet, formerly Roy Thomson, went broke several times in his native Canada before going on to own *The Times*, *The Sunday Times*, Scottish Television and the odd North Sea oil well.

1.4 SPORTS AND PASTIMES

You should take care to maintain the most important piece of equipment in the firm, your mind and body. You need to keep reasonably fit to take the strains placed on you. No need to run a marathon, or to run at all, but eat and drink sensibly, take frequent, moderate exercise and get the sleep you need. Try not to give up all outside interests despite the pressure on your time, so as to give yourself a change and a break. If you play golf off a low handicap, prepare to see your handicap rise. You will not have the time to keep it down. And angling, or any other time-consuming sport, may have to go. One reason for the popularity of squash among businesspeople is that it gets the week's ration of sport over very quickly. But swimming, cycling and walking are probably kinder to your body.

1.5 WHAT SORT OF PERSON ARE YOU?

Most readers may by now be asking themselves if they really have got what it takes to start a firm. So here is a little quiz, to see how you measure up. The idea is to test how you see yourself, and then quite separately to get someone else to mark you. The other person needs to know you quite well, to be relied on to be mercilessly honest, and should therefore probably not be a close relative. The items in the lists are in no particular order. As far as possible they should be related to how you perform at work or in other organisations you may belong to. They might be the TA, a political party, a PTA or just the crowd you go camping with. The important thing is to see how you perform when tasks need doing and decisions have to be made. So someone who knows you just from the pub would probably not be much help.

A. *You ought to score high on most of these:*
- getting your own way when you want to, without offending too many people;
- spotting potential snags and problems, and getting round them;
- revealing your feelings only when you mean to;
- having a fairly quick mind;
- getting your message across;
- being technically competent to the necessary level;
- seeing opportunities for improvement;
- leading rather than being led;
- not being put off by setbacks;
- having good general health;
- being prepared to have a go;
- will to succeed.

B. *Optional extras that can help a lot:*
- family support;
- management experience;
- experience of getting things done to tight deadlines;
- skill with figures;
- problem-solving skills;
- experience of persuading people in your work;
- being used to getting many things done at once;
- family background in business;
- experience in your chosen field of business;
- highly priced, scarce, specialised skills;
- lots of money.

Overall these lists are meant to give a picture of the main characteristics of many successful businesspeople. They are not comprehensive, as some industries have very specialised requirements. The balance between the items is different for everyone, and there is no one standard success formula, thank heaven. What can be said for certain is that a shrinking violet who never has a new idea, or always folds up when opposed and is a bit slow on the uptake will have a hard time establishing a business.

So think carefully and long, and listen to the advice of honest people who know you well, before taking the plunge.

1.6 FOUR TYPES OF PEOPLE WHO START BUSINESSES

Many people who set up firms fall into one of four groups: technical specialists or craftspeople, experienced managers, salespeople, or administrators. That is not to say that everyone has to be in one of these categories, just that a lot of people are. Here we will look at each type of person in turn.

The technical specialist or craftsperson

Many businesses are started by people who know how to make or mend things. They are often – but not always – good at it, possessing some highly marketable skills which other people are eager to buy.

The problems that they face usually fall into the following categories:

- Poor sales skills, so that they fail to convince customers that the full asking price should be paid.
- Not realising how valuable their output is, and charging too little.
- Assuming that they are forced to go into manufacturing, whereas it might not be necessary: someone else might take that on.
- Poor appreciation of what customers really need, as opposed to what they *say* they want.
- Indulging their desire to make things to high standards, whether or not that is what people really want.
- Having an inflated idea of how special their product is.
- Assuming that what they like to make is what customers want to buy.
- Treating selling and sales skills as things that can be looked at only if there is time left over.

If it were possible, one of the most useful experiences they could have would be to work on a 'spieler's' market stall for a few weeks. Even watching one for half an hour would be valuable. They would quickly see how a little imagination can re-present a mundane product as something special, which raises the price that people are prepared to pay and their eagerness to buy it. They would learn about the importance of communicating the advantages of a product clearly and in terms that the customers have no trouble in understanding. The lesson would also teach them how to spot winning products quickly and to readjust losers to get them sold. Not everything they saw would be immediately applicable to their own businesses but the attitude of mind would rub off. That attitude tells them that:

- The offering needs to stand out from the crowd.
- The same product can be offered in many different ways.
- People are attracted by special offers.
- Enthusiasm is attractive and convincing.
- Offers are often more important than products.
- Offers should be unique, or at least seem to be.
- Cost of production is rarely related to what people will happily pay.
- Successful salespeople steer the interview along a predetermined course.
- Asking customers questions keeps them involved in the sales story.
- People feel reassured when they buy from a busy seller.
- Attractive display and presentation are very important.
- Customers expect to be asked for an order.

This does not mean that sales presentations need to verge on showbiz, like those of the more colourful street traders, but modesty, expecting the product's quality to speak for itself, and a lack of drive will more or less guarantee perpetual problems and possibly cause failure.

If the person with technical skills should decide to run the firm as a partnership, the most useful partner will be someone with sales skills. They should avoid getting together with anyone of a meticulous turn of mind: most technicians and craftspeople can themselves supply all the worry about detail that a small firm can take. What is needed is someone with big ideas and a vision that extends beyond the design studio or workshop. Salespeople can be excellent partners for craftspeople, but can sometimes be overbearing: their skill is to be good at getting their own way, and the good ones can employ the entire range of legitimate methods of persuasion.

The experienced manager

People with years of management experience behind them who decide to start their own firms often come unstuck. Why? Because many of them think that experience and attitudes from big business can apply anywhere. Some do not realise, until it is too late, that *running a small firm is different.*

What are the most common mistakes? They seem to stem partly from the scale, momentum (and inertia) of the big firm, partly from the special outlook that a manager must have in a large company to survive. For example, in big business it can sometimes be dangerous to admit to not

Table 1.1 Different attitudes in small and big business

Activity	Big company	Small business
Collecting money from customers	Someone else's job (unless you are the credit manager)	Your job, and crucial to survival
Return on investments	Often expect to postpone profit for a year or two, as long as there will be a return eventually	Has to be more or less immediate
Overall management of the firm	The job of some remote figure	Your main job
Attention to a narrow specialism	You are paid to be a specialist	You are a *general* manager now, so keep the specialism in its place
Break-even point	Often at a high level of sales	Needs to be kept as low as possible
Profit margins	Preferably fat, but volume makes up for thin ones	Must be high, because there is little opportunity to go for volume
Raising money	Usually the job of someone else, on behalf of a firm that carries real weight	Your job, backed up by little or no clout
Attention to detail	It pays to have three people working on something affecting 1 per cent of £100 m sales	Deal only with important things. 1 per cent of your sales in year one is less than £1,000, most likely
Spending 'small' sums of money	£1,000, £2,000 or even £10,000	Spend nothing, if possible; if not, spend little
Using specialist advisers	On the staff, available free and more or less on demand	Select good ones, be prepared to pay, use wisely and get value for money
Prestige and appearances	Big offices and cars, good furniture are vital	Get nothing that doesn't really work hard for you
Delegation and help	People on hand to take on tasks	You do it or it doesn't get done
Complete understanding of objectives	A few people at the top, with big problems of communicating them more widely	Possible for every employee to have it
Responsibility for going broke	Shareholders and directors	Yours

This is only a selection of some of the main differences between running a small firm and working for a big one. Not all large companies have the slightly muddled attitudes that may be suggested, by any means. But, despite the shake-out of recent years, many still do. The table does show the considerable change in attitude that the big-firm manager must undergo to adjust successfully, build on strengths, and survive.

knowing, so people develop techniques to help them bluff their way past danger and to cover up ignorance. When someone starts a business nobody expects perfection in all departments right from the beginning, and many of the people best able to help will be put off by a know-all attitude. And a lot of very competent advisers are available, and should be used to help in the transition from functional specialist to general manager.

Thus the key challenge is that of converting from a big-company set of attitudes to one better suited to survival as a small-firm owner. The check-list on page 8 shows the main points to watch for. Your experience is valuable, make no mistake, but on its own it does not make you a small-business superhero. Most people in bigger organisations have to specialise to a greater or lesser extent. When a manager sets up his or her own firm they must change into an all-rounder as fast as possible, preferably over-night. Their best attributes may be know-how, confidence and competence, and the enemy over-confidence.

Most small firms are founded by people who have worked in small businesses, and have seen their operations close to. This may be why many fail: it can look easier than it is, and not all small businesses have habits that should be copied. Such people do have a head start in many ways, through having seen at least something of how small firms work. Big business experience has been the foundation of many a small-firm success, but only if the special outlook that it encourages is radically altered to meet this completely new challenge.

The salesperson

Salespeople who start businesses have obvious strengths. That is, if they really do know about selling. Some salespeople are employed to do little more than take orders, or are employed in a narrow field and cannot apply the general principles of selling elsewhere. Most, however, have a good idea of what makes people tick, and of how to get orders from customers. If they have worked for really lively companies they will also have been exposed to many different sales-promotional techniques. Their strength will be exactly what is lacked by the craftsperson discussed earlier.

But, like everyone, many a salesperson has weaknesses which include:

- over-confidence in one's own judgement;
- optimism in situations where fear would be more appropriate;
- too great a belief in one's own abilities;
- underrating the difficulties and complications of production and administration;
- taking on commitments with only a sketchy idea of how they will be met;

- dismissing, ignoring or not seeking cautious advice;
- seeing paperwork as dull (which it can be) and unnecessary (which it is not);
- being inclined to lay out too much money on 'front' – fancy stationery, equipment, clothes, cars, premises and staff;
- being a 'sucker' for other salespeople's offerings;
- steamrolling colleagues who are trying to save them from their own folly.

These may be important weaknesses, but if they can be kept in check the good salesperson's main worries will be about the tax bill. Their ideal partner will be someone who is good at administration and is not easily overcome by pressure. The salesperson must recognise that a lack of interest in paperwork and administration is a significant weakness and can cover for it in the selection of a partner or other associate. He or she should strenuously avoid other 'ideas' people; together they will build magnificent structures with the flimsiest foundations. Above all, they must pay attention to colleagues' views, and allow them due weight. That they are spoken softly does not mean that they are valueless.

All this is important because, contrary to the views of some salespeople, other folk do make an indispensable contribution to the health of a business. The accountant, the production manager, the distribution manager – all may look like pallid personalities to a flamboyant salesperson. Nevertheless they make sure that his or her salary arrives, they make the products, and they get them to the customers. Important though he or she is, the salesperson is only one link in the chain, all the links being equally important. A salesperson going into business still needs someone to fulfil these functions, and someone to exercise a restraining influence on his or her more ambitious excesses. Alone they might become that figure beloved of romantic fiction, the glorious failure. With the right associates they can be a considerable success. The strengths that they bring to a business are the imagination to see new ways of doing things, the drive and determination to carry them out, and an ability to inspire colleagues with their energy and commitment. These strengths are enormously important and only too scarce in small businesses in Britain today.

The administrator

People who have spent a lifetime in administration usually exhibit all the sterling qualities of their calling. They are usually:

- thoughtful;
- quiet;

- cautious;
- meticulous;
- ruthless in pursuit of precision;
- dedicated to exact observance of rules;
- inclined to seek rulings from above about deviations from the norm.

All businesses need access to these strengths, but they are not the qualities of which leaders are made. While the administrator is pursuing the missing £22 to make the books balance, someone else in the business may be making the firm £22,000 by exercising a very different set of skills. Not all administrators are good at their jobs, some having been forced into them by circumstances rather than choice. They may well survive in administration while not employing the more entrepreneurial skills that they might possess. The message for the administrator thinking of going into business is to think hard before doing it. There is no shame in recognising that your talents lie elsewhere and in not going ahead, but the true administrator does not need to be told that: he or she is already doing it.

Let us take a more positive look at the administrator's potential in a small firm: many small firms have no formal systems to speak of, and although the owner may not realise it, may have a great need for the administrator's skills. It is important for the administrator not to apply a standard solution but to talk through with the entrepreneur what *he or she* thinks is needed and to arrive at an understanding of what truly makes the firm tick. Thus, they can help to ensure that the vital processes which really keep the firm going are not adversely affected by being brought under sound control. At the same time controls which will not make any real difference to the firm's efficiency, effectiveness, or survival should be avoided.

The administrator might not make much of a leader or be very good at selling, but is an excellent Number Two to a visionary entrepreneur. Instead of setting out on his or her own, if the administrator lacks the imaginative drive to found a successful firm they could do a lot worse than hitch their wagon to the rising star of some wild individual who has the gift of making things happen. Such people often have no grasp of proper systems, necessary administration, and their associated paperwork. The administrator's contribution to such a person's success could be a vital one, but it will not always be acknowledged. Indeed, there may be more kicks than thanks, but is it not characteristic that the administrator takes satisfaction in being right, rather than in getting the limelight?

In summary, whilst these portraits of four types may sometimes veer towards caricature, they do contain elements of truth. However, they ignore the fact that people can develop. The important thing is to recognise any need for change and new skills, which only careful self-examination can reveal.

1.7 WOMEN STARTING BUSINESSES

The purpose behind this part of the book is to encourage more women to recognise the strengths they have as entrepreneurs.

Is it patronising to devote some space to businesswomen alone? Why not something on male business starters as well, or just ignore the question, treating the sexes as undifferentiated? The answer is that, in my view, most men will go ahead with a project they believe in; indeed, if anything, more men seem to me to need restraining than urging forward. On the other hand, many women will hold back, despite having really worthwhile ideas and plenty of ability to put them into practice. My intention is therefore to discuss the special characteristics of businesswomen in the hope that more might develop enough confidence to explore their potential.

'Many a woman in a position of responsibility wonders each morning if this will be the day when she is found out and exposed as a fraud.' So says a woman I know, an authority in her field who strikes everyone she meets as not only likeable but also full of a confidence justified by knowledge, skill and experience. It is a surprising admission and suggests an extraordinary degree of insecurity in someone who appears to have every reason to feel the opposite. It may account for her great conscientiousness and thus could be related to why she has achieved so much.

I am unable to say whether that feeling is as widespread as she believes it to be. Nor am I qualified to write of women's feelings as such. However, having dealt with many women as students, consultancy clients and colleagues, I can report on what I have observed of the way that most of them go about managing complex tasks.

My conclusions happen to accord with such research into women in business as I have read, so I believe they have objective support. In general I have found most women, when compared to most men, to be:

- harder working;
- more careful;
- more accurate;
- more serious;
- more enquiring;
- more likely to admit to inability;
- more likely to seek and listen to advice;
- quieter and less flamboyant;
- less inclined to push themselves forward;
- better at dealing with people;
- more likely to worry;
- more likely to underestimate themselves;
- more likely to blame themselves when things go wrong.

There are, of course, exceptions among both men and women, but I have found these assertions to be more true than false. What do they imply for women starting in business?

In my experience women are more wary initially and will therefore do their research with greater care and less wishful thinking than many men. Not rating their personal capacities highly, they will seek and listen to advice from others. Being worriers, they will look at every issue from a number of points of view and conduct many 'what if?' analyses in their heads and on paper. Thus, once they decide to go ahead, the decision will be firmly based on sound preparation.

After the research and planning phases are over, when the business becomes operational, women are good at keeping a number of things going simultaneously. They also tend to write things down and make proper records. Their skills in dealing with people also help in getting the best out of customers, suppliers and staff. When difficult choices face them they own up to not being certain of the answer, do research and seek advice, which helps them to make more informed decisions.

In summary, women tend to set up firms on a better basis than men and then run them more thoughtfully. Many men get it right, so there is every reason to think that, if equal numbers of men and women were to start businesses, more of the women's would survive.

As what I have written may give rise to misapprehensions and misinterpretations, let me say that this is not meant as a feminist rant, nor a criticism of men, nor an attempt to court popularity. It is intended solely to report what I have seen over a number of decades and to comment on its implications.

1.8 YOUR PERSONAL FINANCES

A new businessperson can feel like a financial untouchable. Until there is a record of two or three years' successful trading, financial people regard their income as insecure, and see him or her as a risk. This need not stand in the way when it comes to raising money for the firm (see Section 4 on raising capital), but some personal matters should be cleared up first.

If you are in work and plan to buy a house, but have not yet done so, sign up for a mortgage while the lender can still get an employer's reference.

In planning for your business you will allow for some sort of income to yourself to cover living costs and household expenses. This will probably be some minimum figure so as not to put too great a strain on the firm. That makes sense, but it is also wise to make your plans show a rapid rise in your cash drawings from the firm to give you at least the full entitlement of an employee. When employed you are used to seeing deductions from gross pay to meet income tax, National Insurance and pension fund contributions, and perhaps other costs. But there are hidden subsidies to employees that you need to take into account when working out how much your business must earn to make good your lost income. For a start there is the employer's National Insurance contribution, about one-tenth of your gross salary. Then there is the employer's pension contribution. That varies from scheme to scheme, but can be as high as one-quarter of your gross pay. Another tenth is accounted for by paid holidays and bank holidays. Use of a company vehicle is something you will certainly miss. Life insurance? Health insurance? And lunch allowances, and other perks? Somewhere there must be a saint who never misuses an employer's property, but the sinful majority are used to free pens and pencils, Sellotape, phone and photocopier as well. Some of those costs will be built into your financial plan, but others are personal perks that you will either have to do without or afford from the income the business pays you.

All this is explored in detail in Section 3.

1.9 WHAT SORT OF BUSINESS TO START?

If there is one clear rule, it is that there are few clear rules. Small-business success stories include people who have stuck to a field that they know, as well as those who have broken into something quite new. Obviously, if you do not know much about a particular line of business it pays to find out as much as you can. It is surprising how often what is 'obvious' to the insider can be almost invisible to the newcomer. The Army has a wise saying – time spent on reconnaissance is seldom wasted. Whatever you do, avoid the get-rich-quick scheme that requires you to sign up straight away. Take time to map out the territory before leaping in. All this may sound elementary, but too many people repent at leisure decisions taken too hastily. I once met a couple who bought a hotel, sinking their life savings and taking a hefty loan. Only when they were installed did they realise that it was an eighteen-hour-day, seven-day-week business. The tragedy was that they had gone into it hoping to give the wife the quiet life that her health needed.

This is not to say that no opportunity to make a good profit is ever genuine. The message is that probing and searching enquiry is essential in any circumstances, but especially so when you do not know the industry. One of the biggest enemies you will encounter is the natural human tendency to assume that things will work out well, just because that would be convenient.

A further influence on your choice might be the amount of money you can raise or are prepared to risk. If you want to minimise your investment you could look at a business that offers a service, rather than one that makes things, one that settles in cash as soon as the job is done, or even takes a deposit with the order, and does not need special premises. If you must make things it could be worth investigating having them made by a subcontractor at first. That might mean paying a higher price than you would wish, but it will have at least two powerful advantages: most of your time will be free for the vital job of selling, and you will not have to tie yourself down with premises right away. If things go well there will be plenty of time to set up your own workshop – if you find you really need one after all. Or you could set up a service operation concerned with your main line, get to know the users and build a reputation, and later go into the high-capital business of actually making the main line.

If your experience is in manufacturing, do not automatically assume that your business has to make things. Many successful service firms have been founded by people with production experience. For example, there is the engineer who, instead of making cutters for machine tools, identified a need for a quick-response tool-sharpening service. There is no limit to the number of possible approaches, and a little thought and imagination could get you into business realistically, leaving the big build-up for later when you have a track record to satisfy yourself and the bank. Even if your idea seems outlandish at first, remember that sometimes the standard formula wins, sometimes the completely new approach. There are few clear rules.

1.10 TAKING UP A FRANCHISE

Faced by the bewildering range of options available, the aspiring entrepreneur might think that taking up a franchise could be the answer. After you make enquiries, there will follow a parade of success stories and very persuasive sales techniques. No doubt the success stories can be proved to be true, but they might not reveal all that you need to know. The first thing you must remember is that the person selling the franchise might stand to make much more out of the deal than you could ever earn from it.

We shall go into the main matters to be considered in a moment. First, a brief summary of how the system works.

If I have had a bright idea for a business, and for whatever reason I lack the desire or the resources to exploit it nationwide, I might think of franchising as a way of making some money from it. Let us suppose that I have proved that it works in a couple of establishments of my own. I can therefore show detailed costings, prices and profit margins, as well as the site layout (we shall assume, for this example, that it is a shop-based operation) and design that my experiments have developed. I decide to offer it as a franchise. I shall expect people to pay me a lump sum at the outset, and a royalty, probably based on their sales, each year. I might also insist that they buy some or all of their supplies from me, on which I shall take a cut.

You see my advertising, and pay me a visit. I shall probably hold a seminar in a plush hotel, with much razzmatazz and hard selling. You will come away with hope in your heart, hope that the dream I have described, of large sums of easy money, will come true. You are not stupid, but you are now in that most dangerous state of mind – you *want* to be sold to! You are uncertain, and I am offering certainty. For your own good you must break the spell. Otherwise, you might just sign the agreement and hand over a cheque. Put your trust not in the yarn that I have spun, but in your own judgement, that part of you that says, 'There must be a catch in this somewhere.' Your uncertainty is correct; my certainty could well be an act designed to part you from your money as easily as possible within the law.

Franchising is a method employed by some highly respectable companies, who would not dream of behaving disreputably. At the same time, there is little to stop me from making an insubstantial offering in the convincing way that I have portrayed. If you go in for a franchise, you would do well to ask many searching questions of my imaginary operation and trust nothing I say that I cannot prove.

What can you expect from a reputable franchisor in return for your money? The main benefits are:

∎ reduction in risk: tried-and-tested idea;
∎ advertising and public relations support;
∎ predetermined marketing, production and administration package, clearly defined in writing;
∎ package of finance;
∎ continuing support and help with problems.

Not all of these elements are present in all franchise offerings, but the general idea is always the same: somewhere there is a Mr or Ms Big who operates at the national level, while you run your own firm locally, which also happens to be their local branch. The best try to run the show in the spirit of partnership that will build a long-term relationship with franchisees, the worst more or less take your money and run.

Some key questions to ask yourself include:

- Does this particular franchise need experience of the trade, or could anyone with enough drive run it?
- Am I the right type of person for this business?
- What sort of franchise would suit my circumstances – one demanding equipment and premises, or one I could run all by myself, or what?
- Do they want a high initial fee, and a low royalty? Is this suspect?
- Can I finance it? (Costs range from £10,000 or less to over £1 million to set up.)
- Have I evaluated this proposition as carefully as I would my own business idea?

The advisory agencies can offer advice, and some banks employ franchising specialists. The British Franchise Association can give information (their address is in Section 17). As always, care is called for in assembling and judging facts, and imagination needs to be balanced by scepticism. Needless to say, you should get advice from a good commercial solicitor. With any luck, the outcome will be a wise decision.

1.11 YOUR IT STRATEGY

There is absolutely no compulsion for any firm to fill its workspace with computers. Many small businesses still survive quite happily without them. However, the benefits that IT offers can be so great that it is important for you to decide where you stand well before you launch.

Any number of options is available, but the main categories might look like this:

- no IT at all;
- IT used selectively, perhaps for word processing, spreadsheet and database applications for records, forecasting, quotations and correspondence (including e-mail);
- the above, plus a passive website (one that announces what you do but does not take orders);
- IT at the centre of the business with all systems interlinked: take away the IT and the firm ceases to exist.

Any but the first option creates an immediate dilemma. On the one hand, preparation must begin immediately and the entire system be specified and installed before the business starts. On the other, that forces you to choose at a time when you know least about what is needed. Consequently many firms adopt a middle way, starting with a minimum and growing their use of IT as their experience and confidence build up. That is possible in most cases, the sole exception being the final item in the list above. The obvious example of that type, albeit on a large scale, is Amazon; anyone setting up on their model has to install all of the IT for day one, for without it the firm simply does not exist.

Nestling within the greater IT strategy is your approach to using the internet. Again, a variety of approaches are available:

■ a passive website that acts as a sort of poster telling surfers about you and giving your postal address and telephone and fax numbers for contact;
■ an extension of that which allows the surfer to send you a message of limited length, perhaps to order a brochure, to which you can reply by e-mail, fax, post or telephone;
■ a fully interactive site that allows surfers to e-mail you and to place and pay for orders;
■ an extension of that which also integrates your buying, accounting, records and reporting into a single package.

To my mind, today's customer expects all firms to offer at least the second item on that list. Depending on the business you are in, they might also be surprised not to find the third. Customers will not know whether your firm goes as far as the final item, since everything it adds to the third item is internal or upstream of the customer.

Now that burning your own CDs and DVDs is a realistic option even if yours is a very small system, you may consider producing brochures or sales demonstrations in that form. If you do so, you need to be sure that your customers have equipment that will read them. The same applies for video streaming on your website – customers without broadband are unlikely to be able to view it effectively. Of course, if your customers are larger firms, they will have broadband and think you backward if you do not assume it.

Section 5 goes further into these matters.

1.12 SHOULD YOU SET UP A 'DOT COM' COMPANY?

The irrational euphoria that greeted the launch of multi-million pound dot coms, and the subsequent gloom surrounding the collapse of so many, has obscured the fact that there are many niches occupied by profitable small businesses which supply worthwhile services to their customers.

The point that eluded so many of the early dot commers and their featherbrained publicists is that the internet is, in the end, just another medium of communication. Yes, it does bring new dimensions not offered by older media, and it can change the standard equations of costs; but that alone does not absolve dot com companies from observing the basic laws of business. Chief among those are the fact that to deserve orders you have to offer something relevant to customers which they cannot get from their present arrangements, and that you have to earn cash faster than you absorb it.

Fortunately, the losses sustained by commonsense smaller firms have not been through direct investment. They have nonetheless been serious, though largely confined to losses incurred by those amateurish gamblers in the City who found in dot coms a novel way to waste our savings and pension funds.

Two firms that have, in my experience as their customer, cracked the web are MailOrderBatteries.com and The Map Shop. I have intentionally done no research into their backgrounds and have neither been offered nor would accept any favour for mentioning them. I sense that neither is very large, but their dealings with me have been highly professional. One appears to be a straightforward web-based firm, the other a conventional shop using the internet to expand its marketing scope, the so-called 'clicks-and-mortar' model of business.

MailOrderBatteries.com

Once upon a time people might have needed the odd battery for their bike lamp or a torch and not much else. The explosion in electronic consumer goods has led to such a bewildering proliferation of batteries that in many households few weeks go by without one or another needing to be replaced. My acquaintance with MailOrderBatteries.com began when I tried to buy a replacement battery for a camera, for which the high-street photo shop wanted £18. I went on the web and came across some suppliers, sent off enquiries and got replies. Most wanted further details but MailOrderBatteries.com knew what I wanted and quoted £10. The battery arrived two days later and ever since they have been my first port of call. I now have such confidence in them that I am happy to order from their automated catalogue and payment system. I will never make them rich (I hope) but to my mind they have got their business formula right.

The Map Shop

My other love affair is with The Map Shop, of Upton-upon-Severn, a delightful town far from where I live.

I needed some maps of the Netherlands that covered the country in as few sheets as possible, consistent with showing all the cycle routes. Both their website and those of far bigger suppliers listed Dutch maps, but I needed advice about the features of specific maps before choosing. I rang a big firm, which happened to be the map supplier I would automatically have thought of, but was put in a queue. Down went the phone and I dialled The Map Shop. The phone was answered immediately by a woman who not only understood my questions but also had the answers at her fingertips. I duly placed an order.

Not only do they know their own business, but they also seem to have influence with the Post Office: the maps arrived next day. (How do they do that?) And the maps were exactly what I wanted. Now the famous name I would usually think of has been supplanted in my affections by The Map Shop: they have pushed aside a far better-known competitor. Repeat that a few thousand times and their web business should grow very satisfyingly.

In both these cases the firms have got the business fundamentals right. They understand their customer, they know their field and they deliver satisfaction. They appear to see it as their responsibility to get things right by using the internet, rather than using the internet to prop up an unsound business model.

What lessons do these examples hold for the new businessperson? Perhaps there are four:

1. almost any niche may be worth exploring, especially if you know something about it already;
2. not everyone with an apparently impressive presence is invincible (though you'd be brave to tackle Amazon head on!);
3. a great source of business ideas has always been dissatisfaction with the service given by existing firms: the web makes it easier to test them for their vulnerability to competition from you;
4. as important as the website is the customer's experience of your service.

The key message underlying all this is perhaps that, where the web is concerned, the medium is *not* the message. The message is the same as it has always been, ever since Ig sold Ug the first family-size pot of designer woad. What has changed is that Ig's fame need no longer be confined to the environs of his hut, but can be known to woad-lovers everywhere via the internet. The internet is an additional way to reach more customers at less cost: useful, perhaps revolutionary, but the web will not help Ig one jot if he ignores business basics and runs out of stock, doesn't control quality, or fails to collect payment.

1.13 KEY JOBS TO DO

- Understand that the firm's success largely depends on how you use time.
- Ensure that your family understands and accepts the implications of your decision.
- Assess your strengths and weaknesses in relation to running a business.
- Set your personal finances straight.
- Decide on the type of firm to start.
- Recognise that if you are ever going to pull out, now is the best time.

Build yourself a brighter future.

Opportunities to own a Dyno franchise are available now.

Fed up with working for someone else? Then why not construct your own successful business with the help of Dyno, the UK's leading and most experienced franchise operator? You don't need any previous practical experience, just ambition, good business skills and an ability to manage and motivate people.

It's a unique opportunity to own a service business with the full backing of a famous brand. The Dyno name is well known and respected giving our franchisees a massive competitive advantage. And with the support we provide, backed with 40 years of experience, a Dyno franchise offers the chance to launch a business with minimal risk and maximum reward.

Choose from acquiring an established Dyno-Rod drains maintenance business to investing in one of our new franchises: Dyno-Plumbing, which taps into the huge potential of the plumbing repair market, or Dyno-Secure, our burglary repair and glazing service. Or, there's Dyno-Locks, our market leading locksmith franchise.

Whichever you choose, investment levels start at £35k, of which 70% can be financed. And with opportunities available right now, there has never been a better time to break out of your old job, and start building your own business.

For an information pack call us free or visit our website.

0800 316 4604
www.dyno.com

®DYNO

BUSINESS FOR BREAKFAST

Referral is the most effective and often the least expensive method for any company to generate new business because:

- A referral generates 80% more results than cold calling.
- 70% or so of all new business is generated through networking or positive (client or business colleague) recommendation.
- Each referrer holds an average of at least 250 contacts to refer.
- Any contact that a business might need may be only four, or five of those contacts down the line.

Described by their members as being *"definitely the best marketing tool in business!"*, *"an excellent way to grow new sales"* & *"I would have no hesitation in recommending BforB as the best of the networking organisations and a must for any small to medium business wishing to grow."* **Business for Breakfast** provide a forum for likeminded business professionals to meet and pool the resources of their contacts to generate referrals for each other's businesses and share their business experience for the benefit of their collective knowledge. Focus is on QUALITY not quantity of referrals and The BUSINESS FOR BREAKFAST business club format is unique in the market in its distinctive combination of:

- A sensible annual subscription fee.
- Meetings, which are bi-monthly rather than weekly; thus allowing members more opportunity to collect quality referrals.
- A more organised yet more flexible and friendly approach to referrals, providing the right business environment and tools to our members so that they may provide quality referrals, rather than pressure to provide a high number of lower quality referrals.
- Quality training of Executive Teams and Moderators and their empowerment.
- Additional incentives to Executive Teams and Moderators (that lead each individual meeting) to develop their meetings and act in these roles.
- National and potentially international referrals through its developing on-line member services.
- Ongoing development of additional premium training, services, benefits, savings, products and offers for our Members at both local and national level.

Interested in becoming a **franchisee**? Do you have?

- A strong personal sales ability, including one-to-one skills.
- A strong personality and approachability to launch and attend meeting groups.
- Excellent time management and organisational skills.
- A good personal network or networking ability to get initial meeting groups fully subscribed.
- A business background that allows you to satisfy the needs of members, who will themselves be business professionals.
- The ability to work long hours in the initial year of business development

For more information contact **John Fisher** on **0871 7814314**
www.bforb.co.uk

"Business for Breakfast has been a tremendous opportunity to build business communities"
Joe & Mandy Duncan, Business For Breakfast, Manchester & South Lancs

Winning new business

Although starting a business is huge fun and can be exciting, it is also fraught with problems. For many, their new business is the realisation of a long term dream. The proprietors of young businesses are nearly always passionate about their product and convinced that they will be successful in their new venture. But the brutal commercial reality is that passion itself is not enough. To succeed, the business will need a wide variety of management skills; and at the head of the list is the ability to win new business.

It has been said that in business "cash is king". In plain language, this means that the first priority is to ensure a steady flow of customers to generate revenues which in turn will fuel growth.

"Unfortunately", says Perry Burns of specialist consultancy Sales 101, "many businesses fail because they simply don't understand how to relate their enthusiasm for the product to the needs of their customer."

The first step, he suggests, is a full understanding of the market and its needs. A "Unique Selling Proposition" (USP) must be developed which aligns the business offer to market needs. In most cases the new business will have to work hard to demonstrate that it has a real competitive advantage.

There is a real temptation to cut corners in the creation of a sales and marketing plan. After all, as consumers we are constantly exposed to marketing and often feel that we can do at least as well as, if not better than, the professionals. "The truth" says Burns "is that creating a successful sales and marketing engine is a highly skilled task which really benefits from expert advice and guidance."

Sales 101 works with businesses to help them develop winning sales strategies. Specialising in one to one training for busy executives, the firm offers a full range of services to help businesses win more business.

Perry Burns is a seasoned sales advisor and can be reached on **0870 766 2448**

Section 2: Marketing, selling and advertising

2.1 AIMS OF THIS SECTION

'Marketing' aims to find out what the customer wants, and to supply it at a profit. It is the opposite of making whatever you like and then looking for someone to buy it. Good marketing aims to make it easy to get profitable sales, bad marketing may make it impossible. Good marketing can make profits from ordinary products, where poor marketing would cause losses. Without good marketing and effective selling your business will be like a car with no fuel and no driver. It can do only two things: sit there and rust, or run downhill. This section aims to equip you with the basic techniques for getting your business to go somewhere.

2.2 WHAT ARE YOU SELLING?

At first glance this may seem a silly question. You know what you want to sell: let us say it is children's clothes. But that's not the whole answer; it does not fully describe what the customer really wants. The customer may want warmth and weather-proofing, or lightness, or fashion, or value for money, or good wear and long life, or good service (such as a no-quibble replacement guarantee), or twice-weekly delivery, or something else besides. The point is that you need to *know* – not just assume – what your customer really wants to buy, and then sell it to them. Often it is a combination of factors. You need to decide which are important and which are not.

2.3 WHO WILL BUY IT?

The obvious answer is 'Customers, if anyone.' But who is the customer? A jobbing builder might say that the householder is the customer, a toy-maker could say that parents are, an engineer might cite engineering buyers. Certainly all of them are important, but so are the architect advising that householder, the child who doesn't like the colour, the engineering manager who trusts only his old friends at Smith & Jones.

In each buying decision more than one person will have some sort of say, and every time the influence of these often unseen people will vary. One of your tasks is to understand how this works generally throughout your market and, in time, to know what the exact balance is for each of your customers. Obviously, you need to make sure that the people who really influence the decision have heard of you and approve of your proposition, even if they're not the ones you normally meet when you visit the customer. It need be neither difficult nor expensive – you can, for example, simply write to them.

2.4 HOW TO FIND CUSTOMERS

Big companies' markets are made up of huge numbers of people. It is a real headache for them to find effective and efficient ways of telling their customers about the product. On the other hand, depending on the market it is in, a small firm usually finds the job of locating its customers much easier. The first step is to define the 'consumers' of your product, the people who will actually use it. Sometimes they place the order, sometimes someone else (a shop, perhaps) buys from you to provide it to the consumer. The consumer is the king in your business, and you place his or her interests slightly higher than your own. If you look after the consumer you should be able to make a living, but if you don't you are risking a lot.

Suppose your product sells to consumers through the shops. Suppose you supply something that the customer wants, yet the shops resist it. Do you give up, and bow down to the shopkeeper? You could, and in the short term you might be right. But sooner or later the consumer's need that you identified will be satisfied; as you thought of it first, why not by you? The example that springs to mind is of John D Rockefeller giving away paraffin lamps in order to increase the use of paraffin. Many shops hated it because of the effect on the number of lamps they sold, but Rockefeller kept on and founded one of the greatest commercial fortunes in the history of the world. The example proves the point that it can pay off to put consumers higher than the dealers you have to use. But more often than not dealers will recognise it as valid if you offer a better deal for their customers – your consumers.

To deal effectively with consumers you need to group them together: it would be difficult to reach people who have practically nothing in common, and probably impossible to design something that they all liked. Consumers of your product can be grouped together in all sorts of ways. For instance, on the basis of where they are geographically, or whether they use a lot of your product or a little, or by income group, or social class, or age, or leisure interests, or in many other ways. Once you have an identifiable group or groups you have a crystal-clear target for your whole marketing effort. If your consumers seem to fit into more than one overlapping grouping, so much the better. It defines the target more clearly. For instance, if you plan to service small motor-mowers, your main target could be owner-occupiers (not tenants) in housing with between 50 and 500 square metres of lawn (those with less than 50 square metres probably use hand-mowers; those with more than 500 square metres probably use a ride-on type), in the small towns or suburbs (small villages – too costly to reach; town centre – too few lawns), within a 10-mile radius (you aim to dominate your home area and will concentrate here). All these definitions are imaginary. In practice they would come from information on people's lawn-mowing habits gained from many sources.

Once you have decided on your target group(s) you can decide how to reach them, whether by direct selling or through other channels. The eventual aim is to select a group or groups with the biggest profit-potential, and which fits best with your resources. Before that final selection is made you need much more information on your market.

2.5 INFORMATION SOURCES

It is surprising how much information on your market is available if only you know where to go for it. Much of it is in obvious places like *Yellow Pages*. Most large public libraries carry the *Yellow Pages* directories for the whole of the UK. Public libraries often have special commercial and technical sections, carrying a wide range of directories of all sorts as well as information on the bigger public companies and much else besides. Librarians can be incredibly helpful. They are trained for years in how to find out facts – indeed, some people call them information scientists – and can then be put in charge of collecting fines for overdue novels. Those that get into the library's commercial section are in their element and thoroughly enjoy helping you find what you want.

Other people with knowledge useful to you include local authorities (whose estates departments have lists of tenants of their industrial properties); local industrial promotion units, Chambers of Commerce, trade associations, business clubs (who have lists of businesses), colleges, your bank and your accountant, who have knowledge and contacts. But probably one of your best information sources is your own knowledge of your industry, coupled with your own eyes and ears. If you are selling home extensions you will probably look for areas housing young, growing families – the modern, owner-occupied, housing estates which you can see with your own eyes.

The more specialised your target groups of customers are, the more likely they are to be served by magazines, clubs, and so forth. This goes for anglers, training officers, and plumbers, just as much as for the professions and farmers and any other groups you can think of. Their clubs and institutes usually publish membership lists which anyone can consult. The smaller ones have noticeboards and newsletters and the larger ones will be served by magazines: both will give you valuable information on developments among your customers and give you sales leads galore. Some trade magazines run surveys among readers and may sell you old issues that contain survey reports. Most market research surveys are privately commissioned and are not supplied to all comers. Some exceptions include the more lively trade bodies and associations – tourist boards, for example, carry out a lot of research and make it available.

You may find websites with information that looks useful. If you can find it – and the disorganised chaos of the web may make that difficult – it needs careful evaluation. Anyone can publish anything they like on the web, however inaccurate it may be.

Possibly the best sources of really good reports on different markets are by Corporate Intelligence, formerly EIU (Economist Intelligence Unit) and Mintel. Every month they each publish well-researched articles on different markets. Mintel's website offers reports on specific industries for around £1,000; www.EIU.com advertises five-year industry forecasts for $50. Both have much more besides. While it is costly to subscribe direct, many larger public libraries and college libraries do keep some of them as well as other sources. Finally, the Department of Trade and Industry publishes a lot of statistics, which can tell some interesting stories and are kept by large libraries.

2.6 FORECASTING YOUR SALES

This is a vitally important activity. It is also difficult to get right, even when you have plenty of experience in your business, and is therefore a big problem for the new starter. From the sales forecast flow most of the big decisions in the business. It governs how many people you need to employ, what equipment, what size of premises, how much cash. In turn, if any of these is already fixed, it is a limitation on the sales forecast: you would be crazy to sell more than you could make on your equipment, for instance. (No sensible business owner would take that statement at face value, of course. If there was the chance of making more profit than capacity would allow, he or she would try to find a way round the problem. Two examples that spring to mind are upgrading the equipment or contracting out some of the production, but only if it can be done profitably.) Also, the sales forecast sets standards to compare with actual results.

Before any comparison can take place, however, a forecast must first be made. Wishful thinking, 'something will turn up' – forget it. No one owes you a living. No one will give you an order unless you have a proposition that they like and which you have put across clearly. You will have designed your proposition by now and tested it out on a few people in the target market, no doubt, and feel finally that you are getting it right. Now is the time to test it out in earnest. Why not visit potential customers to see what they say? Stress that it is only a research visit, and encourage them to speak critically as well as in praise. It is not a selling call, you are there to learn from them, and since you are not paying for their valuable time the least you can do is listen. Construct a simple questionnaire to remind you to ask all the questions, and get at least 30 replies from people who are truly in the target market. Thirty, the statisticians tell us, is the smallest number that can safely be taken as a sample representing a group. One problem of person-to-person market research is that most people don't like to hurt the interviewer's feelings and will often give a kind answer rather than a truthful one. Others will pooh-pooh your proposition through nastiness or in the hope of driving the price down. Equally, on a research visit you cannot present your proposition as energetically and persistently as on a 'live' call – would you have swayed more people if you had actually been selling? There can be no general answer, so you need to keep your wits about you to assess what people really mean and how they will probably behave, and adjust your forecast accordingly.

Because it is fraught with such uncertainty, the best method for many people is to start the business off on a small scale, perhaps part time, perhaps with someone else making the product initially. Once you have gained some experience it will be easier to forecast sales and you will have greater confidence that the whole operation will work. Some people feel this is so important that they don't mind making no profit, or even a small loss, on this 'test-bench' approach. One vital piece of financial planning can be done at this stage: a check can be made that you can reasonably expect to achieve at least the minimum level of sales to cover the firm's likely costs. (See also Section 3.)

2.7 THE PROPOSITION YOU ARE SELLING

Customers don't buy products, they buy propositions. That is to say, there is much more to the offer you make your customer than just a product at the lowest price. Take an example that everyone recognises, of someone buying a shirt from Marks & Spencer: they sell a lot of shirts, yet their prices are comparatively high – twice as much as the local market traders charge. They can get those high prices because they offer much more than a shirt: there is the convenience of high street shopping, easy self-selection, acceptable styling, good standards of quality backed by a guarantee, no-quibble exchange (or even a refund), helpful assistants, acceptance of credit cards and cheques, and a pleasant, clean environment. Marks & Spencer take much more money from the customer than it costs to provide these extras. What is more, the customers love it. None of that just happened, it is the result of a century of painstaking observation of customers' behaviour and research into their needs, and rigorous analysis of competitors' offerings coupled with a powerful determination to increase profits all the time.

Despite their recent problems, Marks & Spencer were built up on one successful formula, but it is not the only one available (indeed, that formula has had to be adjusted over time). There are many smaller firms selling shirts more individually styled at even higher prices from suburban locations (easy parking), city-centre sites (near concentrations of rich customers) or direct via mail order or websites (there is no need to leave home to buy). So there is no single formula for success, but an attitude of mind that fixes on what the consumers really need (which isn't always what they say they want), and provides it at a profit. And that is where this whole section started.

2.8 WHAT THE CUSTOMERS SAY THEY WANT

There can be a big gap between what customers say they want and what they actually buy. This may be partly because what they want is not available, and partly due to sales skills. But the main reason is that what they say they want, and what they really need, can be very different indeed. An engineer might be anxious to cut his bill for small tools – twist drills and the like. He will say he wants to buy cheaper. If you take that literally and import lots of cheap drill-bits you could look very sick, even if they are only one-tenth of the price of the domestic product, because few engineers would trust their performance. What the customer *really* needed was a lower price for the same quality, or better quality pieces perhaps at a higher price still. Or he might just need a better system for controlling his stores so that fewer go missing – always assuming, that is, that he is getting what he is paying for, and that the high costs are not due to some fiddle involving fake bills for deliveries that were never made. Only detailed understanding of how your chosen market works will enable you to see the difference between your customer's wants and needs.

2.9 WHAT THE CUSTOMER REALLY NEEDS

In the last example above, the customer's real need might have been an overhaul to his accounting system. If instead he had bought some low-quality tools from you he would probably accuse you of selling rubbish, even though the low price should have warned him. So one lesson to be learned is that the price alone is not as important as people make it out to be. What *is* important is the price *for a given level of quality*: another word for it is 'value'. Following Marks & Spencer's lead, you will try to make your proposition more valuable than a competitor's, and to do it for less cost than the extra money that the customer will pay for it.

To see how to add value to your proposition you must know what customers really need. Look at every part of the propositions currently on offer. Do competitors deliver monthly? If you deliver weekly or fort-nightly customers need to carry less stock and can get urgent 'specials' more quickly. Do competitors deliver weekly? Perhaps you could deliver twice a week? Or monthly, making bigger deliveries and charging lower prices as a result. Most of the time customers will assume that the service they get now is all that could ever be on offer. It needs you to ask them the deeper questions to open up what they really need. Until you ask if a more frequent delivery would help their whole business it won't occur to them that it is possible. That, in turn, makes it important to speak to all the right people. The production foreman can't be blamed for preferring the existing arrangements, and for not seeing any advantage in more frequent delivery. The works manager, who has to perform the balancing act between having enough stock but not too much, should see the point straight away. This whole approach applies to the entire proposition on offer, not just to frequency of delivery: look at everything from the cust-omer's point of view and help them to perform better. They will pay you to. And they will rarely pay you for offering the same or less than your competitors, so you need to know your rivals well too.

2.10 WHY CUSTOMERS SHOULD BUY FROM YOU, NOT FROM YOUR COMPETITOR

Apart from monopolies, shortages and blood-ties, customers will buy only because you have constructed a more relevant proposition (that's marketing) and put it across well (selling). There is no other basis for building a business legally. Without that basis there is no point in spending time wondering about finance, equipment, premises, or any other matter. Once the business is launched you do not stop thinking about why customers should buy from you, for you in turn become the target for some energetic, bright youngster who is just starting up. To defend yourself from aggression, and to keep yourself ahead of the established firms you are attacking, you must keep this question under constant review, and continually strengthen the reasons for your customers to come to you.

Before starting up, ask yourself: what will you look like to a customer? Fairly normal, you might say. But you need to look like rather more than that. A lot of hot air is talked about 'image', but there is sound business common sense behind it. See it from the customer's point of view: all they know about your firm is probably sight of a letter, a brochure, a vehicle and a person (you). He or she is interested in profitable propositions, but also busy, maybe harassed. They will decide in a few seconds whether or not to take your proposal further. The risks of being filed in the wastebin are so much less if everything about the firm looks attractive. To achieve that, it is worth using a professional designer. He or she will:

■　look at your firm from its customer's point of view;
■　express its proposition by means of graphic design;
■　ensure a consistent look to all of your contacts with customers.

'All of your contacts with customers' means just that: letterheads, typeface, business cards, brochures, staff uniforms (yes, even a one-person firm can have a few T-shirts or overalls printed quite cheaply), vehicle livery, showroom appearance, and so on. Think, too, of whether or not you wear a suit (if so, should it be dark and formal, tweedy, or what?), or a white overall or dungarees, or whatever. Discuss this with the designer too. Do not think that this is fanciful, or that it need be expensive. Remember the speed with which the customer decides, and improve your chances of success by looking really good. As for the expense, it need not cost much and ought to pay for itself if you do it wisely. You will spend money on some of these things anyway, and by spending as little as £500 more you could get a lot better value.

Before selecting your designer, ask them about the kind of thing they can do for you. Pick the designer who looks at the problem right through to how the solutions will be implemented and how you will use the materials. This goes right down to the level of choosing standard colours – white for letterheads, and vehicle manufacturers' normal colours for vans and so forth – to keep down the cost of putting the designs into practice. If your designer does not look at the problem this way, they must have a really good reason or they are not a true designer. And, as with every supplier, get a written quote first and do not spend a penny more than you must.

2.11 GETTING THE PRODUCT TO THE CUSTOMER

Not a section on transport, but about whether you sell direct to the user or through middlemen. Shops, wholesalers, distributors, factors, stockists, agents, and so on, can do a useful job, but they might not suit your business. They also want a profit for themselves. On the other hand, selling direct to the customer on the doorstep, by direct mail, party plan, mail order, market stalls, or the telephone, does get you the full price but takes time and costs money. A website may reduce the amount of time spent selling, but it costs money to set up and presents problems of its own (websites are explored further in Section 5). Equally, you might be able to do both, allocating the job of selling to different parts of your market to whoever does it best. To help you to decide, consider:

- If you give the selling job entirely to someone else, who will have the whip hand, you or the salesperson?
- Can anyone else be better than you at selling your product?
- Which makes more money for you, selling or making?
- If you decided to drop either selling or making, what would it cost to get someone to do what you drop, taking into account that they might not do it as well as you do?
- If the chips were down, who would survive – the salesperson who refused to hand over the order, or the maker who refused to deliver the goods?
- If you don't do the selling, can you somehow keep up your knowledge of customers' changing needs, other than by relying on the seller to tell you?

Some businesses force you to deal direct with the customer – an emergency plumber who sent out an estimator to look at the job would seem a bit strange. That does not mean that the plumber could not have links with other emergency services who could put work his or her way, but that in this case the operative has also to sell for each individual job. For most manufacturing and service firms, however, the choice of selling direct or through other channels does exist. The way not to make the choice is by personal preference. If you hate being cooped up all day, that does not make you the best sales operative in your firm. If, on the other hand, you just don't like selling, you might still be better employed as an average salesperson than as a disastrous production manager. You have to decide on the basis of what is best for your customers and for your firm, and then single-mindedly carry it out. Your business should give you pleasure and satisfaction but it will survive to do so only if you shoulder the full responsibility for running it. If that sometimes means doing unpleasant things yourself, so be it.

So far this section has assumed that a real opportunity exists to find a sales agent. ('Sales agent' means a freelance salesperson who sells and takes orders, no more, for a commission of usually between 10 and 20 per cent of the value of the sales made. You pay when the customer pays you. Other frills can be added – perhaps they will agree to carry a small stock of your product on their vehicle for emergency restocking, or chase up slow payers, or undertake other services. Agents sell other people's products too.) Sales agents will only sell lines that are profitable to them, which means that either your product must sell easily and quickly, or you must offer an above-average commission. A written agreement needs to be made, laying down each side's duties and expectations. Good agents can be very difficult for the new small firm to find. The places to look are in the back of your trade press, or you can try the Manufacturers' Agents' Association of Great Britain (MAA) (address in Section 17). The MAA is a member of an international organisation that can help find agents in many countries. You could advertise for an agent in your trade press, or ask shops, and ask manufacturers of associated (but not competing) products to give you the name of theirs. Whatever you do, one is unlikely to come running to you in your early days, and the costs of finding one can be well into three or even four figures.

2.12 SELLING DIRECT TO THE CUSTOMER

This method does help you keep a finger on the pulse of what is going on. If your proposition is wrong you don't get orders; if you don't put it across clearly to the right people, the same applies. Simple, direct, brutal. You learn very quickly that something is wrong, but finding out just what it is takes longer. Dealing direct with customers gives you the chance to adjust the proposition, to try new emphases – but don't change more than one thing at a time, and do test each version out on more than a handful of prospective customers before rejecting it. When you sell direct you also have more profit margin to play with than if you were selling through an agent, which hopefully compensates for extra time taken. Even if you have a genuine choice, it can be best to sell direct in the early stages of your business. That way you learn more about your customers and you could have more control over your destiny. If you have never done any commercial selling before this advice can seem frightening. But you have no alternative – you need to know your customers' needs, you are the only person who will take the trouble to discern what they really are, and no one else will be more committed to your success. After all, if your product fails completely, 100 per cent of your business is down the drain. To a distributor it might be only 5 or even 0.5 per cent of their total sales – a flea-bite.

2.13 DEALING DIRECT WITH THE PUBLIC

The most popular methods are:

- *Selling in the home*, used by, among others, Avon Cosmetics and double-glazing firms.
- *Mail order*, either off-the-page selling, where the customer sends in an order on the strength of the advertisement, or sales from the catalogue or data sheet which the ad asks them to write in for (though not sales through the big mail-order catalogues, which get the whole of Section 2.33 to themselves); see also Section 2.34.
- *Direct mail*, which uses letterbox leafleting, leaflets under windscreen wipers or sales letters to selected sales prospects – you don't have to deliver them yourself, but can use the local newsagent; or the Royal Mail will quote a few pence per leaflet for delivery –more in Section 2.35.
- *Website*, giving information to stimulate an enquiry or an order on the spot. Used by an increasingly large number of firms, but not always well. To run a website properly, consult Section 2.43 and Section 5.
- *Market stalls* at craft shows, public markets, agricultural shows and other events.
- *Street selling*, like the fish-and-chip van, ice-cream van, and vegetable van; some forms of street trading need a licence, so check with the police and local authority.
- *Party plan*, used by Tupperware and thousands of imitators.
- *Showroom selling* from your own premises.
- *Mobile showrooms*, often a converted van, trailer or family caravan.
- *Telephone selling*, used more in North America than here, but extremely useful for setting up appointments for demonstrations, and very cost-effective for getting top-up orders once the initial sale has been made (but it should not replace all personal sales contact) – see Section 2.36.
- *Piggyback leaflets*, such as a seat-cover catalogue in every new car.

There are many more – just look around. More media still are being developed, as electronics push back communication frontiers. The great things are not to overlook an opportunity because you cannot immediately see an application in your field, and not to dismiss it because of prejudice. Instead, seek out ideas used in other industries and ask yourself how they could be put to work for you. That approach could make you the inventor of the next big breakthrough.

If you mean to sell through the shops at the same time as selling direct to the public, be careful. To start with, you should sell at the same price, or no less, than the shops. Otherwise they will be annoyed at your undercutting them. Some shopkeepers may be jealous even then, so it is worth thinking about using a different brand or trading name for dealings with shops from the one you use to the public. Some people even use a different address, too. Another method of avoiding the wrath of the shopkeeper is to run ads for the product which say '. . . Available from good [grocers/chemists/etc] everywhere, or in case of difficulty direct from the manufacturer at [address].'

2.14 THE DEALER'S CUT

Every dealer has to cover costs and make a profit, like any other business-person. Moreover, as the supplier, you will want the dealer to be profitable so that they stay in business and keep on buying. Some people get heated about how much profit dealers take, without understanding the costs they have to meet. That is pointless. It is a fact of life and must be accepted and allowed for. If a competitor can sell to a shop or a distributor and allow the normal mark-up, but you find it impossible to do so, one of you is doing something very wrong. Needless to say, you have to be absolutely certain it is not you. *Absolutely* certain, for a mistake like that could be fatal. And before you depress yourself too much, be sure you are comparing like with like. Anyone can sell more cheaply by using the cheapest material and assembling it without real care. On the other hand, it is sometimes difficult to compete head-on with the prices charged by someone who has more and better machines than you. Better not to pick the fight in the first place, but go instead for a gap which that competitor cannot satisfy. If their production is entirely standardised, could you, for instance, specialise in custom-made?

2.15 HOW THE SHOPS CALCULATE THEIR SELLING PRICES

Whether you sell industrial goods through distributors or consumer goods through shops, you need to understand how they work out their prices. Most trades have their traditional profit margins based roughly on how fast goods in particular trades sell, and on what risks exist. They are all worked out in the same way. Take tinned beans: they don't go out of fashion, or go bad, and most families buy them at least once a month. Therefore the shops make very little on them – perhaps 10p in every £1. Some fresh fruit, on the other hand, needs more careful storage and handling, and often cannot be sold on Monday if it is left over on Saturday. Therefore the shop might keep 20p or 30p of every £1-worth sold. High-fashion clothing is an extreme example of risk: the stock can go out of fashion almost overnight, it is easily spoiled in storage, it needs high-rental premises in a good area, expensive decor and fittings, presentable staff, and it is easily stolen. It is therefore not unusual for half of the takings (or more) to go towards shop expenses and profit. In many trades the picture is confused by promotional offers, often inspired by manufacturers who temporarily reduce a price. It is further complicated by people using terms like 'mark-up', 'gross profit' and 'margin' or 'gross margin' as if they meant the same thing, which they do not. An example is provided in Table 2.1.

Table 2.1 How shops calculate their selling price 1

Cost to shop	£10.00	
Shop adds 50 per cent of its cost	£5.00	This is 'mark-up' of 50 per cent on cost; 'margin' or 'gross margin' of $33^1/3$ per cent on selling price excluding VAT. It is also 'margin', 'gross margin', 'gross profit' or 'mark-up' of £5.
Shop's selling price excluding VAT	£15.00	Usually worked out separately as VAT doesn't give profit to the shop.
VAT at 17½ per cent	£2.63	
Price to public	£17.63	The price-tag in the window

Even in this simple illustration there are as many as seven answers to the question, 'What profit do you make on this product?' To make sure that you understand what the answer really means, ask each trader you deal with to take you through the calculations, using the example of something costing £1 or £10 – or £1,000 or £10,000 if you are in that league. Of course, the canny shopkeeper who sees something that customers will pay £17.95 for will not price it at £17.63. It may look like only a few pence to you, but if they sell 100 of them a year the difference in profit is £32, enough to pay the young assistant's wages for a day. So the canny manufacturer – you – takes the price to the public of £17.95 and works back to a price to charge the shop. Taking that same product, now selling to the public at £17.95, our arithmetic looks like that in Table 2.2.

Table 2.2 How shops calculate their selling price 2

Cost to shop	£10.19	(e)
Shop adds 50 per cent of its cost	£5.09	(d)
Shop's selling price excluding VAT	£15.28	(c)
VAT at 17½ per cent	£2.67	(b)
Price to public	£17.95	(a)

Once you know the way the retailer calculates prices, you can work out what was paid for anything in the shop. Using the example in Table 2.2, this is how you do it:

c = a ÷ 1.175 (or divide by 1.15 if VAT is at 15 per cent and so on)
b = a − c
  = c × 0.175 (or multiply by 0.15 if VAT is at 15 per cent and so on)

$$d = c \times \frac{50}{150} \text{ (or } c \times \frac{m}{100 + m}, \text{ where m = the percentage mark-up on cost price)}$$

e = c − d

If any of this seems puzzling, get a bright 14-year-old with a calculator to take you through it. Youngsters handle figures all the time, and are trained to tackle questions like this. It is worth persevering with, for once you understand the formula you can almost instantly know what your competitors are charging your potential customers. If the 14-year-old has a computer, he or she will probably be able to write a simple program to make the calculation for you.

2.16 WHICH SHOPS TO SELL TO

Having a clear picture of the people who will buy your product, you will know the sort of shops they use. In your own town you know where to find those shops, but how do you find them in strange towns? The answer lies in asking the shops you do know about their counterparts, watching for ads in local papers, contacting Chambers of Trade (often separate from Chambers of Commerce), checking through *Yellow Pages* and trade directories, asking trade associations, and plain footslogging.

2.17 WHY SHOULD SHOPKEEPERS BOTHER TO TALK TO YOU?

Not all will. Some – a few – may even be downright rude. But the intelligent ones will see you, as well as the ones who cannot get credit or supplies elsewhere (for this latter category see Section 3.17 on minimising credit risks). As a business owner you will aim to get all successful retailers as your customers, not just the polite ones, so a thick skin and broad back are essential (see Sections 2.22 to 2.29 on selling and sales skills). The shopkeeper approached by a new supplier knows from experience that only one salesperson in a hundred really has what he or she wants. They also know that you may be that person. It is part of the selling task to fan that tiny glow of curiosity to the point where, however gracelessly, the shopkeeper agrees to see you. Moreover, the shopkeeper in your own town who refuses to see you risks losing you and your friends as customers, and so will probably be polite. Finally, the preparation you have done and the planned way in which you make your case, having good answers ready, will earn respect for your business and the way that you manage it.

One key item of your planning will be to avoid visiting shops to sell things when they are busy (market days, weekends, lunch-times) and, of course, on early closing days. While early closing is less common in these times of seven-day trading, it can still be an obstacle. Early closing and market day information can be found in public library gazetteers.

2.18 WHAT THE SHOPKEEPER IS LOOKING FOR

If you know what they want you have a better idea of how to sell to the shopkeeper, or for that matter to anyone. In an ideal world shops would have goods that were:

- demanded by customers without prompting;
- exclusive, at least in the immediate area;
- not affected by season or fashion;
- unlikely to spoil in storage;
- difficult to steal;
- compact and easy to handle;
- faultlessly reliable;
- cheaper than competitive goods.

Shopkeepers would also like the company supplying them to:

- keep plenty of stock of all varieties, colours, sizes etc;
- have an instant delivery system;
- offer high profit margins;
- give plenty of support through free display material, display stands, heavy advertising that mentions by name, contribution to advertising costs and incentive bonuses that require little effort to win;
- offer unlimited credit;
- be entirely dependable and honest in all its dealings;
- . . . and a lot more besides.

Obviously, there are contradictions in all this, so remember that it describes a shopkeeper's ideal world. In the real world it is simply not realistic to expect, for instance, a product that is both heavily advertised and restricted to only one outlet, or for a fresh food product to have indefinite shelf-life. Retailers realise this. So what do they *really* expect, and what should you offer?

2.19 WHAT YOU CAN OFFER

To get two problem areas out of the way first: it is rare that a small firm can make as good a product and offer as good a service more cheaply than other firms. Many would contest that statement, but the small firm that cuts prices is usually cutting something else to pay for it. Even when someone does break the rule successfully two things happen: they are swamped with orders and annoy customers by keeping them waiting, and then the competitors respond with a bigger price cut. That shortens the waiting list, but if he or she has to hit back it cuts profits too.

Offering higher margins to the trade can be a useful ploy short term, but is fraught with danger long term. In effect it is the same as price cutting, something to be undertaken only after the most serious consideration. All things considered, the shopkeeper wants you to offer goods that will keep customers happy. To do that they must offer better value than competitive goods, whilst giving the shop good service and normal margins. Follow these principles and you should not go far wrong. At the same time, look out for low-cost ways of offering distinctly better service in a relevant manner.

A key point to remember is that few shop assistants ever sell anything. There are exceptions, of course, but most let customers browse and buy, confining their own activity to answering any questions, collecting the money and topping up the shelves. Thus anything sold through shops has to be packaged and presented attractively: if the pack does not sell it, nothing else will. Needless to say, the packaging should be relevant to the product and to the way that the consumer sees the product. If the product is fragile it needs packaging that protects; if its main appeal is as a gift it should look like one, and so on.

Display material may be needed to draw attention to the product and invite purchase. This is a specialised area, so get advice from a design or advertising agency with experience in this field. The material can range from a simple pack-crowner (a showcard that fits on top of the pack) to a full-blown display rack costing hundreds of pounds. Remember that if the product is to sell out of the shop it must be easy for the shop's customers to buy. For that to happen they need to see it and understand what it is for. Get a few shopkeepers and a marketing specialist from one of the advisory agencies to comment before you commit yourself finally: they could save you from an expensive mistake. And if you do supply that expensive display stand, make sure that your customer understands that it is only on loan, and signs for it on that basis, and that it is clearly and indelibly marked to that effect. If the customer uses it to display competitors' products, or goes broke and disappears, you then have a chance of getting it back.

2.20 SALE OR RETURN

You may be asked to deliver goods on 'sale or return' (SOR). This means that the shop pays for them only if it sells them, and if it doesn't you can have them back. In some trades this is the done thing – some art galleries, for instance, offer display facilities and little else. But for the vast majority of trades it means one of two things: either the shopkeeper is not convinced enough by your proposition (in which case your sales technique or the proposition itself isn't right, or he isn't in your target market), or he or she has no money (in which case you should avoid him).

People *can* be tempted to accept SOR, particularly when times are hard, but they often find that when they go back to the shop after a month or two the goods aren't there, and there is a dispute about whether they were delivered at all, or about the terms of the agreement, or an outright refusal to pay. If the goods are actually there to be taken back they have often been poorly displayed and have become damaged or soiled, and thus of little use to the supplier. All in all, it is a pretty bad arrangement. Retailers gets a margin partly to cover the costs of carrying stock, and partly to compensate for taking risks with their buying, so why should they get the *whole* margin for doing only *part* of the job? And if they have paid for some of their stock items and not for others, which will they try harder to sell? If you are asked for SOR, decline gracefully and change the subject back to the benefits of stocking your product.

2.21 SELLING TO WHOLESALERS AND STOCKISTS

Much of what has been said about shops applies to these categories, but there is an important extra dimension – their sales forces. There are also salespeople in shops, but either the shop is small or it is divided into small sections. Thus the relevant sales staff in a shop have a good chance to see your products when they are unpacked and displayed (although it is no bad idea to get the manager's approval for you to check with the staff that they do know what is special about your goods: few will bother to find out for themselves). In contrast, a wholesaler's salesperson rarely gets more than a fleeting glance at your new product among all the others, and thereafter sees it by chance, if at all, on customers' shelves. It is therefore vital to get to the salespeople, preferably by a personal presentation to their sales meeting. Ideally, this would be backed up by an incentive scheme (see sales promotion, Section 2.32). If the customer won't let you see the sales staff, at least get the incentive scheme in. That way you have a fighting chance of being seen among the 4,000 or more lines which many wholesalers deal with.

2.22 PREPARING TO CALL ON A CUSTOMER

You will have done some research, however basic (like looking in the window, viewing their website or reading their catalogue), to see if they are really your kind of customer. You may have asked around, and even have taken out a credit reference report. You could have sought out and studied their advertising, which tells you a lot about them and their attitudes. You will be prepared for any eventuality once you get inside the door. But before you even set off on your first day's selling there are certain items you will need. They include:

■ price-lists;
■ terms and conditions of sale (see Section 7.12);
■ order form (or enquiry form if yours is the sort of product that is specially made and quoted for);
■ calculator;
■ pencils (two, sharpened – a single one *always* breaks);
■ pens (two – one *always* runs out);
■ notepad;
■ visiting cards;
■ diary;
■ worked illustrations of selling prices, savings, incentive bonuses, etc;
■ photographs;

- samples
  - comparisons with competitors' performance;
  - advertising plans and layouts;
  - press cuttings;
  - display material;
- a smart case to carry it all in.

All this should be clean and neatly arranged. One good thing to buy is a loose-leaf ring-binder-cum-clipboard. In the ring binder you can put clear plastic sleeves in which to keep your documents and photographs in the right order, and the clipboard holds order forms and a notepad. They usually have pockets for spare price-lists, customer record cards and so on. You may consider putting much of this on a laptop, especially if video demonstrations are important. Think carefully before you do – it is expensive, and can be unreliable.

The importance of neatness and cleanliness cannot be overemphasised. Your customer sees you infrequently and briefly, so do make a good impression every time. If you look scruffy or ill organised your customers cannot be blamed for thinking that you are a little like that all the time, and place their business elsewhere.

2.23 ON ENTERING THE CUSTOMER'S PREMISES

This is someone else's territory on which you are perhaps an uninvited guest, so behave accordingly. You need not grovel, but should behave with dignity and, above all, courtesy. If the buyer, or the person who looks like the buyer, is already talking to a salesperson, don't hang around but leave immediately (unless invited to wait). Come back later when the coast is clear. If there is a receptionist or assistant, introduce yourself and ask if you may see the buyer. Ask for his or her name and initials (and check spelling), and write them down. Even if the answer is disappointing, treat him or her and everyone else you meet with unfailing pleasantness (can *you* recognise a managing director's daughter or second cousin at a glance?). Play safe, be nice to everyone. You may even find you develop a relationship with receptionists whereby they want to help and actually give you hints on how to get to see the boss, but it will happen only if you're nice to them. Avoid over-familiarity.

Give the person who greets you your card, to save him or her from having to remember your name. If it is not the person you need to see, you might write a note on the back of your card such as: 'Mr Johnson' (you *are* sure he spells it Johnson?); 'We should like to acquire a local stockist for our profitable new product. Could you spare five minutes, please, to talk about it? Peter Jones'; 'Mrs Edwards, A small, low-cost swarf compactor for small machine shops. May I have a 5-minute appointment to demonstrate, please. John James'; or 'Mr Harrison, New, locally made, exclusive fashion knitwear. Please can we discuss? Anthony Smith'; and so on. If you find yourself in a waiting room with other salespeople, quiz them discreetly about the customer – do they pay? What ploys do they use to unsettle salespeople? What are their biggest-selling lines? Ask about everything you need to know. Ask about other local firms too. Many salespeople like to show off their knowledge and to help a newcomer – cash in when you get the chance, and get to know better your customer's needs, methods, plans and weaknesses.

2.24 WITH THE BUYER

Respect your customers, their intelligence, and their time. At the same time, recognise that they will not know your product and proposition as well as you do, and to save time they will be tempted to assume that yours are just like the others. Create opportunities to contrast your product with those of competitors. Don't attack or criticise them destructively, especially if the customer uses them at present – to do that would be to attack the decision to stock those items. How to strike the balance? Not, 'Of course, Smith's stuff is rubbish. We wouldn't dream of making cheap garbage like that. It beats me how any engineer in his right mind could run the risk of using it', but rather, 'We take a different view from your other suppliers. They aim their product mainly at the mass market, and we respect that decision, but we try to tailor ours for the special needs of the small precision engineer like you. Mr James, would I be right in thinking that your whole company stands or falls by the quality of its output?' (Pause – wait for the answer – he can hardly say 'No'.) 'Special products like ours do give you the absolutely vital reassurance that your quality will be maintained and, for that huge gain, they cost very little more. Let me show you how it works. . .' Get him to talk about his needs and problems, ask questions and listen, really listen, to the answers. Don't let pass a single chance of showing how your product does meet his needs. Don't fight over his objections, but welcome them – he is taking you seriously and thinking about your proposition – but turn them to your advantage. Be honest. Don't overstay your welcome.

Even if you are a first-rate comic, don't tell jokes until you know the buyer really well, if then. The trouble with jokes is that many of them rely on making someone look silly and are therefore offensive to that someone. So why take the risk of telling such a story to someone whose background you don't know? Forget the idea that you must have a fund of jokes to stand a chance of selling anything. Moreover, jokes take up your customer's valuable time.

Try to avoid giving offence by using first names prematurely. And when you need to know it, do not ask for their Christian name, but for their first name or forename – not everyone is a Christian.

2.25 PLANNING YOUR SALES PRESENTATION

To some extent every presentation to a customer needs planning individually. In different trades the method of presentation may vary, but there are certain basic rules which apply everywhere all the time. To start with, there is the basic framework of your approach, summarised by the word AIDA, the initial letters of:

Attention
Interest
Desire
Action

Your first task is to get the buyer's *attention*. That's easy – this buyer is looking at you, isn't he? But is he concentrating on your story, or still thinking about the chance he missed to make a killing with a special offer this morning, or how soon he can get rid of you to chase up Tomlinson's last order, or how he's going to deal with that awkward memo from the MD, or whether his wife will still be in a bad mood when he gets home? If you fail to focus his attention on your proposition, he will hardly notice that you've been there.

Once you have got his attention, you need to get him *interested* and involved in what you are offering, so that he moves towards the next stage, *desire* for your product. When that's arrived at, the order isn't guaranteed: you have to get *action*, that is, agreement to place an order.

Analyse those gems of selling, good TV commercials. See how they tackle the selling job in the same way, while sticking to a few main points and putting them across clearly. Practise your story and try to perfect ways of getting your points over vividly.

2.26 GETTING ATTENTION

Obviously you can get attention by extraordinary behaviour, but the whole tone of your presentation must match the tone of your proposition. The best way of getting attention will vary from buyer to buyer, and from call to call on the same buyer. A general-purpose approach for someone who is not used to selling might be to boil down the whole proposition to a few questions. The questions should be phrased so as to leave no possibility of disagreement. Example: 'Am I right in thinking you would like to cut down stocks if you dared?' ('Of course.') 'That if you could, you would have fewer space problems, less stock-control trouble, and fewer stock losses?' ('Naturally.') 'I would like to take a little of your time to show you how we can help you do just that, while maintaining – indeed improving – your service to customers.' (The proposition is that you offer faster delivery and better stocks, so that customers don't have to carry so much stock themselves.) The customer is really listening now, as you've hit on an area of interest to all businesses. But she needs to know how you are going to perform this miracle before she can believe in it, so she is eager to hear more, though still sceptical.

2.27 GETTING INTEREST

When he is interested, the buyer will be comparing your proposition with his experience and his needs. That will give him both favourable and unfavourable feelings towards you. You're new, so you will make an effort to give service, but you're also untried and may turn out to be unreliable. Your product will cut costs, probably, but will need capital outlay for certain. And so on. By now, you are telling your story of how the product works, and why, and pointing out the advantages to him. Get him to react to each point: 'Is that right?', 'What happens in your experience, Mr Adams?' Many of the questions you ask in this phase are open-ended, for if he thinks there is a basic flaw in your proposition you want that flushed out as soon as it arises. You can then deal with it, but not if you press on regardless. Watch out for bodily restlessness. It probably means he disagrees, or is dying to say something but can't get a word in, or wants to get rid of you as fast as possible. If you notice it, stop and ask a question. Try to prevent it from happening in the first place by stopping at natural breaks and checking that he has understood, is still concentrating and still interested – again, a question does the trick. The phrasing of questions matters. Not, 'Have you understood me so far?' (ie, you do look a bit thick), but rather, 'I hope I've managed to make myself clear?' (ie, although I do my best, my explanations are possibly not as good as your obviously razor-sharp mind deserves). Now that you have established real interest in the proposition, you need to move him on to wanting it for himself.

2.28 DESIRE FOR THE PRODUCT

The dividing line between each of these sections is sometimes clear, sometimes blurred. But we all recognise a distinction in our own minds between merely liking the idea of a product and actually wanting one ourselves. There are many products that we like and admire and can afford, but that we do not actually want. So it is vital to move your buyer from mere interest to real desire for the product. What is the bridge across that gap? Often it is the buyer's mind making the leap to imagining what it would be like to own the product, and how much better life would be if she did. Most buyers need help in making that leap, in visualising the benefits. Keep and develop her interest and desire by personalising the points you have made and agreed on. 'Now let's look at what it would do for your business, Ms Elton. We've agreed you would save £2 a unit. How many a day do you make?' ('25, sometimes more.') 'So what's that you'd save every day? £2 times 25 – what's that per week?' ('Er, £50 a day, £250 a week.') '£250 a week: £12,000 a year – could you find a use for that?' Could she just! Once that idea has been planted and taken root you are ready to take things to the next stage, of acting on her desire.

2.29 ACTION: GETTING THE ORDER

This is the most agonising part of the discussion for both of you. Your anxiety is easy to understand, and so is his. Up to now everything has been on a fairly theoretical level, an interesting conversation about possibilities. Now you have spoilt it all by asking for an order. Of course, he expected it because he knows you have a living to make. Human beings are able to kid themselves, though, so this is often the place where you really start to sell. Up to now he's been agreeing with you, you've got along famously, but now he has turned shy. Why? Maybe he is not the company's decision-taker but hates to admit it. Maybe there is an objection still in his mind that has not been uncovered and dealt with. Maybe you didn't entirely clear up one point earlier. Maybe, maybe, maybe.

What you need to do now is to deal with the 'I'll think about it', or 'I'm not sure it's really for us', or 'I don't think we can afford it', or whatever way he wraps up the word 'No', as you would deal with any other objection: uncover it, agree that it needs attention, and then proceed to demolish it. All the time you will be summarising the points in your favour, stressing the benefits to him and comparing their towering advantages with the problem he will continue to have if he deprives himself of this opportunity. Whatever you do, don't drop the price, but keep selling benefits. If you really can get no further, he agrees with all you have said but still says 'No' and offers only silly objections, the odds are that there is something he needs to conceal to save face: one of the 'maybe' reasons above might apply. How do you discover it without making him lose the face he is trying to save? How do you say tactfully, 'Does your boss have to OK everything you do?', or 'Are you really so hard up you can't afford even a small outlay like this?', or 'Don't they trust you with purchases of only £200?', or 'Are you really that scared of your wife?' You could try, 'Is there anyone else I would have to get approval from before you were prepared to place the order?', or 'Would you want one of your engineers or financial people to clear it before you committed the company?', or 'We've agreed that you need a couple of Whizzo-X Mark IIIs; is there any way I can make it easier for you to own one? Would instalment payments help, for instance?', or 'You and I have agreed you need "Gleemo" double glazing, but I never feel happy at asking a wife or a husband alone for the decision. Can I call back later and run through it quickly with you both together?' There is no certain formula for success, but this sort of approach should get better results than taking the first 'No' for an answer.

If you possibly can, get him to define what the stumbling-block is, and to agree how it is to be dealt with. 'So the only thing remaining is for Mr Brown to check it over, is it?' ('Yes.') 'And if he's happy we can go ahead and sign you up?' ('That's right.') Fine, if it goes like that. But he might say, 'Good heavens no! There's the Divisional Director to satisfy, capital authorisation to get – we're a long way off yet.' What a blessing you asked! Now you are really learning about the customer's buying and approval system. Ask him to explain exactly how they work, both the official version and the way that he and his colleagues get round them to keep the business going. For instance, he may be allowed to place orders of up to £5,000, but your system costs £6,000: how about invoicing the machine for £4,000 and the conveyor for £2,000? Could he place two orders like that without getting fired? Some companies would punish buyers severely for doing this, while others would not even notice. Your customer will know very well indeed which category his employer is in.

If you get really desperate, you could try one of the 'last-throw' questions: 'If I were your best friend, how would you advise me to get your business?' or, 'What would someone in my position have to do to win your organisation's order?'

2.30 PRICING THE PRODUCT

A minimum aim must be not to sell below cost. Your management accounting (Section 3.2) tells you how to decide what 'cost' is. You will obviously want to make a profit too, but competitors will see to it that you can't raise prices beyond a certain level. That said, there is a general strategy that the small firm is usually forced to follow, of high margins and low volume. That is because the small firm lacks the ability to make large investments in fast-production machinery, but unlike its bigger counterpart it finds it easier to ensure high and consistent quality because of the owner's personal involvement in all aspects of design, production and administration. Because you cannot make many items, you have to charge a lot for each one; and because you are able to make quality goods people will pay your high prices. One further general rule is not to cut prices to break into the market or increase sales but, if you must give something, add benefits (which usually cost less than discounts). Giving away money in the form of discounts is very expensive indeed.

There can even be merit in pricing your product higher than a competitor's so that you can give a discount to match the lower price with your obviously superior product. Then there is the question of credibility. Who would believe in an 'exclusive' perfume at market stall prices? Or real champagne at £1 a bottle? Your market knowledge will tell you what part price plays in the buying decision; the point to be absolutely clear on is that few customers buy anything on price alone. Most buy on value, and for you that means offering extra benefits at high prices. If in doubt be ambitious in your pricing: it is easy to drop prices if you've gone too high, harder to raise them if they're too low.

2.31 BENEFITS

These can be of two basic types: benefits built into the product, and benefits outside it. Both are important, and to different degrees in different markets. One way of offering the second type is by introducing a practice from another market to one which has never seen it before. That can mean you have a winning combination, even though your product may be no better than other people's. Examples of this approach would include:

- *Snap-On Tools*, whose franchised van salespeople call regularly on engineers, just as the bread van calls on the corner shop.
- *Book clubs* who sell via ads or websites direct to the public rather than through shops or catalogues.
- *Tupperware*, who sell plastic containers direct to the public by party plan rather than through the shops.

Each case sells quality merchandise, though in a way that is unusual in their market. They have been different in a way that appealed to the customers, and it has made them very big indeed. You don't need to be vast to take a tip from their success. In every case they gave the consumer benefits by breaking the 'rules' of the trade rather than by inventing better mousetraps. It is probably no coincidence that they all have reputations for quality.

The examples of benefits shown below are not meant to be complete, but they do show the contrast between the things you can change with difficulty, by redesigning the product, and those you can change relatively easily. You can take it further to enable you to keep the same product looking constantly fresh, by ringing the changes on items from the second column. The final word on benefits is that they must be relevant to the customer. A no-quibble replacement is not much good for film used by a war photographer; £1 million insurance against food poisoning has little appeal to the crisp-eater.

Examples of:

Built-in benefit

- better-looking materials;
- more resistant finish;
- better performance;
- needs less maintenance;
- more reliable;
- lasts longer;
- cheaper;
- easier to maintain;
- cheaper to run;
- more versatile.

Outside benefit

- faster delivery;
- longer guarantee;
- no-quibble replacement;
- free replacement while servicing done;
- easy-payment terms;
- ten per cent off this month;
- buy at your fireside;
- smarter showroom, nicer people.

2.32 SALES PROMOTION

If your product is the cake, this is the icing. If you want to give the customer more good reasons for buying than exist in the lists above – here's your chance. You might call on a customer three or four times, getting a refusal each time. But you need that customer. How can you give *just* the product story each time? Certainly you give the product story – even if she says she remembers, the odds are she has forgotten some key point. But you need something to add sparkle. How much easier you, and she, will find your visits if one month there is a free first aid kit with the product, the next month a voucher worth 20 per cent off essential maintenance items, the next a £25 rebate off a purchase of two, and the next the first year's maintenance contract at half price. OK for industrial suppliers, you may say, but I sell knitwear to high-class shops and they don't go for this. Not true. How about offering to share the cost of a fashion show? Or paying for printing leaflets for them to send to their customers, publicising your new season's range? Or offering a free knitted bonnet with every three pullovers? Or lending them, free, a window display of expensively photographed enlargements of models wearing your product? All it takes is to see things from your customer's point of view – what will help him or her to operate better? If you constantly work hard at answering that question you will keep on improving as a sales promoter and marketer.

Of course it costs money to do this, but that need not be a problem: you take account of it in your pricing.

2.33 SELLING THROUGH MAIL-ORDER CATALOGUES

While they are much like other customers, the very big ones do have their own special practices which the would-be supplier must know about. There are around 30 large catalogues operated by perhaps a dozen firms. If you include Argos (which prints a catalogue but also has shops) they range from the big one-catalogue firm to major companies which own several catalogues, each with its own name.

Selling to them is different from selling to other customers in these respects: they will carry out a preliminary selection nine months or more before the catalogue is due out (so don't go to them in September with Christmas goods), and two or three months later make their final selection. To take part in these processes you are required to fill in extensive forms each time, part of which is a price quotation. Whilst it is not easy to forecast prices nine months in advance, you have to, for they will hold you to that forecast. Samples will be required from the selections, which they expect either to return or be invoiced for. If yours is lucky enough to be selected, further samples will be required, which they pay for. They usually require you to quote for transit packaging; that is, the outer pack that protects your product in the post. That can be useful if the product normally has an expensive package: you can substitute a strong brown corrugated mailing box. Equally, some products can be put in a padded bag – discuss this at the outset with the buyer, and be guided by him or her. They require you to guarantee very rapid delivery of repeat orders, too. Finally, they will usually want a 50 per cent margin on sales, ie, for a product that sells at £10 plus VAT they will expect to pay £5 plus VAT. In return, you get (sometimes) massive orders, straight dealing and fast payment – usually in 14 days from your invoice.

In addition there is a growing number of specialised catalogues selling all kinds of merchandise. Some are aimed at particular groups of members of the public, others at business. They can be very valuable outlets, and all have their particular terms for doing business.

2.34 SELLING BY MAIL ORDER

This is quite different from the process described in Section 2.33. It involves you in advertising direct to users, whom you invite to order your product either 'off the page', ie, from the ad or website itself, or to send for a catalogue. It is a very useful method in many ways, with the following features:

For	Against
▮ direct communication with user;	▮ pay for ads with no guarantee of results;
▮ no dealer to pay;	▮ at mercy of press circulations;
▮ usually cash with order;	▮ at mercy of Royal Mail prices;
▮ can reach many consumers fast, even in minority-interest markets;	▮ at mercy of Royal Mail and press unions;
▮ can turn demand on or off by adjusting advertising expenditure;	▮ results sometimes unpredictable.
▮ reaches consumers that other methods miss;	
▮ can operate from home;	
▮ over time, builds up a mailing list.	

Mail order can be applied to industrial and consumer goods. It works best where the product has a distinct appeal to a particular group who are served by specialist press. Anglers, for instance, or touring cyclists, or mothers of very young children: all these and many more have their own low-circulation magazines in which you can advertise fairly cheaply. There are also the special mail-order sections of newspapers, particularly in the Saturday editions of dailies and the Sundays. Some special considerations apply.

First, you have to decide between 'off-the-page' or catalogue sales. If you have a single product, or a 'flagship' product with a simple, clear reason for buying, off-the-page selling may be better. If so, you will need to satisfy the requirements of the Newspaper Publishers' Association's Mail Order Protection Scheme (MOPS); see www.mops.org.uk. The NPA were worried about the number of dishonest or incompetent mail-order advertisers who took customers' money but failed to deliver, so they decided to allow off-the-page ads only after they had checked up on advertisers. It is nothing to worry about, but needs taking into account in your timetable, and means yet more form-filling. One point to watch: when you enquire about advertising, the newspaper or magazine might not mention the MOPS scheme. Check with them whether this is forgetfulness or because they are not NPA members (nearly every paper is), or because you do not need to conform. Ninety-nine times out of a hundred it is forgetfulness. How difficult it would be for you to be geared up and ready to go, and then find they refused to accept your ad until you had been cleared.

The response you can expect from display ads (where you pay for a space), as opposed to 'lineage' (pronounced 'line-age') ads (where you pay by the line or by the word) is said to be between 1 and 2 per cent of readership. This may be a useful guide, but should be taken with a pinch of salt. Your own experience is the best guide in this field. To get experience there is no real substitute for going and doing it.

A website can be set up to fulfil either function – to stimulate enquiries or make sales. Often, this is the first approach considered by a new firm. This issue is dealt with in Section 2.44 and Section 5.

You may also find that your business comes within the provisions of the Consumer Protection (Distance Selling) Regulations, 2000, which were set up to give more safeguards to customers.

2.35 SELLING BY DIRECT MAIL

If a name and address list of potential customers is easily found, why not write a sales letter direct to them? To service big firms' direct mail needs there are various 'list brokers' who sell mailing lists of people with different characteristics – for example, earning over £100,000 per annum, or boat owners, or amateur computer enthusiasts, or opticians; the range is endless. The small firm can use list brokers, or can usually start off at no cost by consulting the *Yellow Pages*. Royal Mail is keen to encourage direct mail and makes various offers, as well as publishing useful guides, for example, on the art of writing effective selling letters. Direct mail does offer the chance to apply some bright ideas, for you are not restricted to sending only letters. A sample of the product or a ticket to a demonstration, or a voucher encashable against the product, can be good 'hooks'. One excellent mailing idea of some years ago is often cited: the *Guardian* newspaper wanted to get a limited number of people – mainly men – from big advertising agencies to a presentation. They sent invitations to the selected few, together with a couture silk handkerchief. The letter told them that if they came to the presentation they could collect a matching silk tie. Virtually every invitee came. But a bigger and less clever mailing would rarely get more than 1 to 2 per cent response.

In these days, if you are mailing to VIPs, it is best to check anything bigger than a letter with the police. Your prize mailing will lose some impact if it is opened by the Bomb Squad in a controlled explosion.

2.36 SELLING BY TELEPHONE

As a way of setting up sales calls the phone can be very useful. For example, if you sell to farmers, why not phone through the *Yellow Pages* to ask if and when you can come to demonstrate your product? Be aware that some trades are usually available only at some times of the day – farmers, publicans and restaurateurs are examples. Still others are not available at some times of the year – Blackpool boarding-house keepers are just not there in January, but are usually taking a well deserved cruise.

2.37 SELLING BY PARTY PLAN

Many small businesses find this to be a very profitable way to sell. The most successful seem to be selling goods for the home or family, priced up to £100 per item.

Most party plan operators seem to be potters, knitters, wood turners, clothing and soft toy makers. Not all of them stick to the 'rules'. One haute couture clothes designer organises fashion shows in the homes of the well-to-do, at which customers can try on all sorts of clothes after they have been modelled. Her garments cost well into three figures. It is party plan selling really, but her clients would run a mile if she called it that.

To start a party plan operation you need to recruit 'hostesses' (they usually are women), the people who will invite friends and acquaintances to the 'party' to be held in their home. Normally they are paid by a share of the takings – usually around 10 per cent of the night's sales. This is often paid not in cash, but in merchandise to the value. You find hostesses by the following methods:

- knocking door-to-door, or paying someone else to;
- distributing leaflets inviting potential hostesses to ring you;
- asking around your contacts, especially those who belong to clubs and groups;
- advertising in the local paper;
- asking people who are engaged in direct selling – the Avon lady, for instance;
- contacting other small firms who sell by party plan.

The last may seem difficult to do, but the advisory agencies and small business clubs should be able to make introductions for you. The sensible party plan operator is happy to tell hostesses about other good-quality operators, for keeping the hostesses happy and keen is important. You need to build up a good network of hostesses, because none of them can hold a party every week just for you: they would soon run out of guests.

You will need to budget for two items of expenditure. Everyone attending should receive a free gift, preferably a useful or decorative item made by you and carrying your name, but if that is not possible it could equally be a glass of wine. It will help the hostess if you give her some leaflets about your products, on which she can write the invitation to the guests.

It is considerate to include in your range a few small items that can be bought cheaply by guests who really want nothing, but feel that they do not want to let the hostess down.

Guests buy for cash at the party, or place orders and give a deposit. In the latter case, you will need order forms and receipts, which could be combined into one document. Some system will also be needed to control delivery dates, since some goods will be bought as presents for which the timing of delivery is critical. When you deliver the goods you collect the balance of the payment.

As with other direct-selling methods, you collect the full retail price, with no problems of running invoice and credit control systems, and cash on delivery. Also, you build up a mailing list that can be used for later direct mail selling, which should be quite effective as it comprises people who are, presumably, already satisfied customers. Furthermore, some of the people who attend parties as guests are willing to become hostesses.

Party planners find that they often need to operate in pairs. While someone is demonstrating and selling well, they do not want to lose the audience's attention because they have to pop out to fetch something from the car. At well-attended events, two people can be kept at full stretch taking orders. If there had been only one of them, some orders might have been missed, and one or two pieces of merchandise could have disappeared unnoticed.

2.38 WHERE TO ADVERTISE?

It all depends on what you want to say, to whom, and what effect you want to have. If you do not yet know this precisely, do not advertise until you have sorted it out completely. Some people place ads because they feel that they should, being unable to think of any other way of getting known. Do not join them.

Magazine publishing is very competitive and this has produced one or more magazines aimed at nearly every interest group imaginable. This helps the small firm in two ways: if you can't afford the sheer outlay on national newspaper advertising (few new businesses can), you can select part of your market and advertise to it in its special magazine; also, you can target your ads precisely on the people most likely to buy. So don't forget the wide range of advertising media available to you. Nearly every trade has not only magazines aimed at its consumers, but also those aimed at its dealers, and often quite separate ones aimed at manufacturers.

The best way of getting information on this is to consult BRAD (*British Rate and Data*) at the public library or online. BRAD is published monthly and each issue contains a complete list of all British advertising media, including every magazine and newspaper. The online version allows enquirers to buy information instantaneously. Against each is shown all the information an advertiser could want: the advertising office address and phone, circulation, readership, editorial office (handy for sending news releases), as well as details which your advertising agent or artist needs to know about the printing process used, costs of ads, extras offered (and their cost), discounts, and so on. Obviously all this is important, but you do need to go to your friendly neighbourhood bookstall and look at each magazine you might use.

Check through this list:

■ Is it the right setting for your product and message?
■ Do they bury ads like yours where nobody will see them, or do some appear with, or opposite, journalists' stories?
■ Will your ad look like all the others, or at least not stand out? Or will it be properly distinctive (be honest!)?
■ Do long-term small advertisers – the ones you have seen around for a long time – use it? They usually know what they are doing, so the odds are that it works for them.
■ Will customers instantly get some idea of what you offer from the sort of ad that you can afford? If not, you risk getting poor results.

2.39 BUYING AN AD

Having decided on the medium to use you may need to satisfy MOPS requirements (see Section 2.34). Check. There will probably be a choice of 'lineage', 'semi-display' and 'display' ads. They look like those on page 56.

The advertising sales department of the paper will send you their 'rate card' (ie, price-list). It, and BRAD, will contain strange terms like:

rop, or run-of-paper	–	meaning 'we'll put the ad where it suits us'.
facing matter	–	opposite editorial articles, which are what most people really buy magazines to look at (except perhaps for *Exchange & Mart* and other ads-only media) and not lost among other ads.

ifc/irc	–	inside front/rear cover – thought to be plum spaces; also covers are often printed on better paper than the rest of the magazine, so ads look better.
scc	–	single column centimetre: one cm deep, one column wide. Advertising costs are often quoted per scc.

Sometimes rate cards are *very* negotiable. Don't be afraid to make silly offers – there are many examples of people getting half-price advertising just by asking.

There are two basic printing methods, letterpress and lithography (litho), used for magazines and some papers, and a system similar to letterpress for other newspapers. Letterpress is basically similar to the child's printing outfit – you pick out the letters you want to use, assemble them in the right order, ink them, and then print. The only time you need anything more is when you want some special lettering or a picture. Then a 'block' has to be made photographically, for which an artist will prepare 'artwork'. Litho, on the other hand, requires your whole ad, words and pictures, to be made into artwork, which is laid out with the artwork for the rest of the page and then photographed to make a printing plate. This shows where the inevitable cost of extras comes from. There is your artwork, of course, which newspapers and magazines will often helpfully offer to prepare for you. Beware. You may pay central London rates (which can be extraordinary) for the work, and it will be out of your control. So when they produce something that isn't quite what you wanted, you can either accept it, or risk missing the paper's deadline and pay expensively to have it put right. Far better to get it done locally, but be careful to check one vital point: will the artist's work be accepted by the paper?

In addition to the cost of artwork, there is the cost for the plates or blocks the paper makes. Best to check with the advertising salespeople, in advance, what those costs are likely to be, to avoid nasty shocks later. Your artwork will need to be with the paper by a particular deadline called the 'copy date'. If it is not, you could miss that issue (but still have to pay!). The paper should send 'proofs' of your ad for you to check finally. Go over them with a fine-tooth comb. Obviously you will look to see that there are no spelling errors, that the address is right, and so on. But also look for blobs, damaged letters, wrong spacing, and if necessary call for corrections. That is, after all, why they sent you the proofs.

If you start out as, or develop into, a fairly substantial advertiser (say, £200,000 a year expenditure) you should look at the small local ad agencies. They may charge more for artwork than the local moonlighting artist, but they will negotiate and book space and act as commonsense advisers in the confusing world of advertising. The ad booking and advice is

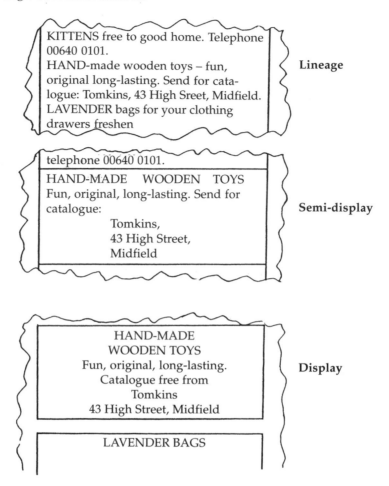

Figure 2.1 Lineage, semi-display and display ads

usually paid for by a discount allowed by the media (which you can't get – only approved ad agencies can). How to select an agency? Go to see them, let them come to see you, and find out if they talk sense. Always see more than one, and don't take any of them on if you're unsure.

When you design your ad, make the *proposition* the most prominent part of it, not your name.

2.40 MEASURING ADVERTISING'S EFFECTIVENESS

The first thing to remember is that one ad is unlikely to work. The effect of advertising accumulates over time, so that you could expect to build up to a reasonable level of response by your fifth. The man who told the author that he'd tried an ad and, because he got no replies, concluded that advertising was a big con, hadn't given it a chance. He sells capital equipment to local authorities, by the way. Advertising could open the door for his sales staff, or give their sales-talk more credibility by eliminating the response, 'Never heard of you.' It was most unlikely to generate enquiries direct to him, because his market doesn't work that way. So make sure you've taken on board the first paragraph of Section 2.38: get clear what your ad is supposed to achieve, and that you are not attempting something it cannot reasonably do. Defining objectives for your ads, and measuring the results, is a lot easier with direct-response ads than with others. If your ad calls for a coupon to be clipped, an order to be placed, a catalogue to be requested, it's easy to measure how well it worked. For that reason many small firms confine themselves to that sort of advertising. If you follow that example, you will quickly develop a pattern from ads in different media. One might cost you £1 per enquiry, another £1.30. But don't stop your records there – watch the sales you make to those enquiries and you may find that the first gives you a sale from every five enquiries, yet the second gives one for every other enquiry. The ad cost per sale, which is what really matters, will be £5 for the first, but only £2.60 for the second. Naturally, you could know this only where you are selling direct and not, for example, sending out catalogues with lists of stockists. Then you would simply never know which of your ads worked best. You might try keeping records like the one shown in Table 2.3, but amended where necessary to fit your trade. From this you will be able to develop the analysis shown in Table 2.4 for each ad you place.

Then, over the course of a year, say, you could add together the total results of each medium in which you advertised, as a tool for deciding which gave the most cost-effective results over a period of time. If you really wanted to know where your customers are, you could try taking (say) a three-month period and dividing customers up regionally. What's the point of that? Well, there are some significant regional differences, although TV culture is bringing us more together – for instance, there is much more soap and soap powder used in the south than in the north. Not because northerners are dirtier (one hopes) but because the hard water

Table 2.3 Example customer record

Customer Record						
Name	*Town*	*Ad medium*	*Issue date*	*Sent catalogue*	*Order received*	*Order value*
Dickens	SE11	Parents	Mar 05	28.2.05	11.3.05	£7.50
Jameson	Sheffield	Good Housekeeping	Apr 05	18.3.05	–	–

Table 2.4 Example ad analysis

	Parents	Good Housekeeping
Advertising media record (This was not a real campaign)		
Date	Mar 05	Apr 05
Cost of ad	£610	£828
Production cost	£110	£126
Total cost	£720	£954
Catalogues ordered	193	337
No of sales	108	124
Sales value	£5,854	£7,798
Adv cost per catalogue	£3.62	£2.84
Catalogues per sale	1.78	2.72
Cost per sale	£6.66	£7.70
Average sale value	£54.20	£62.88
Ad cost % of sales	12%	12%

in the south requires more soap to be used in washing. Perhaps your product is like that, for some reason you've not even dreamt of? Regional analysis would help highlight it, so that you could then concentrate more on the regional editions where you sell best, and save money.

2.41 PUBLICITY

Anyone can get their name in the papers. Journalists are hungry for 'copy', as they call the text they write and, like any of us, they prefer dealing with the opportunity that comes to them rather than the one they have to go out ferreting for. So how do you present them with an opportunity? First, consider what journalists write about. Read their stories. What 'peg' was the story hung on? Chances are that most are about something new, the end or start of an era, personal achievement or heroism, the fall of the mighty, a horrifying ordeal or incident, a miraculous change, conflict, a particular slant on some topical subject – and so on. Any active young business can find aspects of its operations that fit (some of) these categories. For instance:

∎ new firm formed;
∎ new premises opened;
∎ business expanding – more jobs;

- new trainee taken on;
- trainee passes exams, gets award;
- big order;
- new products taken on/developed;
- first/hundredth/thousandth order;
- worked overtime/weekends to get job out;
- to show at exhibition;
- results of showing at exhibition;
- first/second/etc anniversary;
- government grant;
- new executive;
- new machine;
- open day.

Not all your stories will get printed in the form you'd like to see, but it's cheap and can be very effective. People tend to believe what journalists write – they've no axe to grind, have they? – whereas they won't swallow your advertising uncritically. That's not to say you shouldn't advertise, but that editorial publicity complements your other efforts. How do you get in touch with journalists? Note the names of the people who do your sort of story in the press and on TV and phone them. You can get their firms' addresses from BRAD (see Section 2.38) or *Willings Press Guide* in the public library. Don't forget local, national and trade press, local and national media, BBC and independent TV and radio. Assemble a list and send out a 'news release' to them all whenever anything noteworthy happens.

2.42 WRITING A NEWS RELEASE

This is not difficult, if you follow some basic rules. You need to be able to answer most of these questions: who, what, why, when, where, how – and what next? Sort the answers out into the most important (to the reader) first, and least important last. That gives you the structure of your story, and all you need to do now is write the words. Keep it to one side of a sheet of paper, break it up into paragraphs, and enliven it with quotations – no matter that the person didn't actually say the words as long as you clear it with him or her. For example:

Factual draft

Who?	Tom Jones, former steelworker, and wife
What?	Opening a quality grocery shop
Why?	Fulfils lifetime dream, made redundant

When?	Next Monday, special hours
Where?	38 High Street, Midtown
How?	Using redundancy money, bank loan and advice
What next?	Free tasting, WI demonstration.

This can then be developed into the news release shown in Figure 2.2. This example is only one of the many ways of writing up that story. Remember, too, that if the paper wants to cut it, it will start from the bottom and simply lop off a sentence or paragraph, so that's another reason to get the important bits in first.

Now a word on layout. It pays to be as professional as possible, to save the journalist time and trouble. Start off with the clear words 'PRESS RELEASE' or 'NEWS RELEASE', and the date. Sometimes you have to send it to the weeklies or monthlies well in advance of publication, yet you don't want it printed prematurely by the dailies who may be under the same roof. The way to avoid this is to print 'EMBARGO TO 27 JUNE PLEASE' (or whatever date you want) at the top right, where 'Immediate: 27 May' is on the example. Then comes your headline and the story. Set the printer at 10 words to the line, or so, and double space. This gives the journalist the chance to estimate the number of words in the story, and thus the space it will take, by counting the lines, as well as leaving spaces for any corrections and changes he or she wants to make. At the end of the story put the word 'ENDS' two lines down in the centre of the page. On the bottom right-hand side, print 'Further information from' and your name, address and telephone number. You can't claim to be a trained journalist, but you will get a few stories printed if you send your news releases to the editor (no need to address it personally) of each paper, magazine, or programme you want to reach. If you deal overseas, don't forget the BBC World Service at PO Box 76, Bush House, Strand, London WC2B 4PH, and the Central Office of Information, www.coi.gov.uk who do a lot to publicise British developments to the world.

2.43 PROMOTING YOUR FIRM IN THE INFORMATION AGE

Here, we look at how the most recent aids to business can be used by the new firm to enhance its sales. It duplicates some of what appears in Section 5, which deals with the whole sweep of IT and its potential application to your firm. In this passage I concentrate specifically on the promotional aspects. Why leave it to the end of the section? The answer is simple: most people – entrepreneurs and their customers – are used to the paper-based way of doing things, so it makes sense to cover that first. For many firms,

NEWS RELEASE   Immediate: 27 May

New Delicatessen in Midtown

A lifetime's dream will be fulfilled next week when Tom and Sheila Jones open their new delicatessen and village shop for the first time. 'It's a huge step for us,' said former steelworker Tom, 'but we know there's a real demand for quality food in the area. Other places have some of the things a good cook needs, but we've tried to put every-thing under one roof.'

True to their word, Tom and his wife Sheila have stocked the shop with food from all over the world, as well as special aids for the discerning cook. Redundancy pay and a bank loan helped, as did advice from their accountant. The shop, at 38 High Street, Midtown, opens its doors at 8 o'clock sharp on Monday morning. 'As a working woman myself, I know how annoying it is to find the shops shut when I get out of the office,' said Sheila, 'so we decided to open at 8 am and close at 7 pm every weekday.'

The first of many events planned is a tasting of French wines and cheeses, with no obligation to buy. Others planned for the future include special demonstrations for Townswomen's Guilds and Women's Institutes.

ENDS

Further information from:
Tom and Sheila Jones, Midtown 987654,
38 High Street, Midtown.

Figure 2.2   Example press release

it is still a valid way of doing business and, despite many predictions of its imminent demise, it stubbornly declines to die.

As with any recent development, enthusiasts have made claims that cannot be justified. However, there is clearly the potential to revolutionise the workings of many small firms. For example, take the case of a small bed-and-breakfast on a remote Scottish island. Until recently, its enquiries came almost entirely from its entries in directories and referrals from tourist information centres. As a result, it secured some advance bookings – mainly from UK customers – but overseas visitors rarely heard about it. A few hardy souls took the ferry from the mainland and came across them by luck. Therefore, sales forecasting was difficult. Since it set up a simple website, enquiries have come in throughout the year and from all over the world from people who wish to visit the island. It is also able to provide a link to the ferry company's website, which provides a timetable of ferries and a booking service. Upon visiting the website, a potential customer learns about the bed-and-breakfast, and any worries about how to actually get there are overcome. Firm advance bookings now account for the majority of business.

Another example may be found in a maker of designer clothes for children. She had been caught in the trap of being unable to afford colour catalogues, yet needing to publish them in order to have any business at all. Even then, the schedules for photography and printing meant that she had to fix the season's range too far in advance. Occasionally, the fabrics on which she depended had been taken out of production after the catalogue was printed; sometimes she had a new idea, but it was too late to be included. Today, by publishing her designs on the web, she can update them at a moment's notice and – to her surprise – is getting useful orders from overseas. She is considering creating a catalogue on CD ROM featuring her designs and those of other small firms who sell to her market. She reasons that the people who buy her clothes will probably like her taste in accessories, shoes, books, toys and so forth. She may even feature celebration cakes. If this venture is successful, her firm will have evolved from a clothing manufacturer to a specialist supplier of a wide range of fashion goods for children. This would broaden the appeal of the business and give her further opportunities for expansion, yet would retain the essentially personal nature of her clothing business, which would be lost if the company became too big.

As well as being used to sell, the web is a great tool for market research. Using the web, you can research three areas:

■ what your current and potential competitors are up to;
■ what your current and potential customers are doing – this may lead to better ways of serving them;
■ associated areas of business, worldwide, to give yourself new ideas.

The first point is something that an alert firm makes a point of scanning weekly. When the monthly trade paper was the main source of information on competitors, life was easier. Now, the web is where new developments first appear. Unfortunately, checking on the web does involve rather more discipline than a scan through the trade magazine in front of the TV, but bear in mind that your competitors will be looking at your website and plotting how to do better. If you don't keep up to date at least weekly, they could steal your business.

2.44 SELLING VIA THE WEB

From the wide range of options available to you, the two extremes are:

■ provide customers with information about your business, but do not offer anything else – invite them to e-mail, telephone or write for further information; or,
■ offer a full service, covering enquiries, orders and payments.

The simple information model is cheap and easy. However, it still requires careful thought and planning. The main decisions will be how your home-page is designed in order to grab the customer's attention and what to put (and where) on other pages. There are many opportunities to use photography, video and sound – but always bear in mind that every extra feature slows things down for the customer. Anticipate your customers' questions and feature a page with frequently asked questions (FAQ) providing the answers. It is extremely important that the language used is crystal clear – remember that some of your readers may not have English as their first language.

You may be tempted to use some very advanced features that look exciting when the web designer shows them to you. Before using them, be sure that they will load on your customer's computer and that they will not slow the process down. Remember that the designer's demonstration will take place on his or her superb machine, but that many of your customers may be working with something running at a third of the speed. People are impatient with any page that takes more than a few seconds to load and will go off elsewhere if yours is too slow.

Depending on the nature of your business, you may want customers to contact you or leave their details so that you can contact them. In either case, by far the most effective method is to provide a facility to e-mail you – telephoning or writing will mean many fewer enquiries (you may, of course, decide that you want to deal only with those committed enough to go to all that trouble, but it may be a risky course). If you do provide an e-mail facility, remind customers that some e-mail messages may not get through some internet service providers' 'fire walls' and be lost; explain how they can tell.

Once your customer has e-mailed you, it is only the start of the process. E-mails need to be answered. It is easy to forget them until late in the day, so the best thing is to read them as the first task in the morning and again at fixed points during the day. This is one of the areas in which websites often fail. Sometimes, customers who just need to clear up a point before ordering contact the company by e-mail, but are ignored. By the time the questions do eventually get answered, they have long since taken their custom elsewhere.

E-mail as a means of dialogue with customers can also be built into the more complicated second option of a full online service. Its use would be confined mainly to catering for people wanting more information before ordering, answering queries about using the product and fielding complaints. Unfortunately, perceptions of the lack of security surrounding payments made via the web, coupled with some customers' need to check important points with you, means that the system will not run like a well-oiled machine while you are able to leave the office and explore the golf course. This means that enough telephone lines and telephone operators have to be available to deal with whatever volume of calls comes in. Forecasting the volume of calls can be a difficult business. What will you do if your site attracts 200 calls an hour? What will you do about people who telephone from a different timezone, expecting an answer while you are tucked up in bed? For many firms, it may therefore be better to start with the simpler option in order to learn the level and nature of enquiries, and once these have been established, then consider adding further features.

One final warning: never, ever, do mass e-mails to people who you think might buy from you. You may get some sales, but part of the etiquette of the internet is that junk mailing (or 'spam') is not practised. People who flout this convention can get 'flamed' – that is, bombarded with vast quantities of unpleasant revenge e-mails, which clog up their server's memory and take ages to sort through and delete.

2.45 KEY JOBS TO DO

- Research and understand your market.
- Select your marketing strategy – exactly what will you sell, to whom, by what means and in what quantities? How will you differ from competitors? Why should people buy from you?
- Develop your promotional strategy – how will customers hear about you?

- Select your sales strategy – how will you get orders?
- Select your distribution strategy – how will orders be executed?
- Develop your pricing policy – what do you charge, what discounts are available and why?
- Build up forecasts of sales volumes that can be used later to calculate the value of sales and the cost of goods sold.
- Develop numerical benchmarks against which you will measure performance.

This is the road to business success

Opportunities in the Uk and Ireland.

Pirtek hose centres provide a vital mobile hose replacement service to a market estimated to be worth £600 million in the UK. If you are looking for an opportunity to run your own business, we are looking for commercially minded people who would like to take a serious business forward. Capital required in the region of £50,000.

Call Alistair Wiggins on: 0208 749 8444 for an information pack.

- **Market leader • 14 year track record**
- **Growing market and support**
- **International and British franchise award-winner 1997 and 2000**
- **Professional training**
- **Strong branded product**

Number **in Europe**

Pirtek UK Ltd,
35 Acton Park Est.,
The Vale, Acton,
London W3 7QE.

www.pirtek.co.uk

PROFIT FROM OUR EXPERIENCE

Section 3: Finances and financial control

3.1 AIMS OF THIS SECTION

To survive, a business must make profits; everyone knows that, and this section deals with how you plan that part of your activity. Equally important is the need to control cash, actual money in hand, which is rarely given the prominence it deserves. The difference between the two is great, and of enormous importance. If you sell something for more than it cost, you have made a profit, even though your customer may not yet have paid you for it. Even if your customer eventually keeps his promise to pay, you cannot pay today's bills with promises. For that you need cash, and this section shows how to forecast how much cash you will have, and when. Costing is covered in two forms suitable for most small firms. This section is very important, as it deals with matters of survival. If you do not feel at home with figures you need to persist until you understand it. Many inexperienced businesspeople underestimate their costs and lose money. A very high proportion of the firms that go broke are profitable, but just run out of cash. One characteristic of most successful firms is that their managers have a very tight grasp of financial matters. Not only do they plan, but they also monitor their actual performance to see when and where they begin to stray from their plan. That enables them to take corrective action before things get seriously out of hand. They also learn from their inevitable mistakes, getting better and better at running their businesses.

3.2 COSTING

Sell something for more than it cost and you make a profit. It sounds easy, and it need not be all that difficult provided you estimate your costs correctly. This is a deceptively simple statement, for while it is easy to cost the materials used in a job, it is more difficult to divide up general overheads like rent, telephone or electricity. Yet they all have to be paid for just like materials. There are umpteen different costing systems and thick books on the subject, but here we shall confine ourselves to just one method, of most use to the very small business where labour is likely to be the biggest single item of cost. It is known as the 'absorption' method. Quite simply, you add up the cost of materials consumed by a product, add a figure that covers general overheads, plus another that pays you a wage, and you have the cost:

	materials consumed (including wastage)
plus	general overheads (rent, vehicle, phone etc)
plus	wage(s)
equals	cost

At this stage we ignore the capital outlay on machinery and tools for doing the job. They have to be paid for, but are dealt with in a particular way.

To recap, materials are easy to cost. The more difficult items can be made easy to handle if they are expressed as an hourly rate for work done. The rate needs to be set at a level that should, over a year, pay the annual running costs and give you the wage you need. A costing done on this basis might look like this:

materials		£24
overheads ⎫		
wage ⎬	2 hours @ £40 an hour	£80
cost ⎭		£104

It really is as simple as it looks, provided you count all the hours you spend, and your hourly rate is right.

Don't forget that 'cost' to you isn't necessarily the same as the price you charge your customers: see Section 2.30 and Section 3.3.

3.3 CALCULATING AN HOURLY RATE

First, work out all your running costs as you will for the profit-and-loss budget (see Section 3.11). Do not include capital costs, that is, the costs of buying things that you mean to keep and use rather than sell as soon as possible. Such things are machines, tools, jigs, patterns, vehicles, office equipment, computers, any work done to bring the office or workshop up to scratch, and so on. Do include repairs and running costs, though. The way you allow for capital items is through 'depreciation'. Depreciation is a cost which allows for the amount of the item's useful life that is used up in a year. For example, if a machine costs £500 and will probably need to be junked after four years of the sort of use you will give it, you are using up £500 ÷ 4 = £125-worth of it each year. Of the various ways of treating depreciation this is the simplest, known as the 'straight line' approach. Include interest on any loans you plan to take out.

Now to move to the next stage, calculating how many hours you will work. People starting a firm usually set out with determination to work a lot of hours to get it going. Of that large number of hours, however, most will be spent selling, fetching, carrying, doing paperwork, estimating, chasing suppliers and a host of other things. They all need doing, but it is hard to share out the time you spend on them fairly between your customers. The simple answer is to calculate on just the hours in which you work productively, that is, making or doing things that you can charge for. This productive time is easy to share out because it is only ever done on individual customers' jobs. In most one-person firms it is very exceptional to find more than 20 to 25 productive hours being worked per week. The owners are often working 60 or 70 hours a week, but their uninterrupted time at the bench is only about one-third of the total. By all means set yourself a more ambitious target, but do your financial plans on this cautious basis. Whatever you do, avoid that common problem of the new starter, of thinking that you can charge for 40 hours week in, week out, and clear up everything else in half an hour at night in front of the TV set. There may be odd weeks like that but the average will be quite different. Some weeks you will take off altogether for holidays, sickness, and Christmas, so your 25 hours a week can be multiplied by 48 working weeks to show 1,200 productive hours in a year. Thus you have 1,200 hours in which to get back your overheads and a wage. If you need £30,000 a year in your hand to feed, clothe and house the family, the firm will have to pay you about £35,000 before deductions. If the running costs of the business are £20,000, that gives a total of £35,000 + £20,000 = £55,000 to be earned.

Table 3.1 sums this all up. It then goes on to work out the hourly rate, which comes out at £45.83. Do not be tempted to round it down to £45.00. The 1,200 × 83p that you stand to lose comes to £996, nearly £19 a week,

Table 3.1 Working out an hourly price for work 1

Productive hours
25 hours a week × 48 weeks a year = **1,200 productive hours a year**

Overheads to be recovered

Family income (gross)	£35,000
Business overheads	£20,000
Total	£55,000

Hourly rate to be charged
£55,000 ÷ 1,200 hours = £45.83 per hour

---

and the only place it can come from is your wage. The overheads will cost the same however little you charge, so it can only be your wage that suffers. Better to round it up to £46. If you are aghast at the idea of asking that much for your work remember that many firms not only ask but get it. The arithmetic cannot change, so any competitor who undercharges will live in poverty while you survive, and will probably be the first to go to the wall when hard times come. The ways of reducing the impact on your prices are:

- keep interruptions under strict control, so that you increase your productive hours;
- work intensively, so that you turn out more in an hour than your competitor;
- use modern aids wisely, for the same reason.

In many small businesses, getting the hourly price for their work right – not too high, not too low – and making the best use of the time available, are the main keys to profit. Bear in mind, too, that 'cost' is not necessarily selling price. It is only the lowest price at which you can afford to sell. If you can get more on some jobs you will undoubtedly charge accordingly.

3.4 CAUTIONS ON SECTION 3.3

The beauty of the rate calculated by this method is its simplicity. If you are not careful that could conceal a danger. The snag is that all the assumptions have to come true in real life. That does not condemn the method, but emphasises that you need to monitor what actually happens to see in

Table 3.2 Working out an hourly price for work 2

Productive hours
20 hours a week × 45 weeks a year = **900 productive hours a year**

Overheads to be recovered

Family income (gross)		£35,000
Business overheads		£20,000
	Total	**£55,000**

Hourly rate to be charged
£55,000 ÷ 900 hours = £61.11 per hour

---

good time if you are going off the rails. For instance, if you manage only 20 hours' productive work instead of 25, and you get only 45 weeks' work, what happens? Table 3.2 shows that the rate has to rise to £61.11.

That is a rather ambitious rate for many businesses, though not for all, but charging it may kill the firm off before it even gets started. What would be more likely is that the firm would have charged its £46 an hour, with results that might look something like those shown in Table 3.3.

Table 3.3 Working out an hourly price for work 3

Income 900 productive hours × £46 an hour =	£41,400
Business overheads remain the same	£20,000
Family income whatever is left over	£21,400
Desired income (gross)	£35,000
Shortfall in family income	£13,600

This would not be a comfortable position to find yourself in.

Moreover, productive hours is not the only factor that can vary. The same applies to every item in the calculation. Too few weeks worked, overheads higher than forecast, personal wage higher than allowed for, all could scupper your plans equally well. If you use this method you therefore need to budget your costs with care, and then to keep track of each one to be sure it does not stray from target. So a simple method of recording your aim and your achievement is called for. The three crucial figures are your invoiced sales, your overhead expenses, and the productive hours worked. Overheads can be monitored on your cash-flow forecast (see Section 3.10) so there is no point in doing it again. There is nothing to stop you from carrying out other checks, but these are the ones you need to stay in control of your hourly rate. If you feel at home with graphs and charts it can be done that way, but the simplest route is to draw up something like Table 3.4.

At the end of each week you fill in the actual sales you invoiced, and compare it with the target. You complete the running total of actual sales and compare that with the target. Thus you will be able to see at a glance how you are performing. If you are on target, fine; nothing to worry about. If you are well over or under you need to see what effect it will have on your cash flow, whether it is likely to come right quickly, or whether or not you need to rebudget. At least you will know before you have a crisis on your hands, unlike those poor souls who only realise that things are wrong when it is too late to save themselves. A similar check can be kept on the number of productive hours worked.

The last point on costing systems is to keep them under review as your business grows. As with other important financial matters it should be discussed with your accountant before you adopt any system, or before you change one.

Table 3.4   Keeping track of performance

Invoiced Sales, Year 1

		TARGET £		ACTUAL £	
Month	*Week No*	*Week*	*Running*	*Week*	*Running*
Jan	1	–	–		
	2	100	100		
	3	200	300		
	4	200	500		
Feb	5	100	600		
	6	100	700		
	7	150	850		
	8	150	1000		
Mar	9	400	1400		
	10	400	1800		
	11	400	2200		
	12	400	2600		
	13	400	3000		

Taking on an employee helps to spread the load, of course, so that you can reduce the hourly rate that you need to charge. That does not necessarily mean that you will cut prices, but that the chance may exist to make a bit more profit. The effect of taking on an employee might look like Table 3.5.

Table 3.5   Working out an hourly price for work

Productive hours
17 hours from owner (less than before because supervision takes time, and selling the extra output takes longer)
33 hours from employee (44 hour week, 75 per cent productive)
—
50 hours a week × 48 weeks a year = **2,400 productive hours a year**
═

Overheads to be recovered
Family income	£35,000
Business overheads	£20,000
Employee's cost to you	£20,000
Total	**£75,000**

Hourly rate to be charged
£75,000 ÷ 2,400 hours = £31.25 per hour

Before you rush off to take on staff, remember that this lower cost may not come about easily. First, you will be hard pressed to do 20 productive hours' work at the same time as supervising your employee so well that he or she is productive for at least 30 hours a week. Furthermore, instead of having to find a mere £55,000-worth of income a year before the firm makes a profit, your target is now £75,000 (see Table 3.5). Ways of considering this further are covered in Section 3.19.

Before we leave this topic it is worth looking at what will happen if the best possible outcome occurs. Suppose the firm manages to sell the whole of the 2,400 productive hours at the figure of £45.83 per hour: what will happen? See Table 3.6.

This is a very good position to be in, and it shows why firms want to grow.

If your firm is more complex than the one portrayed here, you may feel uncomfortable with the simplicity of this costing system. Another one, of equal simplicity, but reflecting better the realities of the multi-product firm, is described in Section 3.20.

Table 3.6 The best possible outcome of calculating hourly prices

Income	
2,400 hours × £45.83 =	£109,992
Income target	
As before	£75,000
Profit	£34,992

3.5 THE IMPORTANCE OF CASH

To most people 'cash' is just another word for money, wealth or riches. To an accountant, a bank manager or a business owner it has a special meaning. Cash is money that is available to be spent, that is banknotes, deposits in your bank account or in some other easily obtained form. Cash is the only thing that bills can be paid with. If you had a million pounds' worth of jewels you would be rich, but the Inland Revenue could not accept them in payment of your tax bill. People you owe money to can be unforgiving if you do not pay on time, so you need enough cash available at all times to pay the bills that are falling due. It would be wasteful to keep more than you need, as any excess could be tucked away earning interest. But too much cash, and a little lost interest, is far, far better than too little cash. If you run out of cash your creditors could foreclose and put you out of business very quickly indeed.

3.6 HOW TO RUN OUT OF CASH

It is one of the easiest things to do. The most popular methods are:

- delaying the sending-out of invoices for work done;
- losing notes of what work has been done, or delivery notes for goods sold;
- not chasing customers for payment;
- avoiding opening credit accounts with suppliers;
- going out of your way to pay cash as quickly as possible;
- buying large quantities of materials to get discounts;
- buying equipment and vehicles for cash instead of getting a loan;
- taking on staff who are unable to work fast enough or to quality standards;

- keeping on staff for whom there is not likely to be any work;
- never checking things that you sign for;
- never getting a signature for goods that you deliver;
- laying yourself open to theft;
- taking on prestige premises when they are not necessary;
- buying fancy insurance policies;
- not cultivating the bank manager;
- never planning ahead to foresee your cash needs;
- never recording performance and comparing it with the plan;
- taking a really big order, especially from a slow-paying customer.

That list is far from complete, of course. But no more than a couple of items from it should serve to cripple or kill most businesses, large or small.

The last item on the list might deserve an explanation. On the face of it, a big order is very desirable. But, if payment will not be received for a long time after the order has been delivered, and if materials, labour and overheads have all had to be paid for in the meantime, the bank account should be quite empty long before the cheque eventually arrives. Too often in such cases the receiver or liquidator is the one to pay it into the bank.

3.7 HOW TO CONSERVE CASH

This obviously involves doing the complete opposite of Section 3.6 above:

- An order is not regarded as complete unless it agrees acceptable payment terms as well as price, delivery date and so forth.
- A sale is not complete until payment has been collected – customers can be less than keen to pay you, so a few techniques may be useful: see Sections 3.13 to 3.18.
- Pay your bills only when you must, and not before – it is sometimes hard for a new firm to get a credit account from a supplier straight away, so you could be asked to pay cash for six months while you establish a track record – see Sections 9.5 and 9.6 on these and other purchasing negotiations.
- When you do buy supplies, buy only enough for immediate needs – do not buy 15 weeks' supply for £1,500 if you can get two weeks' worth for £250. Although it costs more per item, you hang on to £1,500 – £250 = £1,250 of cash that can be used to pay other bills or reduce the overdraft. This is a question of balance, but if there is any doubt in your mind, play safe.
- Avoid the desire to be monarch of all you survey, to own everything. The easiest money to borrow is finance for property and equipment,

the solid, tangible things. Less easy to borrow is money for working capital, cash for your day-to-day needs. It would therefore be foolish to tie up all your own money in equipment and then have to borrow working capital. It is better to borrow for the equipment, and fund working capital from your own pocket as far as you can.

■ Surplus staff can cause a major outflow of cash. It is fine to employ people for as long as they can earn the cost of employing and housing them, but if business falls off you have an unpleasant but necessary decision to take. While you have a responsibility to your staff, both as a human being and as their employer, you have an overriding duty to yourself, your family, suppliers and customers to stay in business so that you can meet your obligations to them. That is easily said, and it makes it no easier when you are confronted by a weeping employee whom you have sacked through no fault of his or her own; but for the sake of business survival you have to go through with it.

■ Avoid surrounding yourself with the sort of things that 'successful' businesspeople are expected to have: opulent premises, expensive cars, decorative receptionists and secretaries who are underemployed, and the like. Most of this nonsense has more to do with TV and Hollywood than real life. If you can work realistically from home or a £30-a-week chicken shed, why take on a £300-a-week office or factory?

■ Theft and fraud are obviously to be avoided, but every week one seems to read of some trusted bookkeeper who went off the rails with several thousand pounds of the boss's money. It is better not to trust people completely, but to have systems that show where money and other property has gone, and checks to make sure that the records are truthful. A shiver goes down the spine of a business consultant every time a client says, 'I don't understand figures, so I leave all the books and records to X to sort out.' If X is a chartered accountant, all well and good, except that the client is paying the equivalent of graduate wages for labourer's work. If X is simply a private person it means that the business is probably out of control and at risk of being defrauded. It is also unfair on X, for if something goes missing through a genuine mistake there may be no proof that X is not guilty, so that suspicion falls on an entirely innocent person. In another way, leaving it all to X to do is risky. It is most unlikely that X will grasp, or even be interested in, all of the firm's key survival factors. So X will watch what he or she thinks is important, which though sincerely meant may be quite irrelevant.

3.8 WHY BOTHER TO FORECAST YOUR CASH POSITION?

Because cash is the chief factor governing your survival short term, it must be worth trying to forecast how much you will have and when. It brings two main benefits:

■ You can foresee the danger of policies which could run your cash down, and decide whether or not to change the policy or borrow to cover the cash shortage, which is usually temporary.
■ Banks feel a lot more relaxed about requests for loans if you can show how you decided on the sum that you are trying to borrow, and how it will affect your cash situation.

3.9 WHAT MAKES UP A CASH-FLOW FORECAST?

What we are trying to forecast is the amount of cash likely to be on hand at particular times. To do this four pieces of information are needed:

■ what points in time we are forecasting for;
■ the expected flows of cash into the business;
■ the expected flows of cash out of the business;
■ the timing of the inflows and outflows.

As for timing, a business in real trouble might forecast its cash position daily. More usually these forecasts are made for month-ends. What inflows and outflows will there be? Inflows will come from your own investment, loans, sales of goods and services, and very occasionally from the sale of a capital item – an old vehicle, for example. They are therefore based mainly on your month-by-month forecast of sales. Outflows will be calculated on equipment purchases, your monthly purchases of materials, overheads and the wage you draw, and occasionally payments of taxes. The list of overhead costs that you use is the same as that for the profit-and-loss budget (see Section 3.11), with the exception of depreciation. Depreciation does not involve a movement of cash, so it is ignored for cash calculations. Although the basic information is much the same, there is a vast difference between a profit-and-loss budget and a cash-flow forecast, as shown in Tables 3.7 and 3.8.

Let us suppose that Tom is a busy teacher, but around Christmas time he makes some small mahogany boxes which are much in demand as Christmas gifts. It is now November, and he is puzzling over the difference between his profit-and-loss budget and his cash-flow forecast.

Last month, October, he paid cash for £400-worth of timber, screws and other materials. Half of the boxes will sell for cash to colleagues from school, and a local gift shop will take the rest this month but pay in February. He expects to make 200, and to sell them at £20 each. Fortunately his accountant sister-in-law calls in, and quickly sorts out the puzzle by working out a profit-and-loss budget and a cash-flow forecast.

Table 3.7   Tom's profit-and-loss budget

Profit-and-loss budget: end December	
Invoiced sales: 200 × £20	£4,000
Materials	400
Value added	£3,600
Overheads: trivial	–
Net profit	£3,600

Table 3.8   Tom's cash-flow forecast

Cash-flow forecast: October–February	Oct	Nov	Dec	Jan	Feb
Income					
Cash sales	–	200	1,800	–	–
Sales to shop	–	–	–	–	2,000
Total income	–	200	1,800		2,000
Outgoings					
Materials	400	–	–	–	–
Cash flow for month	(400)	200	1,800	–	2,000
Cumulative	(400)	(200)	1,600	1,600	3,600

Note: Brackets signify minus quantities.

What Tables 3.7 and 3.8 show is that Tom's profit does turn into cash eventually, but only in February. The bottom line of the cash-flow table gives the position month-by-month. Before he gets his money back he is quite badly out of pocket.

Table 3.9 What to include in profit-and-loss budgets and cash-flow forecasts

	Profit and loss	Cash flow
Sales invoices	All issued, whether or not paid	Only shown when payment expected
Materials	The value used to make the goods sold	Shows value bought when payment due
Overheads	The share for the period, whether or not invoiced or paid	Shown when payment expected to be made
Depreciation	The share for the period	Not shown – no cash moves
VAT	Ignore it if you are VAT-registered	Show it

Most people would have carried out only the profit-and-loss calculation. If Tom and his family have lots of spare cash that may be enough. But if they are at all short of cash it is vitally important that he and his family realise that the profits will not all be spendable until well after Christmas. This particular example of a cash-flow forecast is easy enough to do in your head, but in a real-life business there are dozens or hundreds of transactions going on over a period of time, far too much for mental arithmetic to handle.

In real life, therefore, *cash* and *profit* can be very different things. Each therefore needs a separate forecast. Otherwise you could join the thousands of other unfortunates who were making profits, but ran out of cash without realising until it was too late.

3.10 DRAWING UP A CASH-FLOW FORECAST

A simple example may help to explain the principles. John runs a very straightforward business selling apples from a market stall. On his first day in business he does the following:

- borrows £200 from his granny, interest free on the promise of repaying her as fast as possible;
- buys a market stall for £100 cash;
- pays the council £10 for a day's pitch on the market square;

- buys apples for £90 cash;
- sells half the apples for £80, all in cash.

At the end of that Monday his profit-and-loss account looks like Table 3.10.

Table 3.10 John's profit-and-loss account for Monday

	£
Sales	80
Cost of goods sold	45
Value added	35
Overheads	
Rent for pitch	10
Profit	25

But where are the £45-worth of apples he still has, and the stall worth £100? And for that matter where is the £80 we know he has in his pocket? The answer is that the profit-and-loss account records only the sales, and the expenses relating to those sales. It could not show where stock, or cash or equipment is. The 'missing' items will appear on the balance sheet, an entirely separate document. The balance sheet pretends that you stop all the buying and selling for a split second and record where money is tied up at that moment. It also shows where the money in the business has come from. At the end of Monday, John's balance sheet looks like Table 3.11.

Table 3.11 John's balance sheet

Where the money came from	£	*Where it was at that moment*	£
Loan from granny	200	Fixed assets (stall)	100
Retained profits	25	*Current assets*	
		Stock at cost (apples)	45
		Cash (day's takings)	80
	£225		£225

This way of showing a balance sheet is now old-fashioned, but it is easier for beginners to understand – so don't worry if balance sheets you have seen are laid out differently. They all mean the same thing.

You do not need to concern yourself further with balance sheets at this stage of your firm's development, so we shall leave them there. The point in mentioning them is so that you can see that they are basically simple documents, to illustrate the sort of information they contain and to confirm, yet again, that profit is only one of the two key matters you must deal with. Therefore, the young business needs to monitor its profit-and-loss account but need not worry about the balance sheet. Instead it pays hawk-like attention to its performance against the cash-flow forecast, which is a more flexible way of controlling and concentrating on the high-risk areas of the balance sheet.

To return to John. It is now Tuesday morning and he sets up his stall in the market again. He pays the council's superintendent another £10, and sells the rest of his apples for £80. The result of Tuesday's trading is shown in Table 3.12.

Table 3.12 John's profit-and-loss account for Tuesday

	£
Sales	80
Cost of goods sold	45
Value added	35
Overheads	
Rent of pitch	10
Profit	25

For the rest of the week he repeats the same pattern, ending up with 6 x £25 = £150 by Saturday night, all in cash. Having made £150, and being a nice young chap, John thinks of paying off some of Granny's loan. He knows he must keep some cash back to pay for stock on Monday, to pay the council, and to pay his £30 weekly keep. So he does a cash-flow forecast. He works out what cash he can expect to come in and when, and what he will have to pay out and when. Follow what John wrote down; even if it looks a little difficult at first it is not complicated. As usual, brackets mean a minus figure.

Table 3.13 shows that the result of Monday's trading is expected to be a fall of £50 in John's holding of cash, even though he will have made his

Table 3.13 John's cash-flow forecast for week 2

	Mon	Tue	Wed	Thu	Fri	Sat
Cash taken in day (a)	80	80	80	80	80	80
Cash paid out at start of day						
– keep	30	–	–	–	–	–
– rent	10	10	10	10	10	10
– apples	90	–	90	–	90	–
Total cash paid out in day (b)	130	10	100	10	100	10
Net cash taken in day (a – b)	(50)	70	(20)	70	(20)	70
Cash in hand at start of day	*150	100	170	150	220	200
Cash in hand at end of day	**100	170	150	220	200	270

* He will start the week with £150 left over from previous week
** The figures on this line become the 'cash in hand at start of day' for the following day.

usual profit. That profit, plus another £15, will be tied up in apples for sale on Tuesday. So can John pay off Granny? Bearing in mind that he must start each day with enough cash for his outlays that day, he looks to see what he can pay Granny and when. He will start week 2 with his £150 (the next to last figure in the Monday column above) and he must finish the week with at least £130 for his outlays at the start of week 3. Try working out what he can pay, and when. The answer is in brackets at the bottom of the next page. If you found that a little challenging you will see why John did it on paper and not in his head. The calculation is not difficult – it is only simple addition and subtraction – but there are so many steps to it that you cannot do it in your head. John could easily have taken the short cut and paid out of his profits. Had he done so he would have run out of cash and out of business. As it is, he still owes Granny £60 but he is still in business. Having established the principle of how the cash-flow forecast is drawn up, we can move to an example – in Appendix 1 – that is meant to be a bit more like real life. Although it may look very complicated, its framework is identical; there are just a few more items to list, add up and take away. Again, do not be put off by it but work through it at your own pace.

3.11 PROFIT-AND-LOSS BUDGETING

The title of the document may be misleading. It would be difficult to budget for a profit and a loss at the same time. It would probably help if the name were changed to 'profit *or* loss' budget. But it is not likely to be, so please accept the traditional name. What the profit-and-loss budget (hereafter referred to in the accountants' shorthand of 'P&L') shows is the sales invoiced during a period of time, the cost of labour and materials in the goods invoiced, and the difference between those costs and the sales, known as 'gross margin'. It then goes on to show the overheads, that is, the costs of the business which cannot be easily charged to particular products (rent, rates, postage, fuel and so on). Finally it subtracts that from gross margin to show net profit before tax.

This may be a good point at which to remind ourselves of the essential differences between the three basic accounting documents, as illustrated in Table 3.14.

Table 3.14 Differences between profit-and-loss accounts, balance sheets and cash-flow forecasts

Profit-and-loss account	Balance sheet	Cash-flow forecast
Sales invoiced in the period, whether or not the customer has paid.	**How much** money is tied up in the firm. **Where** it is tied up.	**Income** – shows how much, and when, cash is expected to arrive.
Expenses incurred in the period, irrespective of whether the bill has been paid.	**What** were the sources of that money. **Depreciation** is shown.	**Expenses** – shows how much cash is expected to be paid out, and when.
Depreciation is shown. REFERS TO A PAST PERIOD	REFERS TO A MOMENT IN TIME	**Ignores** anything that is not an actual movement of cash – like depreciation. REFERS TO A PERIOD IN THE FUTURE

(Answer: This week, John can pay £50 straight away, £20 on Monday evening, £50 on Wednesday evening, and £20 on Friday evening. If he tries to do it faster he runs out of cash – so he still owes Granny £60 at the end of the week.)

If the heading to the first of these three sheets were changed to 'Profit-and-loss budget', it would represent a forecast; an 'account' is a report on something that has happened already. The other references would also change to reflect expectations, and the last line would change to 'REFERS TO A FUTURE PERIOD OF TIME'.

When you are looking at the budgeting exercise in Appendix 1, introduced in Section 3.10, one point will jump out of the P&L. There is no mention of gross margin, some impostor calling itself *value added* appearing in its place.

'Value added' is what it says, the amount of value added to raw materials. It appears instead of gross margin because gross margin is arrived at after charging some labour; no labour is charged in the calculation of value added. The value added approach is simpler and thus seems to make sense in the very small firm where the exact split of productive time to unproductive is hard to tell in advance.

At the end of the year you, or your accountant, will produce a P&L account, a key piece of information for the tax office. It is also useful to you, as guidance on how you did against your plan. If you follow the controls suggested in other parts of this section you should not need to do it more frequently until your business grows and becomes more complex. At that stage a computerised accounts package will make it simple to produce a monthly P&L account. You will then have a very sensitive measure of whether you are straying from your plan, as a prelude to taking corrective action.

To confirm the way the P&L is made up, you do not write down items that you expect to be charged for in the period, as you do for cash-flow forecasts. Instead, you show the expenses you have actually used up in the period. The electricity bill is a good example. Suppose you know you will use £100-worth of electricity a month, the bill coming in quarterly. You received the last bill a month ago and plan to pay it this month. This month's cash-flow forecast will show an outflow item of £300 for electricity, but the P&L will record £100, the amount you reckon actually to use in the month. So the cash-flow forecast for next month will show nothing under electricity, but the P&L will show the usual £100.

Another steady overhead, or with luck a rising one, is the proprietor's wage. Some people might be uneasy to see that shown as an overhead, preferring to have the boss live off the profits. I prefer to do it this way because it forces us to remember that the boss and family expect some sort of income from the firm. If there are profits over and above that, all well and good, but we must plan for the boss to get a wage in order to minimise the risk of getting nothing.

Keep an eye on the ratios, too, as well as the absolute amounts of money. In the case of the Yule Fuel Company in Appendix 1, value added was just over 81 per cent of sales. If it turns out to be less, or more, than budget the owner should find out why. The same goes for the main overheads, and overheads in total. Ratios are a key part of your early warning system for alerting you to matters requiring attention.

3.12 CREDIT CONTROL

If you must give customers time to pay bills, it makes sense to allow the facility only to those who are likely to pay, and to get them to stick to the agreed terms. That is what credit control is about. If customers pay late, there will be a hole in your cash flow. If they fail to pay ever, there will also be a hole in your profits. The only sure-fire way of avoiding these problems is not to give credit, but to get paid cash with the order, or cash on delivery.

3.13 AVOIDING GIVING CREDIT

Every business that gives credit looks with envy and admiration at another which succeeds in getting cash with orders. In some lines of business it is difficult to avoid granting credit, but many firms do manage to do so. Once you start, you are stuck with it, so it is worth looking at alternatives. Many businesspeople will say it is impossible not to give credit, but it is not as clear cut as that. If you can pull it off you will avoid a great deal of administration and worry. One advantage of dealing direct with the public is that they expect to pay a deposit, or sometimes the whole cost, at the time of ordering, and the balance on delivery. Can this ever be done when you are selling to businesses?

You probably can if your product or service has any of the following characteristics:

- *Small outlay.* Nobody really minds paying the window-cleaner's £20 from the petty cash.
- *Emergency.* If the only way the big problem can be solved quickly is to pay cash.
- *Scarcity.* The only person providing something that everyone needs can get cash payment.
- *Uniqueness.* If the complete package that you offer really has outstandingly attractive features, people might swap their desire for credit for their desire for those features.

From that list, which has to do with what you are offering the customer, it becomes clear that credit is a marketing tool. Thus the decision on whether or not your policy includes offering it is partly a marketing decision. A further marketing point is that you can argue that cash on the nail saves you a lot of administration and bank borrowing. Therefore you pass those savings on. If customers want credit they can have it, but at higher prices.

If you are dealing with the public, think about accepting credit cards. They cost you about 5 per cent of the sale, but the customer can buy without the need for cash, and your cash is virtually certain.

3.14 GIVING THE MINIMUM AMOUNT OF CREDIT

You may have wrestled with the problem of not giving credit (Section 3.13 above) and lost. You now want to consider minimising it. After all, credit is an interest-free loan made on trust, often to a complete stranger. First, it is worth seeing if you can reduce the sum at risk. A deposit with the order would help. This works best when you are making something specially or obtaining it to special order. The customer can see your point of view, that if he does not come back to collect the thing you could be stuck with something that nobody else wants. Anything between 20 and 50 per cent probably seems fair to the customer, depending on the circumstances. Alternatively, you may be able to use the engineering industry idea of 'materials on free issue'. There the customer buys materials for the job and issues them to the subcontractor at no charge. Whether or not you are in engineering, could that idea be used in your business? Admittedly, the main reason for it in engineering is to give the big firm the benefit of quantity discounts on materials, but it has useful side-effects on the small firm's cash flow.

3.15 SETTING THINGS UP TO GET PAID QUICKLY

Many businesses simply put 'payment 30 days' on invoices and expect that to do the trick. Most customers ignore it and pay after six weeks or more. Can anything be done to guarantee quicker payment? Guarantee – no. But a lot can be done to encourage faster payment, and it often works. The time to lay the foundation for good credit control is at the time of negotiating for the order. That is when you can find out if this is one of those firms with a fixed policy of always taking 90 days' credit. If at that stage you detect this policy you can either modify your quotation or decline the order, but if you had not introduced the subject you might not have spotted it until you had accepted the order on their terms. Usually, though, payment terms are negotiable. By asking for cash payment seven days after delivery you might get it. You will make fast payment seem like an important issue – not too difficult because it is – which will only emphasise the importance of the concession when a customer forces you to accept a promise of 30-day payment, instead of giving the discount he or she is demanding. Now that it is accepted *before* the firm order is placed the promise of payment is as much part of the deal as the price. Thus you will have exactly the same right to kick up a fuss if the customer does not pay on time as he or she will if you overcharge. Record the payment terms along with all the other details on the order confirmation that you send.

After you deliver, invoice immediately by first class post, or best of all, deliver invoice and goods at the same time. If you get into the habit of leaving a couple of days between delivery and invoice that can too easily slip to a full week. Once that happens you will find that you have too many balls in the air to get back to instant invoicing. Customers will take time to pay anyway, so it seems foolish to handicap yourself further. Invoices should carry:

■ the information required by law (see Section 6.9 on disclosure of business names);
■ the charge and how it is arrived at;
■ the date of issue, which is also the tax point for VAT-registered traders;
■ any information that the customer requires, such as an order number or stock number;
■ payment terms, shown prominently.

Statements are required by some customers. They are summaries of the transactions with the customer over an appropriate period of time, say three to six months. They are usually sent monthly, and show:

■ all invoices issued during the period that the statement covers, those due (or overdue) for payment being marked accordingly;
■ payments received during the period;
■ the outstanding balance on the account.

In view of the rising costs of administration and postage, many businesses now send statements only to those customers who insist on them. They can be a help to the customer in checking that his idea of what he owes you coincides with yours, and that you have registered the payments that he has made. They can help you, by drawing to his attention overdue invoices. But you can chase overdue invoices just as effectively without issuing statements, so that alone is not sufficient reason for instituting them.

This is an *invoice*. It is simply a bill for goods supplied or services rendered.

ABCD Ltd			
		700 High Street	
		Anytown AN1 1AN	

Invoice

Smith & Co
698 Cook St
Anytown

No: 217/05
Date and
Tax Point: 11/3/05
Your Order: 92/2709/pr

Quantity	Description	Each	Value
8 cases × 24	Widgets no. 2050 ½"	£12.50	£100.00
	Goods		£100.00
	VAT @ 17½%		£17.50
	Total payable		£117.50

PAYMENT DUE 30 DAYS FROM INVOICE DATE
Registered in England no 123456
VAT no 111.2222.33
Directors: A Allen, B Brooks, C Cliff, D Davis

ABCD Ltd				
			700 High Street	
			Anytown AN1 1AN	
To			*Date:* 31/3/05	
Smith & Co				
698 Cook St				
Anytown				

Date	Invoice	Value	Payment	Balance
Brought forward				180.00
18/1/05	103	55.00		235.00
27/1/05	118	123.00		358.00
3/2/05	124	81.00*		439.00
5/2/05			180.00	259.00
28/2/05	183	97.00*		356.00
7/3/05			55.00	301.00
12/3/05	217	117.50		418.50
26/3/05			123.00	295.50
Balance carried forward				295.50

ITEMS MARKED* ARE OVERDUE – PLEASE PAY NOW
Registered in England no 123456
Directors: A Allen, B Brooks, C Cliff, D Davies

This is a *statement*. It summarises the activity on this customer's account. The invoice shown above (no 217 for £117.50) is the last one on it. The information it gives is taken from the firm's books, and enables the customer to see if his books agree with yours. Most people get something similar every month – a bank statement.

Figure 3.1 Example invoice and statement

3.16 COLLECTING MONEY FROM THE SLOW PAYER

This is a game that involves applying pressure with personal pleasantness. If that does not work you turn to tougher tactics. Anyone with due items on his account is asked to pay before further deliveries are made, or at least to make a firm promise of payment. Customers with overdue items definitely have no more supplies until they have paid off all items that are due for payment or overdue. Anyone who has not paid seven days after the date that an invoice was due for payment should be telephoned to check that there are no problems or queries. Customers can rightly withhold payment for faulty goods, but sometimes they are tempted to use that as an excuse to stop paying you anything at all. In fairness, it is also a way of getting you to attend to the problem fast, assuming that the complaint is genuine. In any case, by the end of that telephone call you will have identified a problem that you did not previously know of, will have sorted out how it will be dealt with, and will have agreed how payments are to get back on track: 'I shall drop everything to be with you at 8.30 on Friday morning to put the faulty one right. Can I work in a corner of your warehouse? . . . Will you have a cheque in full settlement, ready and waiting?' Write, fax, e-mail or telex to confirm.

If that fails you can try one last telephone call or personal visit, sounding more sorrowful than angry. You supplied the order, in good faith, on time, and as ordered apart from a minor problem that you raced over to put right. You have spent pounds on letters, stamps, phone calls, visits, interest on the debt, and lost time. Yet they refuse to pay or keep putting you off. Your bank manager has stopped accepting excuses from you, and demands hard cash. Will your customer help you?

Because not everyone can be shamed it might not work, but if they do not pay they have only themselves to blame for what happens next. Almost certainly, threats are unlikely to work, especially if they are old hands at this game. Nor should you visit with 18-stone razor-scarred 'business associates' and a Dobermann, or snatch goods to the value of the debt. That would probably constitute illegal harassment and theft, and could put you on the wrong side of the dock in a criminal case.

If the debt is for less than £5,000, the next move is to the county court where the officials will be pleased to introduce you to the small claims procedure which can be settled by arbitration without lawyers or a court appearance, and it costs very little.

Look up 'courts' in the phone book, ring the local county court and ask for advice. They are helpful people, and will tell you how to go about it, but they cannot, of course, give you any advice on your chances of winning. For a large sum, or where a lot of argument is on the cards, you should think about getting a solicitor to conduct the case. Before committing yourself, tell them the facts and let them ask questions. Then ask for an estimate of costs. This may be difficult to get, so you must be prepared to ask for the lowest possible figure, the highest likely figure, and a reasonably pessimistic idea of the probable cost. This is essential so that you can weigh up the costs against the benefits to be gained by winning. Ask about the chances of the loser paying the winner's costs. Not all solicitors are equally energetic and effective in commercial matters, so before choosing one it could be worth asking around among your bank manager, accountant, and other contacts. Ask a debt recovery specialist (see 'debt collectors' in the *Yellow Pages*) to quote, too. They can be surprisingly cheap and effective, so that it may be worth giving them the whole of your overdue debt-collection business, whether or not you could conduct some of the cases yourself. Check with your insurance broker to see if your type of business qualifies to be able to insure against these sorts of legal costs.

3.17 MINIMISING CREDIT RISKS

Anyone who gives credit to a vulnerable customer is obviously asking for trouble. The sort of firm that is the greatest risk is a very young firm, say under two years old; the ailing subsidiary of a big firm – sometimes the owner lets it sink, accepting no responsibility for it; the customer who applauds every line in your sales story, and places a much bigger order than expected – you admire your salesmanship until your demands for payments come back marked 'gone away'; and the customer whose works, store or shop is surprisingly empty – they may be packing up, or unable to get supplies elsewhere because they owe so much. If you are selling to the public there may be similar signs – bare cupboards, lack of furniture and so on. However, unrestrained opulence may mean huge debts, so it is not an exact science. Therefore some checking is necessary.

Members of the public with a record of financial unreliability are probably on the files of at least one credit reference agency. Debt recovery specialists often have links with such firms, so that could be another reason for contacting one – see Section 3.16 above. Credit reference agencies are thick on the ground, and most are better at some things than at others. Some might specialise in members of the public, others in retailers, and so on. Even a few discreet local enquiries can tell you a lot. 'Everyone' knows about old Smithy's 17 liquidations in 12 years, except you. Bank references can help to spot the out-and-out rogue. Your bank makes a written request to the customer's bank for information, and the answer comes back in a form of words that means little to the outsider, but which your bank will decode for you. In effect, it puts them in one of three categories: we know nothing against them and they conduct their bank account properly; we are not happy with them but they might survive;

or, they are very risky. Those are oversimplifications, of course, and no bank reference is infallible. Therefore back-up checks are needed. You might also ask the customer for the names of other suppliers to whom you can apply for a reference. Two should suffice, but remember that every business, however dodgy, probably has two suppliers it must keep sweet in order to stay in business at all. When you take up references it is probably best to phone at first. If they deal with these requests that way you will get a quick answer, whereas if they ask you to write in you will be able to get a name or a department address to write to. If you write, ask specific questions: how long have they traded together, how has the account been conducted, what credit limit do they allow him, and any other matters that you feel you need to know. Try to keep it short, as you are asking a favour of them, and do enclose a stamped addressed envelope. When you are with the customer, it might be worth having a form with you which you complete along with the order form. It would serve to remind you of the questions you need answers to in order to run a proper account with him. It would include information on:

■ trading constitution – sole trader, partnership, limited company;
■ names and addresses of partners or sole trader;
■ authorised and issued capital and registered number if a limited company;
■ country of registration of limited company;
■ trade referees;
■ bank branch and address.

You might use that list selectively, not using it at all for BP, but seeking all that information, plus perhaps information to enable you to check on the directors personally in the case of a small limited company placing a very large order. Another way of reducing your risk over a large order is to offer to split it into a number of smaller orders delivered more frequently. That way you can hold back the second delivery until the first has been paid for, and so on.

Incidentally, if you are ever asked for a credit reference, be careful. The safest course is to say that it is your policy never to give references. If you want to be helpful to a good customer by giving a good reference, stick to the facts of your business relationship with them. Do not be tempted to praise them to the heavens; just say that they have always paid you on time. If you go further than the facts, and they do not pay the other supplier, you could find yourself being sued for misleading that supplier into giving credit. If you are asked to give a reference for a rogue do not treat it as a chance to get your own back, but simply say that you are not in a position to give a reference. That way you avoid a court action for damaging his or her character.

3.18 CHASING LARGER FIRMS FOR PAYMENT

People in small firms are often frightened of chasing their big-firm customers too hard. Yet big firms can (sometimes!) be easiest to get money from. This is because some, though not all, do have a conscience and do not mind paying your bill anyway – after all, it is probably petty cash to them. None of them will want a bad reputation among suppliers, although many will feel that might is right. Also, some are so diffuse that the accountant you chase for payment hardly knows the buyer who is your direct customer – indeed, they may be hundreds of miles apart, and too busy to communicate over small matters. Therefore it may be possible to chase the accountant very hard without word of it ever getting back to the buyer. It goes without saying that you need to spy out the land carefully before assuming that to be the case, but there certainly are many big firms like that.

In extreme cases, where all else has failed, you can try the ultimate weapon – publicity. Imagine the fuss if an MD were to see the factory railings covered with placards as he or she drives in to work. The first thought would be that there is some union trouble. Then he or she sees the wording: 'XXX plc puts small firms out of business', 'Wife, child and XXX plc to support', 'XXX plc debts unpaid for 5 months', 'TV and Press invited for 10.30 am: XXX plc injustice', and that sort of thing. It has most of the ingredients that the media love. You might even make the national papers if you dress in rags and chain yourself to the railings, but that is not really what you are trying to achieve. What you really want is to get paid. It could well work, but it could equally misfire, by making them really determined to cause you maximum inconvenience before they pay you, and by putting other customers off using you for fear that you might do the same to them. That is why it is suggested only as a last resort, when you have nothing left to lose.

To save you having to go that far, there are one or two techniques to try beforehand. You could include in your terms and conditions of sale (see Section 7.12) a punitive rate of interest on overdue accounts – something like 10 or 20 per cent per month would be enough to make most people sit up. You do not intend to charge it unless forced to, and will be happy to waive it for a cheque in tomorrow morning's post. You might be shouted at a bit, but you might also be paid. That method can be risky too, so perhaps you should use it only on customers whom you regard as risky. You may prefer to rely on the Late Payment of Commercial Debts Act. Under it, firms with less than 50 staff can add interest at bank base rate plus 8 per cent per annum. That percentage can change by ministerial edict. In addition, you could write a personal letter to the customer's MD at home, asking if he or she is aware that this is how the firm behaves towards local small firms, and whether it is official policy to be deceitful. The company promises to pay in 30 days, but does not, forcing small suppliers to borrow at much higher interest than the bigger firm pays in order to save it from borrowing. The MD will be aware that withholding these small sums gives only a tiny advantage, yet to you they mean the difference between survival and failure. The long-term result will be that specialist small suppliers that the large company needs to survive will either go out of business or take on work from the large company only in the last resort. Either way, the firm will be less efficient as a result. Instead the MD could have you competing hard to supply the company if instructions were given for very small suppliers to be paid within 14 days, assuming the delivery to be in order. All very politely, of course. Many large-firm managers see the point already – the CBI, whose members include most large firms, has written to its membership to remind them of the difficulty that slow payment can cause small suppliers. So there are pressures you can put on big firms that companies in your own league would probably ignore.

Never charge interest to members of the public unless you are registered under the Consumer Credit Act.

3.19 HOW LOW CAN SALES FALL WITHOUT CAUSING LOSSES?

This is a useful piece of knowledge, and easy to work out. You have done your P&L budget, and a nice profit shows in the bottom line. Just suppose you do not hit your sales target – should you give up, or are things not that bad? Until you have worked out your *break-even point* you just do not know. The break-even point is the level of sales that will make enough gross margin, or added value, to cover your costs, but not to show a net profit. Table 3.15 works out a break-even point.

So if sales reached only 80 per cent of budget, that is, £72,000, the firm would not actually lose money, but would, of course, make less profit. The cash flow would be adrift, and would need re-forecasting as soon as the trend was apparent. Holiday plans might be changed but there would be no need for despair just yet. In case the method of working it out is not obvious, this is the sequence to follow:

1. Budgeted value added ÷ budgeted sales × 100 = ? per cent.
2. Overheads ÷ ? × 100 = break-even sales.
3. Break-even value-added = overheads.
4. Break-even materials = break-even sales – break-even value-added.

Table 3.15 Working out a break-even point

	Budget		Break-even (figures rounded)
	£		£
Sales	90,000		69,000
Materials	30,000	(33 per cent of sales)	23,000
Value added	60,000	(67 per cent of sales)	46,000
Overheads	46,000	(Remains same)	46,000
Net profit	14,000		–

It is worth dividing your annual figure for break-even sales into weekly and monthly figures. Then you can keep a close check on whether or not you are earning a profit each week.

Another way of showing this is on a simple chart, like the one in Figure 3.2. First, the vertical axis is set up to show £, and the horizontal to show the quantity produced (or productive hours worked, or any other relevant measure of output: usually the bottleneck factor is selected, that which cannot easily be expanded). Then the level of overheads is drawn: by their nature they hardly change whatever the level of sales, so they are labelled 'fixed costs' and shown by a horizontal line. Next, the variable costs are shown. As the name suggests, these vary with the level of sales in the business. In our example they are just materials and nothing else.

If those two costs are added together they produce the figure for 'total costs' – there can be none other than fixed or variable costs in our example, and in most small firms. To show this on the graph is very simple. The line for variable costs is picked up, and laid down higher up, so that it now starts from the point of origin of the fixed costs line. The last line to be drawn in is that for sales. The chart is now complete, as shown in Figure 3.2.

We can now examine it to see what messages it has for us. We can see at a glance where the break-even point is, and how much profit or loss will be made at different levels of sales.

A further beauty of this kind of chart is that it is easy to redraw for different situations. For instance, the business owner might want to know what will happen if the firm takes on a supervisor at a cost of £20,000 a year, freeing the owner to get out on the road to do more selling. How much more turnover would have to come in to justify the decision? How bad would things look if only half of the extra sales needed came in? Another application might be in helping to weigh up merits and draw-

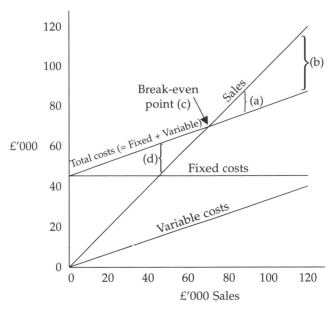

Profit is the surplus of sales over total costs, so that:

(a) there is a profit of £14,000 at £90,000 sales;

(b) there is a profit of £34,000 on sales of £120,000;

(c) there is neither profit nor loss, since total costs and sales are equal, at £69,000 sales – this is the 'break-even point';

(d) at sales of £50,000, there is a loss of £12,000.

Figure 3.2   Graph showing the break-even point

backs of different premises. Which will be more profitable, to operate from the cheap ones that are a bit too small, or the costly ones that are likely to be more efficient? And, once again, what are the effects of under-performing? How low could sales be allowed to fall before the firm started to lose money? These vital issues are seen more clearly in the light of a break-even chart.

Careful examination of the chart also shows up one very important principle for the new starter: keeping costs variable, rather than fixing them straight away. However good your sales forecast and your estimates of cost, the one thing you can say with certainty is that they will be wrong. The best forecasts are those that are least wrong. Your worst forecasts will probably be in the early days, before experience has taught its lessons. How stupid it would be, at the time of greatest ignorance, to tie yourself to fixed commitments that may prove to be not what you really need.

In practical terms this means not tying yourself immediately to owning vehicles and machines, if you can hire someone else's spare capacity instead; not taking on leases until it is really unavoidable; not taking on staff if a subcontractor can be used, and many other ideas besides. Doing this may cost a little more per item in the early days, but it could help you to avoid expensive white elephants. The more you can keep your break-even point down, the more flexible you are. That does not mean that you never make investments in fixed assets, but that you postpone the decision until you really know that it is right.

3.20 COSTINGS FOR MORE COMPLEX SITUATIONS

The system described in Sections 3.3 and 3.4 caters well for most situations. However, the moment you begin to run a range of standard products, or the volumes in the firm change and matters become more complex, your costing system needs to be a little more sophisticated. Perhaps the best system then will be the one known as contribution costing. In essence, contribution costing is saying: 'we can't allocate every item of cost to a product to help us to ascertain its full cost, so let's not even try: we'll allocate just those things that clearly belong to that product and put the resulting profit into a pool out of which we'll meet the overheads and make a profit'. It's quite simple, as Table 3.16 shows.

Table 3.16   Example showing contribution costing

Product:	X	Y	Z
Direct materials (£)	10.00	15.00	25.00
Direct labour (£)	2.00	18.00	5.00
Total direct costs (£)	12.00	33.00	30.00
Average sales value (£)	30.00	55.00	40.00
Contribution to overheads and profit, per item (£)	18.00	22.00	10.00

'Direct' materials and labour are those costs that obviously belong to the product itself. In the case of a screw it would be the metal put into the machine and the staff cost of the machine operator. All other costs – telephone, stores, lighting, vehicles etc – would be paid for out of the 'contribution' made to overheads and profit.

Now, this clearly relates to financial planning, so we shall take it on a stage. The key thing you don't know is whether those contributions will be enough to cover the overheads you will actually incur, and show sufficient profit. The next task is to multiply the contributions by the forecast sales of each item, which produces the total contribution (see Table 3.17).

Does £107,000 cover your needs? If so, fine; if not, can you change volumes, prices or costs, or reduce overheads? You will need to do one or more of them until what you plan to earn meets what you plan to spend.

Table 3.17 Example showing the total contribution

Product:	X	Y	Z	Total
Contribution to overheads and profit, per item (a) (£)	18.00	22.00	10.00	
Sales forecast (units) (b) (£)	2,000	3,000	500	
Total contribution (a) × (b) (£)	36,000	66,000	5,000	£107,000

Two major advantages of this approach have to do with its flexibility. It enables you to play with forecast sales volumes and with predicted costs, to see what effect changes to each might have. In addition, you can see clearly how influential each product is, as a way of helping you to focus on what really earns your keep. In the example above, product Y is by far the most important earner, with product X in second place. In comparison, it hardly matters what you do to product Z, it earns such a tiny proportion (less than 5 per cent) of the total contribution. If that tempts you to discontinue it, beware – the £5,000 it is expected to contribute will have to be earned from somewhere. That last point is a useful caution to anyone thinking of dropping a product that seems to be making a loss. If there is no better prospect to replace it with it might be worth keeping on for its contribution to overheads alone. (That assumes that the sales value is actually greater than its direct costs, of course.)

3.21 KEY JOBS TO DO

- Decide on a costing system – relate this to pricing (Section 2).
- Calculate hourly charge rates for labour.
- Set up a system to monitor performance.
- Decide your policy on granting credit.
- Forecast your cash situation.
- Prepare a P&L budget.
- Calculate your break-even point.

Section 4: How and where to raise money

4.1 AIMS OF THIS SECTION

There has been so much publicity for funds for small business that it sometimes looks as if someone is trying to drown you in easy-to-get money. This section aims to offer a guide through the maze with a few warnings about what they do not tell you – unless you ask.

4.2 GRANTS

First it is important to distinguish grants from loans. Grants are monies given to you with no expectation that they will be paid back – a gift, in effect. A loan, on the other hand, has to be repaid at some time, depending on the conditions on which it was made. The only exception to this general rule is that some grants are given to encourage some activity – providing jobs in a depressed area, for instance. If you take on staff, get the grant and then sack them, you may be required to repay all or part of the grant.

The main grants generally found useful by new, small firms are discussed here. They are:

Allowance for new starters in business

People who have been registered as unemployed can get help under the New Deal from their Jobcentre. The rules vary by age group, but can allow them to collect their benefits while trying out their business idea, so as not to lose all income. Moreover, in some cases grants and a subsidy can be paid to employers, including the self-employed.

Local authority grants

Many grants are given by local authorities in different parts of the country, usually tied to job-creation. Details from Town, County or City Hall, or small business agencies.

The Prince's Trust

This organisation gives grants and loans as well as advice to people under the age of 30 who start businesses. Amounts are usually between a few hundred and a few thousand pounds. They are in the telephone book.

Department of Trade and Industry

This department offers a range of help based on targeting particular opportunities or problems. It is well worth enquiring if you are one of the following:

■ young and unemployed (it provides the 'New Deal');
■ a member of a disadvantaged community or group (you may be eligible for the 'Phoenix Fund' of the Community Finance Initiative);
■ undertaking R&D – applying for their smaller schemes can be remarkably simple;
■ have innovative ideas (they can help with the costs of consultants' investigations);
■ in an area of the country that attracts European Social Funds or European Grants (ask your local Business Link).

There are others, of course, so it is well worth consulting the advisory services before you start up. It is also worth keeping in touch with the grants scene as your business grows, for many more are on offer to the expanding firm. Many grant schemes disqualify people who start the work and then apply, but some work in retrospect.

4.3 WHY BORROW?

Perhaps this sounds like a silly thing to ask, but many firms do set up without borrowing a penny. Usually it involves the customer paying cash with order, the goods to send him being bought on credit or with this cash. Even if such a firm does need to borrow, it will not need much. These ideas are not pure fancy: the great boom in supermarket expansion was financed in exactly this way. If a new shop could be opened with all the stock bought on a month's credit, and if that stock turned over every fortnight or three weeks, all the stock would have been sold and the profit taken before a single item had to be paid for.

Avoiding borrowing is so important that it deserves thinking about. If you can devise a formula that works, you could save the price of a good holiday for two every year in bank interest alone.

Even if borrowing does look inevitable, before you sign for a loan take stock of your personal assets. Sell the caravan and boat – there will be no time to use them, and they will only deteriorate and lose value if you put it off. If your house is bigger than you need, sell it and buy something smaller, releasing some capital and lowering your household expenses. If you live in a high-priced area, move to a more modest neighbourhood and invest the difference in the firm. If you can couple these moves with an increase in your mortgage even more cash should be freed, but it may mean some shopping around among lenders to find one which will allow it. It will also mean a rise in your outgoings to cover the higher repayments. If possible this needs to be done while you are still in a job and can still get any necessary employer's reference to back your mortgage application.

4.4 WHAT SORTS OF LOANS ARE AVAILABLE?

To take the banks first, because they are usually the best source – most comprehensive and flexible – there are basically three sorts of money available: short-term overdrafts, designed to cover day-to-day or month-to-month gaps in your cash flow; medium-term loans (up to five or seven years), best for buying equipment; and long-term (seven to twenty years) mainly used for buying property. There is, of course, a whole range of finance companies and secondary banks, not to mention money-lenders, also trying hard to lend. Many of these are rather tough and ruthless and are the sort of people you should do business with as a very last resort, probably only if you are in business already and in real trouble. They should be used only in very special circumstances if you are trying to start a firm up.

One simple pointer is to see how easy it is to borrow. If all the lender seems interested in is whether they have security for the loan, beware. If they are interested in discussing your project in detail so as to use their experience to help you and to understand the nature of your plans, that is better. If they ask for a written plan and discuss it critically and constructively with you, they are the people you want.

Why, you might ask, favour the lender who makes it hardest to borrow? The answer lies in another question: which do you think will put you in the best position – the lender who will let you have whatever you want, knowing they can bankrupt you to get their money back, or the lender who uses their experience to help you to avoid business pitfalls and to develop a wise business plan, as well as lending what you need? The former is a sort of large-scale pawnbroker, and the latter is a proper banker. That is not to say that the proper banker will not seek some tangible security, but that it will not come first – their main security lies in a customer running a viable company that can meet its obligations. It is not easy to borrow money from banks. They have demanding requirements which make it imperative that you approach them only with a properly thought-out case, presented in the way that they expect to see. Even then the lending is far from automatic.

4.5 SPECIAL FORMS OF FINANCE FROM BANKS

There are special schemes for new starters and very young firms offered by various banks. European money (loan or shares) may be available in some areas. The scene is constantly changing and it is worth shopping around to see what is on offer.

4.6 SECURITY FOR BORROWING

A bank will often ask for security for a loan, for if you fail they want to get their money back. On loans of under a few thousand pounds they are unlikely to feel it necessary. Borrow more and they will probably ask for some security or collateral. This can take almost any form, but for most people it means pledging their share in the family home. Written approval from your spouse or life partner will be needed, even if the house is not in joint names, because a few years ago a bank tried to evict the wife of a man whose business had failed so that they could sell the family home. She took the case to court, claiming her right to live in the house, and the court found in her favour. So now the banks understandably require spouses to sign away that right in advance.

In all the excitement of planning your business, it is important to remember just what you are putting at risk. You might be able to avoid this by reading Section 4.7, or relatives may lend, or they may guarantee loans.

4.7 THE GOVERNMENT LOAN GUARANTEE SCHEME

There has always been a lot of discussion between banks and small business organisations over how difficult or not it was to borrow from the banks. The banks said they lent money to any viable project presented to them. Small business organisations, on the other hand, maintained that the banks were obsessed by tangible security. They said the banks would lend only to people who had assets and were prepared to pledge them as collateral. This locked out a lot of people from getting into business, so the argument went, and only the government could break the stalemate. The government did act, by launching the Small Firms Loan Guarantee Scheme (SFLGS). In effect it is an insurance policy covering most of the money you borrow. It applies to most firms with an annual turnover of up to £3 million (£5 million in manufacturing), and the amount loaned and costs depend on the age of the firm. The premium is an extra loading on your interest rate. It works like this:

	Aged up to two years	Aged over two years
Loan:	£5,000–10,000	£5,000–250,000
Guarantee:	70%	85%

The extra interest is 2 per cent a year, so that if you are paying 12 per cent interest to the bank you will pay 14 per cent in total. It is certainly not cheap, but if it is the only way you can realistically plan to borrow what you need, it may be worthwhile. Most high street banks offer it, as well as a number of others. There are some restrictions on the types of firms supported.

4.8 NON-BANK BORROWING

HP (hire purchase) or credit sale agreements are available to businesses and are often much more expensive than bank borrowing. HP or 'finance' companies, as they like to be known, do offer rather more than the three-year loans on cars or furniture that most members of the public associate them with. In fact, you can borrow practically any amount from them for up to seven to ten years, but they will be very concerned indeed to have adequate security cover. They also offer equipment leasing, under which you – in effect – hire the asset and never own it.

There are other sources, such as merchant banks, a category that includes 3i (formed by a consortium of banks and the Bank of England), who will generally invest only to make as much money from you as possible (and why not?), leasing agreements and factoring (the finance company pay, say, 80 per cent of your invoice the moment you send it out, and when the customer pays you get, say, another 15 per cent; sometimes they take the credit risks too. They hang on to the rest as their reward). These are not always appropriate to the very young company, and your accountant's advice is needed. He or she might also know a private investor willing to buy shares in your firm, sometimes known as 'Business Angels', in order to get tax relief under the Enterprise Investment Scheme, which Inland Revenue leaflet IR37 explains. This is very complex, so both sides should seek advice from accountants.

In Wales and Scotland the Development Agencies have some funds for small business. They can help to put you on to the right form of finance for your project, as well as giving up-to-date information on the lending situation in general.

4.9 INTEREST RATES

There is a nasty little trick resorted to by some financiers who should know better. They sometimes quote a 'flat' rate of interest, which sounds very attractive, but it is not quite as good as it seems. Suppose you borrow £100 at a flat rate of 10 per cent for a year, repaying £25 per quarter plus the 10 per cent interest – £10 – at the end. That is fair enough, you might say – but it is not, you have been cheated. The £10 interest would truly be 10 per cent only if you borrowed the £100 for the whole year; but you did not, you paid back £25 every quarter. In other words, you borrowed £25 for three months, £25 for six months, £25 for nine months, and £25 for a year. Thus, a true 10 per cent interest on that £100 loan is £6.25, not £10 (see Table 4.1). A £10 charge is in fact a whopping 16 per cent interest rate. How do you tell? Look for the small print, and if there is none (or if it is a verbal quote) ask if the 'true rate' or 'annual percentage rate' (APR) has been given. By law, they are obliged to tell you and to quote the true rate of interest.

Interest rates can be 'fixed' or 'floating' – 'fixed' speaks for itself; 'floating' ones move up and down with the bank base rates. 'Base rate' is the basic rate to which a few percentage points are added to quote rates to borrowers. Small firms normally borrow at 3 to 4 percentage points over base rate, and the largest at one point over – the extra over 'base' is related to risk and administrative cost. Thus, if base rate is quoted at 5 per cent, small firms will usually borrow at 8 to 9 per cent.

Table 4.1 Example showing interest on a loan

Borrowing Interest				
£25 for ¼ of year @ 10% p.a.	=	£25 × 10% × ¼	=	£0.625
£25 for ½ of year @ 10% p.a.	=	£25 × 10% × ½	=	£1.250
£25 for ¾ of year @ 10% p.a.	=	£25 × 10% × ¾	=	£1.875
£25 for whole year @ 10% p.a.	=	£25 × 10% × 1	=	£2.500
£100				£6.25

4.10 OTHER FEES AND CHARGES

Bank charges are negotiable, despite what the price-lists suggest. When you are enquiring about opening your account, shop around and make it clear that you want low-cost banking as well as a good service. Query the charge per cheque, the cost of interviews, and other charges (especially if you trade internationally – a fixed charge plus a percentage for processing export documents can play havoc with margins). When borrowing money, you will probably have to resign yourself to paying any legal costs the lender might incur (eg solicitors' fees and Land Registry dues for register-ing a charge on your house) but you could possibly negotiate a reduction or complete waiving of 'arrangement fees'. At any rate, whenever you deal with the bank or anyone else it is always worth asking if there are any extra charges you do not know about. And it is not just fees payable here and now that you need to look out for: there can be penalties for not spending the whole loan after they have agreed to lend it to you, and for repaying it early. Some business-support agencies have negotiated low arrangement fees for their clients with some banks.

4.11 SELECTING A BANK

Banks as a whole can look fairly forbidding, but the important thing to remember is that they are only shops. They rent out money, and sell money transmission and storage services.

Choosing which bank and which branch to deal with is very impor-tant. While they all look more or less the same they do have different services and attitudes. Even within one banking firm, branch managers can differ a lot. What do you need to look out for? Well, as a new starter you are probably better off with a small branch where you will deal direct with the manager. In larger branches you will deal with a trainee manager who may be very bright but perhaps does not have the breadth of business experience to be very helpful to you. The manager has all sorts of limits to observe, and in a small branch he or she may have to refer decisions up the line for approval if they involve more than a certain figure; this is called a 'discretionary limit'. When you shop around before deciding where to bank, try to go for branches of a size that will serve you best. For instance, if you expect to do a lot of exporting you will probably need a bigger branch, and almost certainly not one of the small banks. In some banks, you may have no choice but to deal with the Small Business Advisor.

Look at the range of services offered: before you meet the manager make sure you have read all that firm's leaflets on its services to small businesses in general and on any specialist services you may require. To get them, it is best to write to the bank's Head Office: banks are large and complex organisations and not all bank managers can keep fully up to date on everything that their firm offers. Then, look at the manager – young, with a name to make, might he or she do it all 'by the book'? Or a year or two from retirement and winding down? Does he or she seem to want to help? Is there real interest in your project and does he or she offer ideas? Ask if a career move is expected soon, for few things can be more frustrating than working hard at presenting yourself and your project to Ms Smith only to find that she hands over to Mr Jones before your loan is agreed. It is said that some banks tend to transfer their staff every few years for the same reason as the Foreign Office does its diplomats: it prevents them from 'going native', getting so enmeshed in the local community that they start representing the customers to the bank, rather than the other way around. You will kick yourself to find that if you had asked for £29,900 it could have been OK'd locally, but the £30,100 you actually requested has to go to the Regional Office who will judge it more coldly than the branch manager who, as well as having the figures, also has your magnetic charm to help persuade him or her. So ask what the 'discretionary limit' is, the amount they can approve without referring it upwards. They might not want to tell you, but you can take as a rough guide that it will be about £100,000 in a small market-town branch.

Most important of all to some businesses is the question of what sort of branch they will be dealing with. Some banks have split off their dealings with business from the rest of their transactions, to the extent of creating specialist 'business only' branches. The idea is that the business customer will get a more relevant service.

4.12 PRESENTING YOUR CASE TO THE BANK

In Section 4.4 it was said that a proper banker will seek more than just collateral or security for a loan. What else will they look for? In the case of an established firm they look at the track record. Merely to have survived proves something, and there may even be a progressive pattern of profitable growth. The bank manager will also look for some straightforward explanation of how much is wanted, what it will be spent on, how long it is wanted for and how it will be repaid: in other words, some forecasting is needed.

Because the new business starter has no track record, he or she has to work a little bit harder at putting the case across – it is as much of a challenge to your selling ability as getting an order. You have to prove that you have thought things through and have a good chance of showing the bank a profit on the deal, or they will not be interested. At the same time, you have to convince the bank that you have got what it takes to make your paper plans work in real life. Because most intelligent people ask to borrow money that will make money, most failures to borrow are because of poor presentation. To sharpen up the presentation, some people advocate trying your case out first on a bank that you do not intend to use. It pays to talk your idea over informally with the banks you have shortlisted, taking into account any points the managers have raised during informal discussions. The paper should include brief summaries (no more than two pages on each, and preferably less), on:

- The product or service you plan to provide.
- The markets you plan to serve, competitors, customers, and why customers will buy from you.
- The experience and background of you and any other principal person involved.
- Premises and equipment, with costings.
- For the first year, a detailed monthly cash-flow forecast and a detailed profit-and-loss budget, with outline plans for the following two years.
- A statement of how much you want to borrow, what for, how long you need it for, how you plan to repay.
- Security (if any) that you can offer.

Whatever you do, do not be tempted to doctor the figures to make them look good, but put down what you can reasonably expect to achieve. Getting the money is not the whole job: you will be expected to fulfil your forecast. Let the bank manager have all this a couple of days before your appointment to discuss it. If you do not feel confident in preparing it all yourself, do as much as you can and get your accountant to help pull it all together. Most of the advisory agencies can also help to do this and may cost a lot less.

Finally, do not forget that some bankers still think in terms of lending a pound for every pound that the owner puts in. Thus they are likely to be more impressed by people who have some capital behind them. But financial standing is not all. They will also judge your competence and your character. As one senior banker recently said, 'Banking is a "people" business'. By this he meant that all the paper plans in the world may be fine, but in the end he decides whether or not to lend on what his instincts and experience tell him about the person on the other side of the desk.

4.13 KEY JOBS TO DO

- Investigate grants.
- Decide your financing strategy – how much do you put in, how much will you borrow and on what terms?
- Create and present your case to potential lenders.

Institute for Entrepreneurship

ideas, innovation... future

Entrepreneurship at the cutting edge

The Institute for Entrepreneurship (IfE), School of Management, is a recent venture for the University of Southampton funded by a start-up award from the Office of Science and Technology's Science Enterprise Challenge Fund and Higher Education Innovation Fund.

Our programmes are designed for those who wish to undertake an in-depth study of particular aspects of business venturing and entrepreneurship and who wish to attain a formal, fully recognised academic qualification.

MSc/Dip Business Venturing (MBV) is an innovative, fast track programme that blends practical experience and learning. This formal qualification will prepare you for self-employment and business start-up, for employment in larger, innovative organisations as intrapreneurs developing spin-outs and spin-ins, and other corporate venturing activities or in business and professional support agencies. Available full-time and part-time.

Professional MBV is a part time stream of MSc/Dip Business Venturing and is delivered in block taught semester mode.

MSc/Dip Business Venturing (Social Entrepreneurship) offers specialised knowledge and skills to address the challenges of development and sustainability of social enterprises in a variety of sectors.

MSc/Dip Business Venturing (Entrepreneurship Education) is designed for those who wish to conduct training or teach at Further Education or Higher Education level in the subjects of business venturing or entrepreneurship and/or social entrepreneurship.

PG Certificate Entrepreneurship provides a broad knowledge and understanding of the business venturing process.

MPhil/PhD Programme offers an opportunity to pursue leading-edge, high-profile academic research in a topic of your choice related to the research interests of the IfE. Available full-time and part-time.

For further information and to apply, please contact:
Margaret Westwood at the Institute for Entrepreneurship
Telephone: 023 8059 8899, Fax: 023 8059 8981, Email: ife@soton.ac.uk
or visit www.ife.soton.ac.uk/Programmes-and-Courses/

Open Evening:
Thursday, 19 May 2005, 5.30 – 7.30pm
School of Management, Building 2, Highfileld Campus
Univestity of Southampton

University of Southampton

Institute for Entrepreneurship
School of Management
University of Southampton
Building 25, Level 3, Highfield
Southampton SO17 1BJ

Section 5: E-business and the small firm

5.1 AIMS OF THIS SECTION

There are five main ways in which the technologies available on PCs – and now to an extent on telephones – can benefit your firm by:

- increasing sales through expanding your geographical cover;
- reducing costs through publishing catalogues on the web and on CD or DVD;
- reducing costs and increasing choice through expanding the range of suppliers available to you;
- saving time through speeding up and simplifying communications;
- saving time through making information more readily accessible.

While some of these topics are discussed separately in this book, they deserve to be brought together at some point. Here, we look at them as a whole in order to put the hype into perspective and to provide the basis for your considered judgement of exactly how your firm will best use the useful bits and reject those that may produce profit for somebody, but not for you. The section is not comprehensive – whole books are devoted to the subject – but it should give you a general idea of the issues and some pointers on what to do next.

5.2 PROBLEMS WITH E-BUSINESS

Firstly, it needs to be recognised that a PC costs money and can be an awful nuisance, too. Common problems include:

- *Taking up a lot of your time:* you brief a website designer, who then fails to get it right, meaning you have to invest even more time correcting things.
- *Badly designed websites:* this is often a result of a designer who fulfils his or her personal mission, but doesn't serve the needs of your customers.
- *Unwanted e-mail:* you may be flooded with messages in numbers that you cannot hope to deal with.
- *Missing e-mail messages:* this can happen when you fail to get your messages past another ISP's 'firewall', but are not told it has failed.
- *Digital crime:* you can be open to credit card fraud or people hacking into your system. This could leave you unable to operate your bank account.
- *Lost data:* this can happen when you are prompted to update programs, but are not told that doing so could lose some or all of your data.
- *The need to keep up to date:* you may need to update programs to new versions that take up so much memory that you have to upgrade your computer. This can leave you unable to operate your business while your outdated model is out of action.

To redress the balance, let's try to find some positive reason for using computers in your firm by looking again in the next few sections at the list of five points in Section 5.1.

5.3 INCREASING YOUR SALES VIA THE INTERNET

If you think about the nature of selling via the web, it resembles in many ways the methods of selling by conventional mail order. Let's look at it from the point of view of your customer – see Table 5.1.

Table 5.1 shows why some people see the web in its present stage of development as just another mail-order medium. Moreover, they believe it is one that is less convenient to use and less trusted than conventional sources. Of course, this situation is changing by the day as more people conduct more transactions online. Evidence has been cited that good, off-the-page mail-order advertising pulls in orders from about 3 per cent of the people who read it. According to some sources, a similar percentage of the general population has so far bought over the internet as a whole.

Table 5.1 Customers' perceptions of similarities and differences between conventional mail order and selling via the web

Similarities	Mail order	Web
Are you easy to find?	sometimes	sometimes
Can I see the product itself?	no	no
Can I see a video demonstration, via DVD, CD ROM, cassette or online?	sometimes	sometimes
Can I actually see that you have stock?	no	no
Do I have to pay up-front?	yes	yes
Can I be certain about delivery dates?	no	no
Will delivery be at a convenient time?	not always	not always
Differences		
Am I fearful of misuse of my credit card details?	not usually	decreasingly, but it does happen
Do I need special equipment to read the catalogue?	no	yes
Is the small print easy to find and read?	usually	not always
Is it easy to track you down if I'm dissatisfied?	usually	not always

This comparison encourages us to look at the hard facts behind the hype before any crucial decisions are made. The pundits tell us that business-to-business sales on the internet are likely to be far higher than sales from business-to-consumer.

The question of whether you should take orders over the web or confine yourself to publishing a catalogue on it is not addressed here (for this, see Section 2). Instead, we look at some of the practicalities that you will need to know to help you to decide, and which will help you to make realistic plans if you do go ahead.

5.4 CATALOGUES ON THE WEB AND ON CD OR DVD

Organisations put their product and service information on the internet in the hope of securing a number of useful benefits. They hope to:

■ expand the range of people who hear about them;

- save on printing paper catalogues;
- save on posting paper catalogues;
- make updates possible within days rather than weeks.

Many times, these hopes come true, but many companies find that they cannot do away with paper catalogues completely. Customers may be attracted by a website, but often feel the need for a piece of paper in their hand as written confirmation of its promises. So, the real advantage may lie in expanding your cover of the potential market.

Once you have attracted the customer – either via a website or more traditional means – a CD or DVD can be an attractive alternative to a paper catalogue. The disk enables you to offer a video demonstration of the service in action or the product in use. It can use sound, stills, moving pictures, text and charts. Again, because it is not 'hard copy', it may not be a complete replacement for a written production, but it can certainly be a powerful enhancement.

5.5 PURCHASING VIA THE WEB

Just as potential customers can come across you via a web search, you can use the web to source *your* supplies. For most businesses in their early stages, the things they have to buy in are either occasional purchases (machines, furniture and equipment, for example) or are pretty trivial in the overall scheme of things (stationery or office supplies, say). Nevertheless, there may be useful discounts to be had on the internet, which you can use in one of two ways. You can either buy from the web-based firm or show their offer to your local supplier who may be willing to match it.

If you are in a specialised industry and expect to use large quantities of specific supplies, the web may disclose all sorts of opportunities. However, if you are a specialist in an area of business already, you may already know about the best suppliers.

So, some options to bear in mind when buying via the web are:

- Buy from the web, where serious savings will make up for the time spent tracking them down.
- Use web prices to influence your local suppliers; they may be able to give you service at short notice, whereas most web-based companies will be based further away and will be at the mercy of delivery firms' schedules.
- Avoid using the web for trivial purchases – it will waste more of your time than it can ever be worth. When searching the web, it is tempting to stay on it for longer than you need to – such time would be better spent earning your income.

5.6 ELECTRONIC COMMUNICATIONS

The main two-way communications routes open to your computer used to be confined to e-mail and conferencing. Some firms currently find that publishing parts lists, price lists, availability schedules and other changeable information either on web pages or on disk can improve customer service and cuts costs. The new dimension is added by WAP-enabled mobile phones which can be used to show product features and performance live. Already my local antiques auction is crowded with people using them to send pictures back to colleagues and customers.

E-mail

Increasingly, suppliers and customers expect even the smallest business to have an e-mail address. The advantages of e-mail are:

- *Cheapness (once you have the computer and software):* each message need cost no more than a local telephone call lasting a minute or two. That applies whether it is to your neighbour or to Australia. Consequently, if you need to communicate a lot with people overseas, its effect on your costs can be dramatic.
- *Absence isn't a problem:* unlike a telephone call, you don't have to be present to receive it. This is especially useful if your business operates across different timezones or if you (or your contact) are out of range of telephones for much of the day. The act of telephoning someone in New Zealand has to be preceded by careful calculations of his or her local time, whereas sending an e-mail requires no such consideration – your contact will simply pick it up next time he or she logs on.
- *Written record:* the law in the UK has recently got round to accepting faxed messages as admissible evidence. Moreover, the Electronic Communications Act makes it possible under certain conditions for a signed internet or e-mail document to be as binding as ink and paper. This begs the question of what a 'signature' is. There are several digital signature programs, but until a common standard emerges it might be wise to print and file any e-mails that are particularly important.

Good e-mail software allows you to create an address book of the people who contact you. That can help you to send mass mailings, as well as protect you from the consequences of the automatic deletion of messages after a given time. It can be annoying to want to write to a person who contacted you six months ago, only to find that your sole source of their address is their message, which was automatically deleted after three months.

Security is of increasing concern, given the large number of viruses spread by malicious people. Ask your PC supplier about the security software that is best for your applications.

Conferencing

If your business requires you frequently to consult a number of people and have discussions with them, it may be worth considering electronic conferencing software. The snag is that *all* participants have to have the software installed, but the time and trouble involved in doing this could well pay off, especially if you are operating across timezones.

Basically, an electronic conference is a bit like e-mail. You type what you want to say into your computer, then the system distributes it to all participants. People can respond and kick ideas around, no matter where they are or when they see the contributions made by others. It can be done by plain e-mail by using the 'address book' facility, but if you do a lot of it the convenience of the true conferencing system may appeal. It is possible to set up any number of conferences on any topics with any combination of people you choose to include. Take the case of a specialist geological consultant who is part of a consortium of specialists bidding for work from an oil company. There may be confidential matters of pricing that he wants to discuss only with the principals among his partners; general issues to do with assembling the bid that need to be discussed by individuals among the bidders; and requests that need to be discussed with the oil company alone regarding clarifications of definitions within the tender document. In each case, a separate conference can be created, each with its own membership. Nobody needs to know what conferences exist other than those of which they are a part.

An extra gloss on computer-based conferencing is the potential for the addition of video. I say 'potential' even though the technology exists and is available at reasonable prices, because performance is not yet up to the standard needed by most business operators. The images are jerky and out of sync with sound, but get better the faster your broadband connection. Again, for videoconferencing to work, everyone who takes part needs to have the right hardware (high-speed broadband, fast modem, TV camera, microphone, etc) as well as software.

As distribution of broadband builds, voice transmission over the internet will grow. It means that no call anywhere in the world will cost more than local rates.

5.7 INFORMATION FROM THE WEB

The internet has been widely hyped as an information source. The reality is often different. Often, the information you need is not yet published on the internet. Moreover, unlike printed publications, there are few safeguards guaranteeing accuracy of information on the internet.

Print publishers invest considerable time and money in making a product that is accurate and well presented. Professional librarians act as gatekeepers, buying publications only from reputable sources, so untrustworthy material never reaches their shelves. The idea is that the member of a library is able to trust what he or she reads (subject to the usual caveats about the accuracy of survey information).

However, the process of researching information on the internet is entirely different. There are few barriers to entry, so material of dubious quality sits alongside that of the highest integrity. Certainly, the web can be useful – sometimes amazingly so – but you need to be sure of the trustworthiness of a source before swallowing whole what it may be telling you.

It is worth using more than one search engine when carrying out a search. None of them is entirely effective yet, and you can get quite different results by posing the same question to different engines.

5.8 SETTING UP A WEBSITE

So powerful are the software tools available today that it is possible for an amateur to create and maintain a website. If you are practised at doing it, it would be foolish to pay someone else to do it for you. However, for most people setting up a business, there are other demands on their time from issues with which only they can deal. Thus, you should consider seriously the idea of having someone else create your website for you so you can devote your precious time to other matters.

Here, I assume that you have taken the strong hint in the previous paragraph and want to commission a firm to develop your website for you. While doing so cuts down on the time you spend on it, it does not mean that you can devote no time at all to the project. On the contrary, you will be heavily involved – or you will risk getting a website that does not meet your needs. The sort of supplier you commission will greatly influence the usefulness of what you get. Many website developers are primarily software people; they may be excellent at creating a site that works in a technical sense, but you need a site that also works in terms of being customer-friendly. Not all technical people understand how to do this.

Therefore, it may be worth seeking out a developer that has staff with multiple strengths or one that has come to website design from a traditional marketing background. In either case, you should find that the developer's main focus will be on getting things right from your customer's point of view.

The work of development follows this nine-point plan. If you use a full-service website designer, most of this should be done as part of the package:

1. *Conceptualising.* This involves creating the idea in your mind of exactly what the website is for and to whom it is addressed. Very clear and rigorous thinking is essential. You need to specify precisely which audience you wish to address and what outcomes you want the site to accomplish.

2. *Provision Strategy.* Decide broadly how the service is to be provided. Will you do it all in-house? Will some or all of the services be bought in? Which ones? Will you need extra telephone lines? Of what quality? Who will construct the site, and at what cost? What goals will you set for performance? (This links to items 3 and 4 below – without some idea of desired performance, costs and volumes you cannot decide on the economics of the options you consider.)

3. *Research.* What volume of traffic is it reasonable to expect? How will it be achieved? What bandwidth and hardware platforms does it imply? What are the various suppliers (site designers, web hosts, telecommunications suppliers, payment contractors) offering? In particular, which backup and recovery systems do they operate and what are their implications? How do they handle errors? What maintenance, updating and redesign can *you* do, and at what cost? What if you want to add a new feature at a later date, such as an online ordering and payment system? Are the above companies' helplines staffed well enough to mean you can always get through? What domain names (eg fred-smith.com) could you use? Which are actually available? (Do a search through one of the domain-name search engines on the web, such as www.netlink.co.uk or www.corpex.co.uk.)

4. *Analysis.* Put together everything learnt under item 3 and see if item 2 still makes sense. If it doesn't, rethink it and go through the process again. Keep on doing this until item 2 really works in terms of what you have learnt.

5. *Design.* By this point, you should be ready to prepare a design brief for the designer. Do this, even if you plan to do the work yourself – it is amazing how you can let the main aims slip when you get too involved in the details. Holding yourself accountable against a design brief can be a useful discipline.

The quality and cost of what you get back from the specialists is usually closely related to the trouble you take to brief them accurately and clearly in the first place. To do this at all effectively, you need to get very clear in your own mind exactly what you want the message to convey and how. In addition, you need to know what hardware and software your typical customer has.

Put the brief in writing and talk it over with the designer before finalising it: the designer may be able to suggest more cost-effective ways of achieving your goals, and it would be foolish not to listen to the expert. Equally, you need to be wary of the delight that some designers take in using the latest tools which, though they may create some amazing effects, could be using software that is not fully debugged. Moreover, it may use up more memory than you can afford and could slow disastrously the speed at which your customer downloads. After seeing the demonstration on the designer's machine (which will be very advanced) always try it out on something more representative of what your customers will use. If it is going to crash on a more humble computer, now is the time to find out.

Remember that the fastest that most customers' home modems will manage to download your pages is about 28k per second and that research tells us that people won't wait for more than eight seconds before moving on. This gives you a maximum size of (8 × 28 =) 224k for your homepage. Remember, that is a maximum; the more you can keep it below that the better. Keep language simple and direct. Have a clear structure, with buttons to access other parts of the site always on show. Don't overload each page. Don't use material that constantly moves – it irritates after only a short time. Use pictures only when they help – they slow down the download time dreadfully. Keep graphics simple for the same reason. Although you have delegated responsibility to the designer to meet your brief, it remains your task to see that he or she does the job, so stay in touch and monitor progress.

6. *Test.* Check for spelling, grammar and comprehensibility. Don't rely on just your own judgement but get the most difficult, critical and pedantic people you know to join in, for this is the last chance to get it right before you go live. Look for potential libels. Ensure that the English you use is simple and straightforward for it could be read anywhere in the world. Check that the integration of the site works – buttons really do link to where they should, and fast. Be sure that all of the page is visible (some companies' pages conceal the button for the very link you want). Check that response times – on a machine of the type that your customers will have – meet the specification you laid down. Test the pages on all the popular browsers (software that enables web searches). Check that any hyperlinks are to sites that are still live.

7. *Launch.* Register your domain name (via your ISP or at www.nic.uk or www.netnames.co.uk). (In practice you may choose to do this at stage 3 above, to make sure that someone else doesn't take your chosen name in the interim.) Register with the main search engines. At first you may choose to launch discreetly and ask for feedback on the site from those who stumble upon it. Put the address on every item of stationery, promotional material, any buildings you may operate from and all company vehicles. See if you can get your trade organisation to give you a hyperlink in return for a modest payment. Offer to put hyperlinks to related (but not competitive) sites, in return to links to yours. Undertake any advertising you plan for the site.

8. *Review.* Check frequently how your site looks and works. Listen to customer feedback. Watch your competitors and other sites, to get fresh ideas. See how long it takes to load at peak times, and speak to your service provider if the agreed service level is not met.

9. *Maintain.* Revise the site to ensure that it continues to meet your and your customers' requirements of it.

5.9 WEBSITE COSTS

Some of the costs have been mentioned above. As has been recognised, there is also a cost involved in your time. While you may learn a lot and have some fun by doing it all (or most) yourself, please do consider the need to spend your time where it really counts. If someone else can do the job, any job, maybe they should be allowed to, freeing you to do the things that only you can do.

The complexity of setting up the site can be hugely simplified if you go to a single source, and it need not cost much either. Some local business-advice organisations offer a package of setting up and maintaining a website for around £2,000 plus £250 a year. They also run two-day courses which promise that you will create a fully functioning website. (Knowledge of Windows and Microsoft Office are needed.) Alternatively, you could dip a toe in by buying a package from BT WebWorld (www.bt.com) which will give you a basic, template-based, four-page site for around £500. Later, if that worked well for you, you could consider upgrading it via one of the more complex, made-to-measure packages. Alternatively, for about £25 a mouth, they offer a complete online catalogue.

5.10 CREATING A CD OR DVD CATALOGUE

A single CD ROM can hold 700 Mb, a quantity of information equivalent to about 250,000 pages of text, 15,000 graphic images or an hour of sound.

Thus you can mix and match a number of items for storage – pictures and diagrams, explanatory text, sound and video images (which are the hungriest for space). If that is not enough, a DVD will hold six times as much. The cost of producing a single CD is about a pound, making it far cheaper than any printed medium and much more versatile. It is also a great deal cheaper to update as you want to change the contents.

However, there is a downside – the cost of setting up the content. Text is pretty easy to create but, except in very specialised situations, is not what you expect to fill a disk with. Diagrams can be created at low cost on a computer by anyone with the right software. Simple ones are well within the range of the programs supplied as standard with most office machines. More complex ones may have to be created by a specialist with specialised software. Even so, they need not cost a great deal. In an hour, for which you might pay £80, an expert should be able to produce quite a lot of stunning material for you. To have sound and video you may need actors (you need to be a good presenter to feature in a video, but there is a stamp of authority and commitment from the boss and staff appearing in person), professional filming and recording and perhaps music rights. Even then, the costs are not over. A master disk needs to be created, from which copies can be made. That usually costs up to £1,000. After that, the cost of replication is very low – £1–2 each is typical for quantities of several hundred. Then your disk needs packaging, both to protect it in transit and to confer some impact, something that makes the customer want to open it and play it straight away. It is obviously at a disadvantage to printed media in that you cannot immediately read it without the aid of a machine. It takes a certain amount of trouble to start to read it, and the customer must want to read it enough to push it to the front of his or her personal queue of things to be done. Many of the replication companies offer a package design and print service as well. How much to allow for packaging? It depends on how elaborate it needs to be, but budget a couple of pounds for working purposes, and don't be surprised if it turns out higher. Don't let these costs turn you away from disks – instead, think how much you stand to save on postage as compared with a conventional catalogue.

As the above suggests, creating a disk can be more like producing a film than commissioning a catalogue. The complexity of the operation is not overwhelming, but is certainly greater than that involved in making a catalogue. Moreover, the fact that it can be updated so frequently almost certainly means that it will be. That in turn creates more work. You need to have a clear idea of who will undertake that work, for it can be con-siderable.

Much of what is noted about dealing with web page designers in item 5 of Section 5.8 is equally applicable when dealing with designers of disks – again, you should liaise closely with the designer, making it clear what you want and getting any feedback he or she may have to offer. As with web page designers, you should be wary of designers who use new flashy software at the expense of the usefulness of the disk – remember that most users will have basic machines. You need to know what hardware and software your typical customer has. The user's computer will need a CD or DVD slot, a sound card, a video card and – if moving pictures are used – suitable software.

Once the master is made, production time can be fast: one firm's website offers different prices based on a turnaround of between 3 and 10 days. This makes it possible to think of updates on a monthly – or even more frequent – basis. Each update will call for a new master, but some firms will feel that the edge that frequent updating gives them more than compensates for the cost.

Finally, if people are to make use of it, they need to know that the disk exists. How do you plan to distribute it, and to whom? How will you know if it succeeds? Here we come back to the point at which we started: before setting out, you need to know who it is for and what it is supposed to do.

5.11 KEY JOBS TO DO

- Decide your internet strategy – how you will use it, if at all.
- Decide your catalogue and documentation strategy – whether it will be on a disk or paper-based.
- Decide your communications strategy – whether to use e-mail, conferencing or videoconferencing.
- Decide your acquisition strategy – what you will do in-house and what you will buy in.
- Read *E-Business Essentials* by M Haig, Kogan Page, 2001.

Future-proof your career

One of the most
innovative franchises in the world,
is seeking to develop new business
opportunities across the UK.

This is the ideal opportunity to own an ever-evolving,
cutting-edge business *...and to be your own boss.*

Hire Intelligence will help you rent premium brand, state-of-the-art
IT and AV equipment to businesses.

We provide you with intensive training and access to 20,000 items of
equipment, supported by a proven franchise network and an
internationally proven business model.

Intrigued? Just contact Hire Intelligence.

Hire Intelligence
The Intelligent Choice in Computer & Audiovisual Rentals

Hire Intelligence UK
Ilmer Meadows, Ilmer, HP27 9RD
Sales: **0845 600 7272**
General Enquiries: **01844 342 862**
enquiries@hire-intelligence.co.uk
www.hire-intelligence.co.uk

**BRITISH
FRANCHISE
ASSOCIATION
FULL MEMBER**

Essentials for Starting a Successful Business

Trading Structure

Choosing an efficient business structure will probably be the most significant decision you will make in during the first few years of your business. Private limited companies are the most widely used and are suitable for the vast majority of businesses.

Benefits of a Limited Company

Limited Liability

Forming a limited company will separate your personal identity from your business. Sole traders have no protection against unlimited personal liability for business debt and law suits against the business. Incorporating a limited company will limit your liability to a creditor to the value of the limited company. This safeguards your personal assets in the unfortunate event of the business failing.

Longevity

Limited companies may continue to operate regardless of what happens to directors, officers or shareholders. If a sole trader or a partner dies the business may automatically end or it may become involved in complex legal disputes. Limited companies have an unlimited life and may extend beyond the life of the founders.

Tax

A sole trader pays tax on all income. A limited company pays corporation tax on profits only. Furthermore a sole trader may pay up to 40% on all income. A limited company pays corporation tax of between 19%-30% on profits only. Business Inc provides a complete company formation service to suit a wide range of needs.

Office and Communication

Keeping start-up costs down is an essential prerequisite of starting any successful business. Every penny saved here will go along way to boosting your operating budget.

Virtual Office

A complete Virtual Office package will provide the subscriber/s with a telephone number which is typically answered in the subscriber's company name. Calls may be transferred to another number e.g. subscribers mobile telephone. The full package will also include a dedicated fax line. Incoming faxes are automated to instantly deliver the fax to the subscriber's email address. The complete virtual office should also include an address and mail forwarding service. In most cases it is possible to subscribe to one or several elements of the service. The most attractive feature is of course the saving over bricks and mortar.

Internet Communication & Presence

The internet has emerged as a major outlet for businesses to sell and promote their products and services. The governments Office of National Statistics published that in 2003 UK internet sales reached £23.3 billion. The internet represents tremendous opportunity for small and medium size business because it offers a level playing field between small companies and large corporates. A well designed website and secure email will add significant value to your new business.
Business Inc provides UK company registration and administration services, offshore incorporations in 19 jurisdiction, virtual office, branding, wed design and hosting, merchant accounts, payroll and other business service. See our advertisement in the main opposite the contents page or visit our award winning website www.business-inc.co.uk for further information.

Section 6: Your business name and legal status – limited company or not?

6.1 AIMS OF THIS SECTION

This section describes the different sorts of business constitution available. There is a lot of difference legally between John Smith, the window-cleaner, John Smith Window-cleaners, and John Smith Window-cleaners Limited; each has its advantages and drawbacks, and the law puts different obligations on each. After reading the section you should be able to choose the one that is right for you.

6.2 THE CHOICES AVAILABLE

You can trade as any of these: sole trader, partnership, or limited company. There are some rare variants of those forms of constitution which we shall not deal with. From time to time there is interest in the idea of forming co-operatives. They can be close to being partnerships or limited companies, but it is a specialised field for which specialist advice is available. Here we shall deal with only the three most popular types of constitution.

6.3 SOLE TRADER

This is the simplest form of business, and the way that the vast majority of very small firms operate. The income from the business is your personal income, most business expenses can be offset against it for tax purposes, and tax is paid at personal rates, rather than corporation tax rates. (Recently there has been little to choose between them, but at times in the past they have been very different – and could, presumably, be so again.) Equally, the losses of the business are yours too, along with all the usual risks of business. If the firm fails you will have to pay the debts. On the other hand it is very easy to set up: there is no need to ask permission or get a licence. You just start up. Of course, there are some activities for which a permit is needed, but that applies whether or not they are sole traders – nobody may operate a slaughterhouse without a licence, for example. Sole traders and partners pay Class 2 and Class 4 National Insurance contributions.

6.4 PARTNERSHIP

Partnership is much the same as sole tradership, except that there must obviously be two or more partners. The key point is that each partner takes on responsibility for all the liabilities of the partnership, so if your partner runs off with all the money, you are left to pay all the business bills, not just your share of them. This applies even if the bills were run up without your knowledge. So taking a partner is a bit like giving out a blank cheque, plus permission to help themselves to your house, car and other property. A partner therefore needs to be chosen with care. Even when there is no evil intent, partnerships can still run into trouble, usually because of misunderstandings about how the responsibilities are to be split, and what each partner expects of the other in the way of effort.

To reduce the risk of these problems it is worth taking advice from a solicitor. A lawyer will have seen a lot of trouble from partnership wrangles, and will be able to highlight matters for you both to think about, before the 'wedding'. The advice might be to draw up a partnership agreement, covering the questions that most often cause trouble, and settling now what procedure is to be followed if one of you wants to get out in ten years' time to sail around the world. If these things have not been thought out in advance and agreed while everyone is still friendly, there can be real trouble for the firm when each of you starts fighting for a selfish view of how things should be split. Prior agreement means less bloodshed. Usually.

6.5 LIMITED COMPANY

In a legal sense, sole traders and partners are people who earn income by means of their business activity. Limited companies are legally quite different. In law, a limited company is a 'person', able to employ people, buy and sell things and generally make its own mind up about what it wants to do. It is quite separate from its owners, who are the people who have shares in it, and from its directors, that is, the people who make its decisions for it.

As a separate person, it has sole responsibility for its debts, which frees its owners from that responsibility. Its liabilities are limited to the paid-up share capital – hence the full title, 'limited liability company'. Very many small companies are authorised to issue £100-worth of shares, but only ever issue £2-worth. So if it is liquidated to pay off debts, all the shareholders stand to lose is £2, in theory at least. Yet it could have been dealing in transactions worth thousands of pounds. The only ways in which shareholders can be held liable for the business debts of a limited company is if they have given personal guarantees, rather like a parent guaranteeing a loan for a teenage child. The same goes for directors, with the additional, very unlikely possibility that they could be sued for debts incurred by the company which it could not repay because they had run it negligently. This is the loophole which allows limited companies to be used by unscrupulous people to operate swindles. They place orders for goods which they never intend to pay for. The goods are then sold and the proceeds go to pay the directors their fees. When the suppliers want paying there is nothing left, and the firm goes into liquidation. It is then that the poor old suppliers learn that the fancy offices, carpets, pictures, tables, chairs, office machines, cars and so on were all on lease. As they are the property of the leasing company they cannot be sold to pay off the debts. As the Crown and employees have first claim on anything left that is saleable, there is usually nothing at all left over for suppliers. Done in this simplified way, it would probably get one or two people a jail sentence for fraud, and almost certainly have them disqualified from holding directorships on the grounds of 'wrongful trading'.

There are more long-winded ways of doing much the same thing which might avoid prosecution, hence the wary way in which many small limited company owners find they are treated. Banks, for example, will want personal guarantees from directors for any loan made to a small firm – see Sections 4.6 and 4.7 on security for loans and the government guarantee scheme which might help you avoid much of this risk.

There are costs attached to limited companies which partnerships and sole traders do not attract. Setting the company up will probably cost £100 to £200. By law its annual accounts must be audited by a chartered accountant, which would add between £500 and £5,000 a year to the bill you would normally expect for the preparation of accounts to satisfy the tax authorities. As an employee of a limited company you would pay National Insurance contributions. The company would also have to pay employer's NI contributions. In total this is rather more than the self-employed person or partner would have to pay. Full details are available from the Inland Revenue (address and website in Section 17).

6.6 CHOOSING WHICH LEGAL STATUS TO USE

In the early stages of most businesses it usually makes sense to be a sole trader or partnership. The exceptions might be where large liabilities and high risks are being taken on, when it might be worth looking at limited liability status. As a general rule, however, the decision to go limited is dictated by taxation questions. In the early years it would probably be right to operate as a sole trader or partnership, paying personal income tax on the profits. This is a simplified picture, but it is worth remembering that as earnings grow you may wish to consider a change of constitution to minimise the total amount of tax you pay.

You must not think that the decision is straightforward: like anything to do with taxation it very much needs expert advice from your account-ant. You would feel a bit silly if you took the decision without seeking advice about your personal situation, solved an income tax problem but found that you had created an even bigger problem with, say, capital transfer tax.

6.7 FORMING A LIMITED COMPANY

The usual practice nowadays is to buy a ready-made but unused company 'off the peg' from a company formation agent. They are people who make a living out of forming companies with names that have not previously been used, paying the government duty of £20 to register them, and selling them to people like you for £100–200 or so. They can be found advertising in the *Yellow Pages* and in the business pages of the quality papers. Because the world is running short of sensible-sounding company names, most of the off-the-peg firms have extraordinary names. If none of the names you are offered seems appropriate, you can usually have it changed for a fee, or, to save time, use an appropriate trading name. Let us suppose you buy Quadblank Ltd off the peg (with apologies to any real Quadblank Ltd that may exist). You think that does not sound right from a marketing point of view, so you decide to trade as Victoria Cabinetmakers (with due apologies as before). Your letterhead and so on can say VICTORIA CABINETMAKERS across the top, as long as it says as well, somewhere,

'Victoria Cabinetmakers is a business name of Quadblank Ltd, registered at Cardiff no 12345, registered office 17 Back Street, Blanktown'. There are other regulations to be observed, too. Section 6.9 gives further details.

As an alternative to using a company formation agent you can ask your accountant or solicitor to set up the company for you. That could cost you a great deal more, so check the costs, and what you will get for your money, in advance. Because of the wider service they can offer your local professional advisers might suit your particular case better. They will certainly give you a full account of your duties and responsibilities as a shareholder and director.

6.8 YOUR BUSINESS NAME

Choosing a trading name for your business is largely a marketing question of course. Dirty Dick's Drain Clearing might be acceptable, but Dirty Dick's Interior Decorating would probably turn customers right off. The associations that customers make from the words in your trading title will be one of the earliest of those all-important first impressions. Ideally it will be expressive, attractive and memorable. It might be right for a plumber to use his or her own name, to convey the idea that there is a real person who does the work and stands behind its quality. On the other hand, if the surname is Leakey there might be second thoughts.

For limited companies there are rules about what they can, or cannot, call themselves. Section 6.9 covers names used for trading (such as Victoria Cabinetmakers suggested in Section 6.7) but this section goes on to deal with the actual names of limited companies, whether or not they use those names for trading purposes. The authority governing these matters is the Companies Registration Office (CRO), whose address is in Section 17. Most of the rules are what you would expect. For instance, a company may not use a name that is offensive, criminal, already registered, or suggesting national or local government approval. That means words like 'British', 'Royal', 'National' and 'Board' are out – unless, of course, you could genuinely claim such associations, and get permission from the CRO. Your company's name needs to be quite clearly different from others, and there are quite strict rules about how different it must be. The Companies Registration Office publishes a free leaflet spelling out all the rules, which have only been summarised here.

6.9 DISCLOSURE OF BUSINESS NAMES

If you trade in a name other than your own, you must disclose your name and address on business documents. These include letterheads, orders placed on suppliers, invoices, receipts and demands for payment of debts. You must also display a notice at your business premises 'prominently', in a place where customers and suppliers have access. It should say:

- Particulars of ownership of (your trading name) as required by Section 29 of the Companies Act 1981.
- Full names of proprietors (insert names).
- Addresses within Great Britain at which documents can be served on the business (insert addresses).

Finally, you must disclose this information in writing immediately you are asked for it by anyone with whom anything is done or discussed in the course of business. In practice it probably means you hand them a letterhead.

The reason it is important is that you commit a criminal offence by not complying, and you might find you could not make your contracts stick. To know if you need to comply you must be clear what counts as your own name. Obviously, John Smith can trade as 'John Smith', 'J Smith', 'Mr J Smith' or 'Mr John Smith', and use his own name. If he and his father go into business as a partnership, 'J & P Smith' or 'John & Peter Smith' count as their own names: but so does 'Smith's'. If John starts a partnership with Tom Brown, 'T Brown & J Smith', 'John Smith & Thomas Brown', and 'Messrs J Smith & T Brown' all count as their own names. None of the examples cited in this passage so far requires you to comply with the disclosure regulations: if you copy the Smiths and Tom Brown you just go into business.

Now for the exceptions, the ones that must comply. Examples are 'John Smith Engineering Supplies', 'Midlands Woodworkers', 'Victoria Cabinet-makers' – none of them is the name of a human being or a limited company. Since a limited company is a person in the legal sense, it, too, can use a name for trading that is other than its own name. When it does, it must observe exactly the same disclosure regulations as real persons. Needless to say, you may not use the word 'Limited' unless you are a limited company.

6.10 KEY JOBS TO DO

- Take professional advice.
- Understand the financial implications – costs, NI and taxation.
- Select a constitution.
- Ensure that provisions governing disclosure are observed.

Section 7: Business and the law

7.1 AIMS OF THIS SECTION

This section outlines the main legal matters with which the business owner needs to be familiar. Because the law is such a complex area, it can only be a general guide to the main issues. For that reason, and because there are always new laws and new interpretations by the courts of existing laws, it should be used as an outline briefing. Detailed advice on your personal position can then be given by your own solicitor.

If you know little about the law at present, reading this section will enable you at least to have some idea of why your solicitor may give you particular pieces of advice. It should be remembered that Scotland has its own system. What is described here holds good largely for England, Wales and Northern Ireland. While many businesses never have legal problems, it is worth knowing the rules and limitations that bind business relationships.

7.2 CIVIL AND CRIMINAL LAW

It is important to realise that there are really two legal systems in operation. The criminal law is set by Parliament, the police prosecute people who break it, and the State punishes them. The civil law, on the other hand, has been developed over the centuries by decisions taken by judges in cases where someone with a grievance asked the court to settle it. Anyone can take out a summons against anyone else under this system, and the judge decides on the merits of the case, taking guidance from the principles established previously.

7.3 CIVIL LAW

Your rights under civil law are laid down quite clearly. So are those of your customers and suppliers. You could not get a policeman to take an interest in a customer who will not pay his bill, because Parliament has not ruled against it. But you have a clear right to be paid at the agreed time, which a county court would be pleased to enforce. But what does 'on time' mean? It has to be defined in the original agreement with the customer. The court might even award you damages to pay for the interest on the debt, your costs of chasing for payment and for other losses you might have suffered as a consequence. There is a great deal of civil law, concerning virtually every aspect of our lives in the community. Mercifully, the business owner needs to be concerned with only two branches of it most of the time – contract and tort. To meet your obligations under them you need to behave honestly, openly and fairly, and to act with care in all things.

7.4 BREACH OF CONTRACT

This is part of the civil law of contract. The only time you need to concern yourself with it is when you, a supplier or a customer have broken it. But to avoid that concern it is advisable to know how it can come about and to take suitable action in advance.

Let us say that Johnson and Thompson (J&T) sell nuts and bolts. You need some special sizes from them by 20 June to finish off the order you have from Cox International. Cox have said that they want to build your part into the assembly they are sending out to Nigeria. They must have it by the end of the month or the whole thing will miss the boat, incur extra shipping and dock charges and penalty payments for late delivery. You tell this to the J&T rep who takes your order, and he says that there will be no problem over delivering them to your specification by 20 June. In the event, only half of the nuts are delivered on time, and none of the bolts. The rest of the order turns up on 29 June, but the thread on the bolts is not what you specified, so the nuts and bolts will not match. Cox miss the boat and, after a lot of shouting, they sue you for breach of contract and damages of £80,000. You lose the case and have to pay up. Actually, it does not cost you £80,000, for as soon as Cox sued you, you sued J&T. The two cases were heard together, and the judge ruled that you should pay Cox £80,000, and J&T should pay you £80,000 for breaking their contract with you. In practice, in a case as clear cut as this, no one would waste the time of the court or build up the legal costs. They might threaten, in order to get people to take them seriously, but it would be settled out of court, possibly for a bit less than the sum claimed.

If the J&T rep had only said that he would do his best but could not guarantee delivery in time, he might have protected his firm. If J&T had standard terms and conditions that specifically rejected responsibility for consequential loss, they might escape liability, and you would have to foot the bill yourself for the whole of the £80,000. Unless, that is, you had such a clause in *your* standard conditions, which governed your sale to Cox and might let you out. The print may be small, but its effects can be quite staggering! In both cases the customer would have had to be aware of the condition concerned, or at least to have had the chance to acquaint himself with it, or it might not stick.

7.5 TORT

There are various forms of tort (French for 'wrong'), of which the one businesspeople most often meet is the tort of negligence. This is also part of the civil law. Suppose that your staff have been complaining for weeks about the loose stair-carpet at your office. This morning young Angela tripped on it and fell, breaking her leg in four places. She was working for you during her vacation from ballet school, where she is a star pupil. To make matters worse, she has one aunt who is a solicitor and another who is a barrister.

By not having the carpet repaired as soon as you became aware of the problem you have been negligent, and the aunts will doubtless sue you successfully for £750,000 to cover Angela's potential earnings, pain, suffering and medical costs. Incidentally, you will probably also be prosecuted under the criminal law by the Health and Safety Executive for a few breaches of the laws requiring you to provide safe working conditions. Few small firms could survive the battery of fines and publicity from such a case, or the immense diversion of time from the key task of running the firm effectively. Yet more time might be lost if you are imprisoned – remember that Health and Safety is part of the *criminal* law.

Even if these types of accident are covered by your employer's liability insurance policy, it might contain a clause giving the insurance company some sort of let-out. You are at risk if you behave negligently towards anyone else with whom you have dealings, and your staff can behave negligently in the name of your business: they misbehave, but you carry the can. Apart from negligence, the other civil wrongs are:

- Nuisance – eg making smells or noise, blocking people's driveways with your vehicles.
- Defamation – damaging a former employee's reputation, or competitor's reputation etc.

■ Conversion – selling stolen goods, even if they were bought innocently.
■ Trespass – entering property uninvited.
■ Passing-off – making out that goods were made by someone other than their manufacturer.
■ False imprisonment – eg detaining on suspicion of theft an employee or visitor who is later acquitted.

Those examples of how you could commit these torts are far from a complete list, of course.

7.6 EMPLOYMENT LAW

This specialised area is so closely bound up with other aspects of personnel administration that it is covered in Section 11 on employing people.

7.7 GOING TO LAW

The main aim of any business owner must be to run the firm effectively. That is usually more than a full-time job in itself, so anything that diverts attention from it must be avoided. One of the most worrying, time-consuming and expensive activities known to humankind is the pursuit of cases through the courts. Thus it does not go well with running a firm. Threaten litigation, by all means, and go as far as the courtroom door if need be, but try to get an early settlement of a dispute, even if it is on less favourable terms than you think you could get from a judge. You are then free to get on with what really matters. Never forget Dickens's description in *Bleak House* of the court case in which lawyers' fees ate up the whole of the estate that was in dispute.

If you do sue, first see if you can use the small claims procedure (see Section 7.8). Check that the defendant has the means to pay you – just having a big house is not enough if it belongs to the defendant's spouse. Above all, go ahead only if your solicitor believes you have a very good chance of winning.

The best way of not getting to court, as plaintiff or defendant, is to ensure that all your buying and selling is carried out in such a way that both sides understand what is offered and what is promised, and to have documentary proof, and to deal honestly. In that way you can enrich yourself rather than the lawyers. Even where friends and relations are concerned (or perhaps especially then), you should have written agreements and written records of transactions and undertakings.

7.8 SUING IN THE COUNTY COURT, AND BEING SUED

If you believe you have a claim against someone you can usually pursue it in the county court. For large sums and complex cases you would be well advised to do so only with the help of a solicitor, so it could cost a great deal of money, especially if you lose. Even if you win, you could find that you are awarded damages but not your legal costs of professional help. If your costs are high enough, it is quite possible that even a win will have lost you money. Recognising the injustice of this, the powers that be invented the 'small claims procedure'. Under this, a claim for £5,000 or less will automatically go to arbitration first, and that in fact clears up most cases without the need for solicitors or for a full court hearing.

Arbitration is an informal procedure and less complicated than a full court hearing, being designed to enable ordinary people to seek justice without the need to pay for legal representation. Both sides fill in simple forms and then meet the arbitrator, who is usually a solicitor, and each other, sitting round a table, in private. The court officials will help with advice on procedure and can give you a very readable booklet which explains things simply and clearly. No business should be without a copy, for it also tells you what to do if someone sends you a summons. Your local county court can be found under 'courts' in the phone book.

Most small firms will come across this procedure on the rare occasions when they have to take a slow-paying customer to court to get paid, when no other part of the contract is in dispute. Anything more complex is not for the 'do it yourself' method, but needs proper, professional advice. Whatever you do, do not try to pursue a complicated matter yourself, get into a mess, then go to a lawyer to unscramble the mess. Solicitors do not come cheaply – £80 to £250 an hour is not uncommon – but the good ones are usually worth it. By the way, another fascinating difference between Scotland and the rest of us: in Scotland some solicitors are called 'Writer to the Signet', a charming and dignified title.

In the last few years, the 'contingency fee' arrangement has come into being, also known as 'no win, no fee'. Under it, a lawyer will take on a case for no fee, instead taking a share – perhaps a quarter or a third – of the award in the case of a win. For people who cannot afford any fee, this system makes sense. However, lawyers offer it only when they are pretty sure of success, so even if it is offered it is often worth declining.

7.9 BUYING AND SELLING GOODS

This central part of a firm's activity is governed by various pieces of parliamentary legislation, as well as by the civil law of contract and tort. Under Section 7.4 we looked briefly at one example of how the law of contract could affect a firm. In case the law looks as if it will involve you in worry and expense day after day, things need to be put in proportion. It is almost enough to say that you will never have a brush with the law, civil or criminal, if you:

■ tell the truth;
■ never make promises you cannot keep;
■ keep the promises you make;
■ know what your obligations are and keep to them;
■ know and observe your customers' rights;
■ behave fairly and reasonably;
■ can prove that what you say is true;
■ read and understand what you are signing;
■ make proper use of professional and official advice.

To help towards this, the following parts look at some of the main details that you need to understand.

7.10 WHAT MAKES A CONTRACT

For a contract to be made three things must be present:

■ *Offer.* That is to say, someone has to start the ball rolling by offering something for sale.
■ *Acceptance.* Someone else has to accept the offer.
■ *Consideration.* There must be a payment of some kind, not necessarily money, in exchange.

A contract can be made on specified terms, like delivery within a week but payment in two months' time. It also has 'implied terms' that do not need to be spelt out but are automatically a part of every contract struck. These are dealt with in Section 7.13. For practical purposes the contract exists and is legally enforceable the moment the agreement is reached over what is offered and what the price will be. It is then too late to ask for changes. It does not affect the legal rights of the matter if it is not in writing, but it may be a lot easier to prove what was agreed if it is written and signed. The only common exceptions to this rule are land sales in England, Wales and Northern Ireland which must be written contracts, and in those special cases where the customer is allowed time to change his or her mind if he or she wants to. An example of this is when the customer makes a contract in the home – Section 7.20 gives details.

7.11 TERMS AND CONDITIONS: BUYING

One day you order some goods from a sales rep, who writes the order down and gives you a carbon copy. Instead of that, or in addition, an acknowledgement of your order may arrive a few days later from their head office. You might do no more than glance at it to check that they have got the quantity, price and delivery date right, and file it. Beware! You might just have taken a time bomb on board. On the back are some densely printed terms and conditions, which nobody ever bothers to read. If you did read them, assuming they were not written in incomprehensible legalese, you would quickly see that they say, more or less, 'we can do whatever we like about your order and you have no come-back'. While that sounds too one-sided for comfort, perhaps it does not really matter.

Perhaps it does, though. Suppose that you need 200 three-foot strips of wood. Your supplier operates in metric, and sells two-metre lengths. Therefore you order 100 two-metre strips. Allowing for the 5 per cent you know you will waste, that will enable you to get the 200 three-foot lengths that you need. But when you read their terms and conditions you find that they reserve the right to measure length with a 10 per cent variation. Some, or even all, of the wood could be about six feet long when it is delivered, too short for two three-foot lengths *and* 5 per cent waste. And yet you might still have to pay for it. If all you had told the rep was that you wanted 100 two-metre lengths, hard luck, especially if you had a copy of their catalogue or price-list stating their standard terms and conditions. By placing the order on those terms, you had implicitly accepted all their small print. On the other hand, if you had made it clear to the rep that what you really wanted were the three-foot strips plus 5 per cent for waste, and asked for timber that would fit the bill, you would be under no obligation to pay for the strips that were too short to use. So the first rule is to specify what you want the goods to do, as part of placing the order. The next thing is to issue an official order which you can marry up with the invoice when it comes in, for checking. Your official order has on it your terms of trade, which might say, in effect, 'we are in the right, even when we are wrong'. Those terms would stick if the seller did not send an acknowledgement of order. The rule here is that the last one in wins. So make sure that you buy on your terms, not someone else's, wherever possible. This sort of carry-on does sound childish, but some suppliers' orders do seem to license them to please themselves about how much they send you and when, as well as to vary colour, size, weight, and more besides. Even if the rep promised you that a particular condition would not apply in your case, it is almost certain that somewhere the conditions say staff have no authority to promise that.

The small print usually also tells you how to complain if the goods are delivered damaged or are in some other way not what you ordered. Leave it too long, or register your complaint in the wrong way (eg by phone instead of recorded letter), and they might still be able to make you pay. Fortunately most firms, and certainly the big public companies, are mainly interested in having satisfied customers. But remember that their small print did not get there by accident.

7.12 TERMS AND CONDITIONS: SELLING

This should definitely not be seen as a chance to hit back for all the indignities that suppliers try to impose on you in *their* small print. It is better to see this as part of your marketing stance, an effort to communicate your reasonable expectations and requirements of your customer. As such it will be written in clear language, although it must give you adequate legal protection. To give you a start in preparing your own, a draft set of terms and conditions appears below. It is not there to suggest that there is only one approach, nor that this approach is perfect. It is offered as something to think about and to change into a form suitable for your business. When that has been done you should give it to your solicitor for comment, to make sure that the final form is legally enforceable and covers what your firm should cover. Remember, too, that the conditions must be part of the 'offer', that is, the customer could reasonably have been expected to know about them before placing the order.

Because you are more interested in having happy customers than in having rows in which you can prove you are in the right, you will probably want to make quite sure that your customers have seen them. They could be displayed, prominently marked, at your place of business, as well as printed in catalogues and price-lists, and attached to or printed on the back of order forms, confirmations and so on. If you do print them on the back, it is only fair to the customer to draw attention to them. This could easily be done by means of a notice on the front of the document. Each numbered clause in the list below has comments after it, explaining why it is suggested.

Terms and conditions of sale

1. Descriptions shown in brochures, advertisements, and by way of samples are correct at the time of going to press, errors and omission excepted. They are liable to alteration at any time without notice. *This is meant to protect you from minor complaints about changes in specification, and mistakes in price-lists and catalogues. You might want to change a specification but not throw away catalogues. But it would not override the customer's right to goods that are 'fit for use' – see Section 7.13.*

2. We may revise prices without notice. Prices will be those ruling at the date of despatch. Any invoice query should be made in writing within ten days of the date of the invoice. All prices exclude VAT which is due at the rate currently in force. Quotations and estimates remain current for one month. *Some protection against cost increases that you might have to pass on. Stops you being bound by old quotations. Makes it clear that VAT has to be paid – if you are registered.*

3. All accounts are payable in full within four weeks of invoice date. *Or whatever your terms are – very important to specify clearly.*

4. We cannot accept liability for delay in despatch or delivery. *It is not your fault if the delivery firm loses the parcel for a month.*

5. Orders for goods may be cancelled only with the written agreement of one of our directors. Orders for goods made to special order cannot be cancelled. *Only a director or the owner should give this permission, not salespeople or others. Special orders are usually unsaleable to anyone else.*

6. All orders over £100 will be delivered free within 10 miles. Elsewhere, carriage may be charged in addition to the quoted price. Orders for less than £100 are not normally accepted for a credit account. *Whether you charge for delivery and what you charge needs to be carefully controlled, as does the cost of administering a lot of small accounts. There is nothing special about £100; it is just an illustration.*

7. Shortage of goods or damage must be notified by telephone within three days of delivery, and confirmed in writing within seven days of delivery, or no claim can be accepted. Delivery of obviously damaged goods should be refused. Notifications should give delivery note number, a list of quantities of the products damaged, and details of the type of damage. Damaged goods must be retained for inspection. *This should be written in the light of what your carrier's conditions say. As they will destroy all papers proving delivery after a short time, they want speedy notification of any claim. It is essential for damaged goods to be saved and eventually collected by you to stop dishonest collusion between customers and lorry-drivers, and multiple claims against one damaged item.*

8. Liability cannot be accepted for non-delivery of goods if written notification is not received within ten days of the date of invoice.
   See comments on 7 above: tie in with carrier's conditions.

9. No liability is accepted for any consequential loss or damage whatsoever, however caused.
   In cases of extreme negligence by your staff or yourself this would probably not stick, but your solicitor might want to see it included.

10. Acceptance of the goods implies acceptance of these conditions. These conditions may not be varied except in writing by one of our directors.
    Now the customer cannot take the goods but complain about the conditions. Nor can he or she bully your salesperson into giving unlimited credit, for instance.

11. Under some circumstances we may cancel the contract without notice or compensation. Such circumstances would include inability to obtain materials, labour and supplies, strikes, lockouts and other forms of industrial action or dispute, fire, flood, drought, weather conditions, war (whether declared or not), acts of terrorism, civil disturbance, act of God or any other cause beyond our control making it impossible for us to fulfil the contract.
    Cover for the times when snow blocks the roads and so on. You might even want to add the insurance policy favourites of damage by aircraft, falling trees, radioactive and biological hazards. . . but, there again, you might not.

12. Until they have been paid for we reserve our title in goods supplied.
    When a customer goes into liquidation everything in his or her possession is sold to pay the creditors, even if it has not been paid for. The exceptions are items on lease or hire purchase, or that clearly belong to somebody else. You cannot normally snatch back the last delivery you sent. Clause 12 gives you protection, by saying that they remain yours until paid for. You could show the liquidator this term on the copy of the order form signed by the customer, and walk out with the goods. It will not work, however, if what you supplied has been incorporated in something else. Nor will it work if you cannot identify those items as precisely the ones on the invoice.

13. Any invoice not paid in full by the due date shall attract interest payments. These will accrue from the due date at the rate of 10 per cent per month.
    Unless you have a licence to offer credit you must not charge the public an interest rate, and one this high would almost certainly be disallowed. It is suggested that you think about using a clause like this to encourage payment in line with your terms. You would probably never need to actually charge it as the threat would be enough to make most firms pay up. Any customer who queries it can be told that it does not apply to them, but to people who break their promise to pay on time. Some firms use a figure of 20 per cent, but this might be so high as to break the rules that the terms must be 'reasonable'. At 10 per cent you might be able to argue reasonableness, as it

would compensate for the management time spent chasing overdue debts. What is reasonable will depend to a great extent on the nature of your particular business.

14. If a 'quotation' is given it is a firm price for the job but subject to these terms and conditions. An 'estimate' is our best estimate of the final cost but may be subject to fluctuation due to exigencies of the job which may be difficult or impossible to foresee.
    In some businesses it is difficult to give a price for some work, as time may have to be spent to uncover the root of the problem before a proper quotation can be given. It is fair to the customer and yourself to make this clear.

This is only a list of suggestions. Some may be right for your business, others wrong, and some right after rewriting. Yet others may be needed that do not appear there. Use the list to build your own conditions of sale that reflect the way you want to deal with your customers. Then, and very importantly, let your solicitor put it into proper shape.

7.13 CONDITIONS AND WARRANTIES

In any contract there are 'conditions' and 'warranties'. Conditions are really important matters, so that if one party breaches them the other is entitled to money back, plus damages. Warranties are less important, entitling the injured party to damages only. These can be spelt out, in price, delivery date, quantity, and the matters dealt with in Section 7.12. In addition, there are implied conditions which do not have to be spelt out, but are present in all contracts. They include:

■ Seller has the right to sell (the goods are not stolen, or on HP, for example).
■ Goods comply with description (if reconditioned, not described as new etc).
■ Goods are of 'suitable quality' and 'fit for use' in the way the customer expected (they must do what is reasonably expected of them. A pruning knife will cut quite thick stems, but not fall open in your pocket and gash your hand. A car must go, steer and stop. If you advise the customer that something will do a particular job it must be capable of it. The only exceptions are where the customer carries out the sort of examination of the goods that could reasonably be expected to throw up the fault, or where you point it out. If the pruning knife does misbehave in the way described, the maker may have been negligent. This brings us into the realms of 'product liability', so far not a vitally important area for domestic firms, but those selling in the USA must take professional advice on it. If it is not insured against they face

amazing risks. It is likely to become more significant throughout the EU in the future).

■ Sample corresponds with bulk (assuming the buyer gets a chance to check the sample you supplied against the full delivery, and that the bulk did not conceal some fault that reasonable inspection should have shown, then the sample is required to be representative).

Thinking of all the legal fees that must have changed hands through the years on arguments over the meaning of words, one wonders if 'reasonable' might not have earned more for the legal profession than most. It is so open to interpretation that it emphasises the need in all your dealings, buying as well as selling, to agree exact specifications with customer or supplier. It is not always possible, but can be done more often than not. The customer wants 'a good, sturdy table' – get him to look at some pieces of wood and specify the thicknesses and type of timber he wants. She wants her gates 'rustproofed' – does that mean metal sprayed, hot-dip galvanised, or a coat of red oxide primer? Does she want you to explain the different costs and performances? Now she can really tell you what she wants, you get a reputation for being helpful, and the area for possible misunderstanding is reduced.

7.14 GUARANTEES

In your trade it may be common for manufacturers to give written guarantees with their products that you build into your goods. That is helpful of them, but it does not relieve you of any of your obligations. Whoever supplies the faulty goods is the person whom the customer can demand satisfaction from, whether or not they are the manufacturer. You must therefore put right the customer's problem at your expense, and then chase the manufacturer to put right your complaint. In practice, you might seek satisfaction from your supplier, but whether or not you get it does not affect your obligation to the person who bought from you. Don't forget to point out on your guarantee that it does not affect the customer's statutory rights.

Another important point is that the customer's rights against the supplier do not have a time limit – except what is 'reasonable' in the circumstances.

7.15 EXEMPTIONS

It is a criminal offence to try to deprive customers, whether trade or public, of their legal rights. Thus the shops may no longer display signs saying

'No refunds on sale goods', or 'No guarantees with special offers'. Sales to business customers may be subject to 'reasonable' exclusion clauses, but not sales to the general public. This also applies to goods hired, rather than sold. An exclusion clause may be reasonable under certain conditions, among them being the question of a discount being given in exchange. This is a complex area and legal advice is desirable.

7.16 TRADE DESCRIPTIONS

To comply with this legislation you have to be sure that what you say about what you sell is true, and the whole truth. 'Leather shoes' is a wrong description if the uppers and soles are leather but the linings are plastic. 'Hand made' is either true or untrue, although the Trading Standards Office may be lenient if such a product had a modest amount of insignificant machine work. It is not necessary to go to ludicrous lengths to avoid an offence. A cardigan might contain wool grown in Australia, dye made in Germany, and buttons made in China from American plastics. As long as it was knitted and made up in the UK it counts as made here.

7.17 CONSUMER CREDIT

A customer might ask you the favour of paying you off over a period of time. By doing so you might break the Consumer Credit Act. If you think you might need to offer the public some sort of credit facility check with your solicitor how to go about it properly. If your problem is that your customers do not need to pay you off over a period of time, just that they do not always have enough money on them when they see you, you can accept cheques backed by guarantee cards and credit or debit cards. Your bank will tell you what the procedures are.

7.18 TRADING STANDARDS OFFICERS

Mention has been made of these officials who are the successors to the Weights and Measures Officers. As the name suggests, they are employed to enforce the various Acts of Parliament that affect trading. Before you start trading it is an excellent idea to ask for an appointment to meet one to talk over your proposed business and get advice on what the law will require you to do. They are most helpful, and much prefer to see that you avoid committing an offence rather than catch you when you do. They work for county or unitary councils and metropolitan authorities or their successors. The only snag is that because their area is local, the advice may only be a local interpretation of the law. If a local officer in another part of the country sees things differently from the one nearest to home, it will do you no harm to be able to show that you were acting in good faith, and on the advice of a professional colleague.

Two ways in which their advice can be particularly valuable are over whether or not your business needs a licence or registration, and the labelling of goods. If you sell products in some form of package there are almost certainly very detailed regulations about what the label may and may not say, what must be disclosed, what units of measure may be used (imperial/metric, volume/weight), what abbreviations are permitted, what size of letters must be used – and so on. The Trading Standards Officer will be pleased to explain it all and tell you where you can get your own copy of the regulations concerned.

7.19 COPYRIGHT, REGISTERED DESIGNS AND TRADE MARKS, AND PATENTING

The law gives some protection to your brand names and any devices you may have developed. Certain types of protection can be costly, and the protection given less than expected. Suppose you spend around £15,000 to £25,000 over the three or four years it takes to get a full patent. You expect that to more or less guarantee immunity from copyists. But what happens if someone does copy you? In theory, the law is on your side but you need to be pretty well-heeled to risk a lawsuit. You may be in the right but you cannot afford to prove it, unless you had the foresight to insure for the legal fees for defending it. Fortunately, cynical copying of a patented thing is rare, and there are in any case other types of protection available.

The least protection is given at lowest cost by copyright. You automatically have copyright in anything original on paper – drawings, music, names, words, writing and so on. The protection also includes anything made from copyright drawings. The trouble is that all the copyist has to do to get away with it is to avoid copying a substantial part of your work. Because the near-copy will itself be original it will itself have copyright. To try to frighten the copyist off an item on paper you can put a ©, your name and the date on it. At least it shows you are aware of your rights. If you want to be really careful you can sign and date every drawing, including back-of-envelope sketches, and keep them safely. You can establish the truth of the date you claim by sealing the papers in an envelope and posting it to your bank or solicitor to keep unopened. The postmark is your proof, but you will need to make arrangements with the keeper to make sure the envelope is not opened by mistake.

If you invent a new name for a product you can stop others from using it by registering it at the Trade Marks Registry. You can also search their records to make sure it really is original, or there are agents who will do this for you. Whether you do it yourself or use an agent, think up at least half a dozen names you could possibly use in case your first choice is already registered. Registering your own mark will cost at least £500 through an agent. Unfortunately registration is not foolproof as it is not compulsory for trade marks to be registered. Many which have been established through long use have never been registered but their users have powerful claims to stop you from using them. Much the same arrangement applies to registered designs, which give broader protection than copyright but less than patents. Patents are much more complex and costly, but stitch up your rights more clearly. Registration and patents need the expert services of a patent agent – look them up in the *Yellow Pages* and shop around for quotes.

The whole principle of patenting something revolves around proving that you were the first with it. Therefore it is vital to take advice from a professional before anyone else is told anything. This applies to possible customers and suppliers, friends you might talk it over with, the draughtsperson who might do the drawings, or anyone who might see the prototype. If you have 'disclosed' it in any way your rights may be nullified. The agent will probably advise an initial application, which is simpler and cheaper than a full application but can still run out at over a thousand pounds. That establishes your place at the head of any queue, and gives you a year in which you can work up prototypes and try to find buyers. If it then looks commercially viable you can go ahead with a full patent, but if not you can drop it at less cost. The protection does not last for ever.

The life of a copyright in 'artistic' products is the life of the author plus 50 years; but if that copyright work is the basis of an industrial design, protection runs for 15 years from the first time the product is put on sale.

Designs are protected from the date of application for registration for 15 years, provided the registration is renewed every 5 years. Patents give 20 years' protection from the date of filing the first specification at the Patent Office.

More flexible administration arrangements were introduced early in 2005, which the government claims will make the patents system easier to deal with.

Insurance against legal fees was mentioned earlier. Even for fairly routine work lawyers seem to charge a lot. In the specialised field of patent work the costs of proving infringement can be astronomical. Special insurance policies are available to cover these costs, which are a must for any small-business owner of a patent. Anyone who might be tempted to risk copying a patented article owned by Joe Bloggs would quickly pull back if he got a letter from a large insurance company's lawyers demanding that he stop. Joe Bloggs is one thing, Intergalactic Mutual Insurance is quite another.

7.20 DOORSTEP SELLING – THE 'COOLING-OFF' PERIOD

Under some circumstances members of the public who buy in their own homes or at their workplace have the right to cancel an order, an HP or a credit sale agreement. The law was framed to protect easily swayed people from their enthusiasms, and it is important to draw it to the customer's attention in the correct way. It also applies if you do not normally sell in customers' homes, but the customer takes the order form etc away 'to think about it' and signs it there. The Office of Fair Trading publishes leaflets which are available from Trading Standards Offices and Citizens' Advice Bureaux.

7.21 KEY JOBS TO DO

- Understand the main implications of the criminal law for your business.
- Understand the broad outlines of how the civil law affects your firm.
- Create a set of terms and conditions of sale approved by a lawyer and incorporate them appropriately in stationery.
- Use copyright, registered designs and trade marks and patents as appropriate.

GUIDELINES FOR PATENT MANAGEMENT

Start of a new project

Having identified an idea, conducting a patent search to identify patents already in existence can be a useful research tool. The patent search could reveal that the idea is already known and if so, may give an insight as to possible problems with the technology. This type of information may save time and resources otherwise spent on 're-inventing the wheel' and provide a focus for further research.

The search may also provide an initial indication of likely legal problems in the future when the product is ready for commercialisation. For example if someone owns a relevant patent, you may be prevented from making, selling or using a new product or process. This could be catastrophic for a new start up company.

The patenting process

Ownership

At the beginning of a project it is important to establish who is to be the owner of the Intellectual Property rights relating to the invention. The Intellectual Property rights may include patent rights, design rights and copyright.

In general, these rights belong to the creator of the Intellectual Property unless there is a contractual relationship between the creator and a third party whereby the rights transfer to the third party. For example, if the creator is an employee, then the Intellectual Property rights will normally belong to the employer.

If a company is commissioned to develop an idea through to a commercial product, then ownership of the Intellectual Property rights will be governed by the contractual relationship between the two companies.

When to file a patent application

In most countries it is not possible to obtain a valid patent if details of the invention were in the public domain at the time of filing the patent application.

It is essential therefore that details of your invention should not be given to others in a non confidential way before a patent application is filed.

Although it is possible to file a patent application directed to an idea alone, it is generally recommended that an application is not filed until at least one working example of the idea has been developed.

Modifications to an idea

After filing of a patent application it is common for further modifications of the invention to be made as the process of commercialising the idea continues.

These modifications should be assessed before they are disclosed to others in a non confidential way to see whether the modifications are already covered by the existing patent application, or whether separate patent protection needs to be sought.

Seeking patent protection abroad

At present, patent protection is provided on a country by country basis, so it is necessary to have a patent in each country where protection is required.

Most countries are party to an International Convention which enables the filing of foreign patent applications to be deferred up to one year from the date of filing of the first patent application. This helps to defer the costs of seeking foreign patent protection for up to one year whilst the invention is developed and its commercial value is assessed.

Further systems, such as the Patent Cooperation Treaty, can be used to defer foreign filing costs still further.

Patent Renewals

Once a patent is granted, renewal fees are payable in order to keep the patent in force. Failure to pay a renewal fee results in the patent lapsing. In general, patents have a maximum life of 20 years; after this time the patent expires and the invention passes into the public domain.

Patent Infringement

Generally, a patent provides the owner with the right to stop others making, using and/or selling the patented invention (be it a product or a process).

If a competitor is successfully sued for patent infringement, then they will normally have to pay damages in respect of the infringement, will have an injunction granted against them to prevent further infringement and will have to pay an award of legal costs.

A patent is an asset

A patent is an asset like any other piece of property and as such may be, for example, sold, mortgaged, used as collateral or licenced.

All comments contained in the above guidelines are of a general nature and full professional advice should be sought on any specific problem.

Park View House
58 The Ropewalk
Nottingham NG1 5DD
United Kingdom

T. +44 (0) 115 955 2211
F. +44 (0) 115 955 2201
E. epc@eric-potter.com
W. www.eric-potter.com

Section 8: Premises

8.1 AIMS OF THIS SECTION

Many new businesses need to take on their own premises straight away, others can work from home initially but need to move out later, and some never need specialised premises at all. Land and buildings can cause legal and other problems, but, as always, a little preparation can save a lot of trouble later. This section deals with working from home, the planning permission system, and the main matters to do with finding and renting workspace. The Department of the Environment, Transport and the Regions (DETR) publishes free booklets on various aspects of the planning system.

8.2 CAN YOU WORK FROM HOME?

A surprising number of businesses start this way. Knowledge-based businesses that operate computers and work on the telephone often do so indefinitely. In recent years official resistance to home-based working has weakened, to the point that UK planning Class C3 includes the category 'small businesses at home'. A word with the planning office should help you to decide whether to apply officially (and risk being refused) or to work clandestinely. Some planning offices are better than others at giving advice informally. If you think there is a risk of alerting them to something they might wish to chase up, you are within your rights to ask for general advice and to withhold your name and address.

Many firms do start without official approval. The main thing they have to fear is action by the local authority to close them down, usually sparked off by a complaint from a neighbour. If no one complains the local authority will usually turn a blind eye, as long as the firm does not provoke action – by burning rubbish, having a large number of visitors, making noise or parking the hulks of old cars on the front lawn, for instance. Therefore this can usually be done successfully only for as long as you give nobody cause for complaint.

Some people may be disturbed by the idea of 'industry' getting a toehold in a residential area (and who can blame them?), and might complain to stop the precedent being established, even though you have been a model neighbour. A few are the jealous, twisted types who will complain about anything if it will spread a little misery. This is why many firms who make or mend things keep their activity completely secret. They whitewash the inside of the garage windows and never open the doors when anyone is about. The children's bikes are kept in a garden shed, to save neighbours' children from seeing inside the garage. Their families are briefed on what answers to give to the inevitable questions. Common sense tells them to work quietly, not to let visitors park across neighbours' driveways, to go out to fetch materials rather than have them delivered on lorries, not to store things outside, nor run unsuppressed electric motors during evening TV, or in any other way to be a bad neighbour. Above all, the sensible ones never allow their commitment to establishing the firm to get in the way of remembering that most people do not want to live next door to a busy place of work, and even consider soundproofing the inside of the workspace.

If you decide to work like this, never drop the high standards of behaviour you start off with. Your neighbours are not all fools and some will get a shrewd idea of what is really going on. If you feel that they can be trusted, you might therefore confide in them at the outset. Do not feel that the absence of trouble for the first three months means that you can now start to store things in the garden to make more working space. Do not forget that what you are doing is not legal, and that you are vulnerable all the time. What may be, from your point of view, a small, neat, unobtrusive stack of material in the garden may look to a neighbour like the thin end of a wedge that will turn the whole area into little better than a rubbish dump. Fortunately, you have friends in high places.

Some time ago the government recognised that many small businesses can be run from home without upsetting anyone, and therefore instructed local authorities to stop closing down such activities purely on principle. They can still be stopped from operating if they are nuisances. If the local authority wishes you to stop it will probably ask you to apply for planning permission, which is dealt with in Section 8.5. Development agencies and enterprise agencies might support your cause with the local authority. If you can possibly work from home it will pay you to do so, not only from the point of view of rent and rates but also because you can work hours you would normally spend travelling. Because you may need to incur the expense of legitimate premises at some time you should cost into your overheads the sort of rent and rates you would have to pay outside. By doing that you will avoid a sudden fall in profits or a jump in prices when you do eventually move out.

It is vital that you inform your insurers that the house is being used for business, otherwise some exclusion clause may operate if you have to make a claim. If you are buying the house on mortgage, the firm that lent the money should be told. As with other important communications these notifications should be in writing with a copy for your files. If your property is rented it would be worth asking your solicitor about telling the landlord. You do not want to be told to stop, but you might risk a claim from him if what you are doing invalidates his insurance.

Your solicitor should also be asked about restrictive covenants operating on the property. Not only could they affect your right to work from home, but they might affect the attitude of the organisation that holds the mortgage.

Needless to say, because of the obvious insecurity of premises that lack planning permission, only the bare minimum should be invested in making them usable.

8.3 AVAILABILITY OF SMALL PREMISES

Many young firms expect to be able to find a cheap and cheerful workshop or office fairly easily. Unfortunately, due partly to the redevelopment of many old areas, and the planning control policies of the 20th century, there is a great shortage of them in many areas. Recently a lot of brand-new premises have been built in the 500–2,000 sq ft range both by local authorities and in response to tax incentives. Owing to the high cost of building they have to be let at higher rents than many new businesspeople expect.

In some country areas there may be the chance of using an old barn or some other redundant building, but do not be surprised if you have to persuade the local planning authority to allow you to use the one you have your eye on. Because of this it is important to start the search for premises long before you think it is necessary. Here one of the development agencies may be able to help the rurally based firm: some even give grants to encourage it. Even then, town or country, you might have to settle for what is available rather than what is affordable. Remember too that walls and a roof are only a start. Necessary – and costly – extras include water, drains, electricity, gas, vehicle turning and parking space, road access and security measures.

8.4 FINDING SMALL PREMISES

Estate agents are the obvious people to approach first. Be sure that they keep you on their mailing lists, and get as much information as you can on rent, rates and availability. Unfortunately the cheaper premises will probably not be notified to estate agents at all, but will depend on your ingenuity and energy to root them out. Any local organisation advising firms should be able to suggest ideas of whom to approach. Local authority planning departments can sometimes help, as they know what planning applications have been put in recently. In the countryside, the Country Land and Business Association and National Farmers' Union could know of something or put a note in their local newsletter about your problem. It may also be worth approaching agents for the local landed estates about redundant buildings that they may want to rent out.

When you do find your workplace you must tell the Health and Safety Executive (see the phone book) that you plan to use it. You should also tell the Fire Prevention Officer at the local Fire Brigade. Officials from both departments will come out to your proposed premises to give advice before you sign up. That avoids you finding out about the problems later, when it may be more costly to deal with them.

It is essential to think carefully about your present and future requirements of the building before making any commitment. Specialists are on hand from advisory agencies to help you to explore every aspect before you sign up.

One way of simplifying the task of finding premises is to look for so-called business centres. These offer a secure space within a larger building which may be purpose-built or a conversion; an analogy is an apartment block for small-firm residents. Most offer easy-in, easy-out terms, but are usually vastly more expensive than renting conventionally. Usually, only office-type activity is accepted.

8.5 PLANNING PERMISSION

Using any building or land for industrial or commercial purposes requires planning permission. You can try to get away without it but the odds are that you will get into trouble with the authorities sooner or later. Customers might be less than sympathetic to find that you are unable to deliver because the council has obtained a court order forbidding you to work at your present premises.

Never assume that because Fred used the building before you it must be all right for you to use it. Perhaps Fred moved out due to council pressure. Or, on the other hand, perhaps the building has established business use rights. Or Fred may have been in a different official class of user: as a woodworker he could use it quite legitimately, but, running a sandwich bar, you may not.

The idea of 'established use rights' is that if a building has been used continuously (and that means what it says – no gaps) for a particular activity since before 1965, it is assumed to have planning permission for the activity. This is true even if planning permission has never been applied for. You will obviously not assume that to be so, but will check with the planning department. If they say there is no problem, get them to confirm it in writing: this is very important.

They might ask you to apply for a Certificate of Lawful Use or Development. That is a formal confirmation of the use rights, but it may tie the use down very tightly to exactly what was done previously, which could possibly be different from what you want to do. In that case you would have to apply for 'change of use'. Since each of those applications will cost about £100 to £1,000 for government fees alone, it is best to get advice. If the planning officer seems keen to help rather than hinder, this advice might be all you need. In other cases it could be better to consult a chartered surveyor, architect or solicitor, or one of the small firms agencies. If you choose one of the latter be sure to ask for at least three examples of local planning situations in which the adviser has been involved. The competent ones will have no trouble in reeling off a dozen or more. Those remarks also apply to a conventional planning application.

Six to eight weeks after an application for planning consent the decision will be notified to you. If it is passed it will fall into one or more of these categories:

- *Full planning consent.* The building and land can be used by anyone forever for the activities specified in the consent document.
- *Temporary planning consent.* Can be used by anyone for the specified activities, but there will be a time limit, usually between one and five years. On expiry you can apply again.
- *Personal planning consent.* Only you may use the building and land. Anyone else wanting to take over the place from you will have to apply for a fresh planning consent.

Where a particularly sensitive site is concerned – say, in a residential area or a place of character and beauty – permission may be granted on both a personal and a temporary basis. This can also apply where the activity is one with, from the planners' point of view, a suspicious history. Motor vehicle repair is a good example. Mechanical repairers sometimes leave a mounting pile of old engine blocks and back axles lying around outside, and bodywork repairers have been known to assemble a growing heap of discarded panels and damaged body shells. Giving temporary consent is a way of keeping you on your toes: any misbehaviour could be punished by refusal of your next application for renewal. If you have been a nuisance yet have heard no complaints it would be dangerous to assume that no one has complained to the council.

Both personal and temporary consent can present other difficulties. Financiers will find it hard to agree to lend money over a five-year period to a firm that has the right to use its premises for only two years. Likewise, you could question the wisdom of taking on such a commitment yourself. Similarly, if you have only personal consent for the use of a building you will want to keep to a minimum any investment in putting it in order. Perhaps the landlord will put it right in return for an increased rent? Spending thousands on rehabilitation out of your own pocket would make sense only if you were sure you would use it profitably for many years to come or that you could sell it on with continuing rights of use.

Even if a councillor or planning officer says that planning permission will be just a formality, do not assume it to be true. Many people who have gone ahead on a friendly nod and a wink are a lot poorer as a result.

In addition to the three broad categories laid down there will be detailed conditions attached to the consent. Almost always there are limits on the type of work that may be done, and on the hours of operation. There may be requirements to improve the access in the interests of road safety, to increase the car parking and manoeuvring area, to carry out planting or landscaping, and not to store anything out of doors. They should be taken seriously, but if any would cause you a great problem talk it over with the planning officer. He or she might be able to arrange for it to be varied, or you might have to appeal to the Secretary of State – see Sections 8.7 and 8.8.

8.6 APPLYING FOR PLANNING PERMISSION

There are forms to fill in, of course, but your approach to the planners should start long before you set pen to paper. Officially it is enough to fill in the forms, attach plans and a cheque and send them to your borough or district council. They would then be laid before the planning committee and the decision would come back six to eight weeks after the application went in. Unfortunately the whole system is run by human beings, so you must be very sure of success to do the officially required minimum and leave it at that. The planning officers (permanent, full-time officials) and the councillors (elected members of the council) are very busy people and are as capable as anyone of getting the wrong end of the stick. They are also subject to pressure from events – perhaps someone else they gave planning permission to six months ago has now created an eyesore – and from people like the local busybody who is getting up a petition against your plans. To stop those influences from working against you it is essential to influence the system in your favour. To do this it is best to start with a picture of how the system works.

When your completed form arrives at the planning office it is checked to see that it is filled in correctly and that you have sent in a cheque for the right amount. At the same time the official cannot avoid deciding whether or not the proposal fits current policies. Copies are sent to water, gas, electricity and roads authorities for their comments – you might plan to build right on top of a high-pressure gas main, or cause extra traffic to cross the road next to a lethal bend – and to the town or parish council for the comments of the body elected to represent the neighbouring community. Immediate neighbours are also notified. Thus all sorts of people get to hear about it and, rightly, get the chance to protest before your application is considered officially by the planning committee.

In this situation the main enemy of common sense is ignorance of your real intentions. The forms you fill in give little enough information, so you need to spread more knowledge in the right quarters of what you are really up to. Invite the planning officer to view the site, describe your activities, explain how small and quiet your machines are, say you do not plan to run a fleet of lorries, and so on. In the nature of their work planning officers are bound to be more aware of the small number of firms that cause nuisance than the large proportion that do not: make it clear which group you belong to. You might be given advice on the best wording to use to describe your activity. Many small businesspeople see officials as tiny-minded and obstructive. That is not always the case, and even if it is your view, remember that an official working for you is a lot better than one working the other way.

Next, invite the town or parish council to visit the site to prepare themselves for the application they will shortly receive. Ask the local councillor representing the area concerned to attend, too. Call personally on the people most likely to be affected, near neighbours especially, to explain yourself. Only then are you ready to fill in the forms. With them should go a letter that sums up briefly the sort of operation you plan to run. Then get every organisation you can think of to write in support of your application to the council – trade association, chamber of commerce, small firms' club, small business agency, and so forth. Then, and only then, can you be sure that you have done everything to ensure a fair hearing of your application. Planning committee meetings are public, so you may attend and listen, but not (usually) join in.

8.7 IF YOU DON'T GET THE ANSWER YOU WANTED

The planning committee might give you permission with unacceptable conditions, or refuse an Existing Use Certificate, or even turn you down flat. Do not despair. First stop is the planning officer to find out exactly why, and to get advice on how to get the answer you want. Officials sometimes disagree with the decisions of their committees and can be very helpful in such circumstances. The best course may be to re-apply using a different form of wording to overcome any misunderstanding that you may unintentionally have brought about. Under those conditions your covering letter would explain the changes you have made and why.

Alternatively, or after a second application has failed, you can appeal to the Department of the Environment against the council's decision. Once an appeal has failed there is effectively no higher appeal. In theory you could go to the High Court, but that is very costly indeed. Hence the emphasis on re-applying rather than going straight to appeal.

8.8 PLANNING APPEALS

There are two forms of appeal. The public hearing route is expensive – £5,000–£10,000 might cover a straightforward one – because you need to be professionally represented. The other sort is by written submissions and costs a great deal less. Either way, you must appeal within six months of the date of refusal, or have special permission for delay.

Most appeals involving small firms are written, so that is the method that will be described. The form on which refusal is notified tells you the address to write to for the appeal forms. You fill them in and return them. A copy of your comments is sent to the council who reply with their views, a copy of which is sent to you. An inspector visits the site by appointment to let you and the council see that there is a proper inspection. The inspector may ask questions for you to answer, but neither side is there to argue. Some inspectors carry their professional detachment so far as to decline a friendly offer to hold the end of the tape while they measure up. The whole process normally takes about six months. Once again the best course is not to do the whole thing unaided. You probably need advice from a chartered surveyor, architect or solicitor. Shop around to see what their record of success is in appeals, and to get quotes for the work. It is a specialised area and a lot may hang on the outcome, so professional help is advisable.

8.9 LEASES

For all sorts of reasons, however straightforward a lease may seem, it should never be signed without the benefit of legal advice. Renting a building involves taking on a number of liabilities which are unavoidable, and others that you might be able to get out of. The ones you usually have to put up with include paying the landlord's legal costs as well as your own, and paying the landlord's insurance premium on the building itself. You are free, of course, to arrange your own insurance on your own things inside the building. It may be worth checking with your broker that the insurance premium you are being asked to pay the landlord is reasonable. You may hear the term 'full repairing and insuring' or FRI lease. That means that you are responsible for all insurances and repairs to the building. Fair enough, provided you do not find that it means you are expected to put things right that were already wrong before you moved in.

The way to protect yourself against this possibility is to get advice from a solicitor or chartered surveyor. They might suggest that the building should be carefully inspected and its existing condition photographed, and a schedule of condition agreed with the landlord. That would establish a benchmark for what is your responsibility and what is not. Another good reason for taking advice is that the professionals have seen the problems before, and will protect you from future difficulty. What happens, for instance, if the roof gets wood-worm during your stay? Or if the existing, pleasant, landlord sells out to a really nasty successor? Often that can be more important even than the wording of documents, so it might be worth trying to find out your landlord's plans for the future.

8.10 RATES AND WATER CHARGES

Uniform Business Rates are charged on business premises by local authorities and water companies in a way that is similar to the Community Charge and water costs that apply to houses. The level is set nationally by the government and can be a lot higher than people expect and, to rub salt in the wound, firms get fewer services than householders. Councils are actually forbidden by law from collecting refuse from many business premises without making a separate charge. People sometimes appeal against a rating assessment out of annoyance. It is wise to take professional advice beforehand – you would not want to draw attention to a property that had been under-rated for years, and get the opposite result from the one you wanted. If you use a lot of water or very little it is worth discussing with the water supplier the benefits of having your supply metered.

8.11 KEY JOBS TO DO

■ Decide on your need for premises.
■ Begin investigating availability early.
■ Understand the main implications of the Town and Country Planning system for your firm and any proposed premises it may occupy.

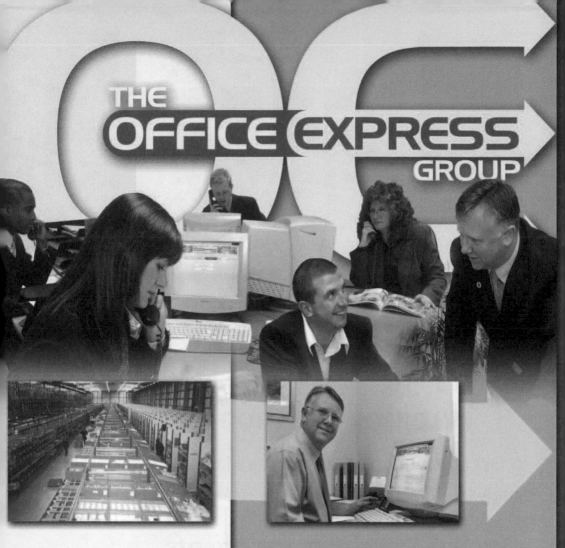

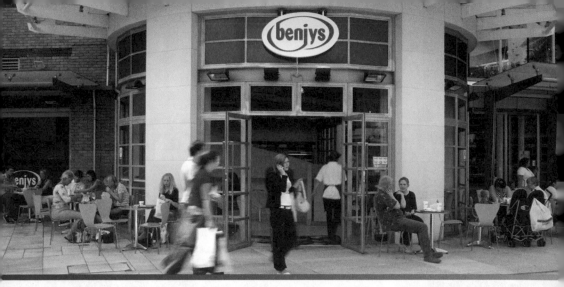

Opportunity

(AN OPPORTUNITY TOO BIG TO MISS)

In fact 3 great franchise opportunities from the UK's leading sandwich retailer:

- **Benjys Development Agents**
- **Benjys Franchise Shops**
- **Benjys Mobile Vanchises**

To find out more about the UK's fastest growing franchise please call our franchise hotline.

Franchise hotline:
0845 33 00 126

or visit www.benjys-sandwiches.com for further details.

Section 9: Management of operations

9.1 AIMS OF THIS SECTION

Although it may look straightforward at first glance, the whole process of providing a service or manufacturing a product can become so complex and confused that you get more and more harassed while getting further behind. Planning and control of your activity are therefore vitally important. Just as you negotiate when selling, you can do the same when buying. Moreover, when buying you can be caught out by unscrupulous people, or just by simple misunderstandings. This section aims to deal with all of these issues, as well as to suggest that, as a first step, it might be best to find a firm with spare capacity to do the manufacturing work for you.

9.2 PLANNING YOUR ACTIVITY

It seems obvious to say that you need to think ahead and to plan, but so many people have gone into business and then found that they rented premises of the wrong size or shape, or that their equipment will not do what is expected of it, or that the time allowed for jobs is never enough, or that they keep running out of materials. If they are honest, they all agree that they could have foreseen and avoided such problems. Of course, there are always extenuating circumstances – we all like to save face and blame anything but our own foolishness.

How do you stop all this from happening to you? You can never avoid errors completely, but a little planning will save a lot of hassle, and make life smoother for you – and for your customers. Also, try to learn from experience: know what went wrong and take it into account next time. To be able to do this, you need records of what happened.

9.3 CONTROL OF YOUR OPERATION

To look in detail at the control methods that you can use, we might start with the firm whose work consists of a number of individual jobs. Each should have its own job card which follows it through the production process. Each job card records:

■ job reference number and description;
■ customer's reference number for the job, and order number;
■ references to drawings, catalogues etc;
■ route to be followed through the production process;
■ completion date estimated for each stage of production;
■ materials needed;
■ special purchases needed;
■ time estimated for in each department or in each process;
■ name of each operative working on this job;
■ packing and delivery instructions.

This sets up the main headings which enable your aspirations for the job to be laid down. To turn the planning document into one that can achieve control, a box needs to be set against each heading in which *actual* performance is recorded. Regular and frequent inspection of job cards enables you to see which jobs and processes are falling behind schedule, so that some sort of action can be taken.

In addition, such a system offers other benefits. At the end of the week the hours recorded by each employee can be totalled to show the productive hours that each has apparently put in. If the hours shown add up to more than anyone has been present for, either you are getting more out of your staff than any boss has a right to expect, or something needs investigating. Likewise for the employee who records far fewer hours than you pay for. If this is your only control over the efficiency of the way you use staff, they will quickly learn to adjust the records so as to make you happy. Nevertheless, though crude, this can be a useful pointer to inefficiencies. Another advantage of a system like this is that you learn where your estimating method is going wrong by comparing estimate with reality. Furthermore, you spot bottlenecks before they occur; job cards that show a requirement for more than you can get out of a department or a machine quickly highlight the need to acquire more capacity, subcontract some work or revise delivery dates.

In addition to controls over individual jobs, you will need to oversee production as a whole. The form of those controls depends largely on the kind of business you are in. Common to all businesses is the need to understand:

- extent of forward commitments;
- spare capacity in each process or at each machine;
- scheduling of the next work to be done;
- holiday schedules;
- maintenance timetables;
- use of capacity against the level budgeted for;
- scrap and rework rates.

If your business undertakes 'specials', additional forms of control will include:

- progress of each job against deadlines;
- availability of special materials needed;
- progress on producing quotations;
- proportion of quotations that turn into orders.

On the other hand, if you make items that are kept in stock, your priorities will be different. You will focus on:

- 'free' stock levels of finished goods (ie total stock, less orders received but not yet delivered);
- materials stocks and reorder lead times;
- making economic batches, yet not over-stocking;
- relating production capacity and stock levels to sales forecasts.

As well as looking at the capacity of your equipment, you should look at that of your people. Do they need to master new skills to handle the work that you expect to be getting? Do they have the tools and working conditions that they need? Does everything they need have a sensible place? Is it in that place? What will you do if a key person retires or leaves for another reason? Above all, do *you* make it easy or hard for them to do their jobs well?

Talk about control systems is all very well, but thought also needs to be given to the way in which information is presented. All those whiteboards, charts and graphs in offices are not there to impress visitors; they are doing a job of work. Not all of the information in your firm should be on public display, but it certainly should be readily available to you at a glance in summary form. Then you stand a chance of running the firm rather than having it run you.

People walking into small firms' premises are too often confronted by muddle and mess. When materials and equipment are needed they cannot be found, causing a loss of valuable time. Spare parts and components get lost and damaged, raising costs still further. As such a firm grows, it sometimes takes on expensive space, rather than sort out the confusion. Yet the simple act of clearing up often releases space to enable expansion to take place much more cheaply.

On the other hand, there are the blessed few firms whose premises are spick and span with everything in its allotted place. The atmosphere of smooth, business-like activity tells you everything you need to know about its management. Compare these two sorts of place, from the points of view of good-quality staff, customers and bank managers. Which is more likely to get and keep the best people? Which will give a customer the better impression? Where does the bank manager feel that he ought to invest his shareholders' money? Neither set-up came about by some mysterious process unknown to mortals, but each was *directly caused* by its manager's attitudes, ideas and methods.

The effect of your behaviour on the way that your staff perform is discussed in Section 11. For the present it is enough to say that your example and leadership are most important. Even the best manager does not get production from staff 100 per cent of the time, however. Earlier discussion of the one-person firm suggested that when you were the sole employee, you would probably manage to produce for 25 hours out of the 60 or so per week you worked in total. This is about a 40 per cent efficiency. Since your staff will not have the same range of nonproductive activity to perform as you do, their efficiency ought to be at or around 70 per cent to 75 per cent. In other words, if you are paying for 40 hours' work, you can realistically expect it to yield about 30 hours' production. To get it to that level and to hold it there demands that you constantly ask of your staff that they set a brisk place. In agriculture they say that the best fertiliser is the farmer's boot; frequent and detailed checks by the boss are what ensure the best harvest. The same goes for production areas.

Once the firm employs a few people, even where they are self-employed subcontractors, it can be worth exercising some direct control over their activities. 'Control' here, as elsewhere, is used in the specialised meaning employed in management circles. That is to say, it does not mean pulling all the strings, but rather knowing what is supposed to be happening and comparing that with what is actually taking place.

The system proposed here is simple but has proved to be effective in practice. Every Friday lunchtime you meet each member of staff in turn for 10 to 15 minutes. They bring to the meeting a list of the tasks they are working on and say where they are on each task now, and where they expect to be in a week's time. You discuss with them whether or not they are being over- or under-ambitious and they make any amendments to their plans that you agree between you. They then produce a fair copy, which they leave with you.

The following Friday lunchtime you both discuss progress against plan before looking ahead to the plan for the coming week. By these means, you ensure that they are kept busy on the tasks you regard as important and also, by recording actual against proposed achievement, build up an archive that helps you to come to a fair view of performance, longer term. That feeds into performance reviews at year-end or, where the employee is failing to deliver, into the disciplinary system.

Thus, by devoting no more than 15 minutes a week per employee to formal planning and review, you keep on top of what is going on, how each staff member is performing, and make a contribution to being seen to manage people fairly. It need not occupy an increasing share of your time as the firm grows, for once you have appointed supervisors or section-heads there is no need to interview every member of staff; instead you confine yourself to applying this technique solely to those responsible individuals.

Staff are the scarcest and most costly item in many small firms. It therefore makes sense to keep them working even when demand falls. In some markets sometimes prices have to be cut. If your business is like this, it is worth talking to a production specialist with a costing back-ground, or an accountant with production experience, about the various methods of costing. Some of them might throw up an opportunity for an occasional tactical price cut to keep the factory employed. Expert advice is essential, for this is a risky field.

In considering the way that your people use their time, do not avoid looking at all aspects. Your effect on them has been mentioned, but you might also consider the rules that you lay down for:

- *Hours of work.* Could 8 to 5 be extended to 8 to 5.30?
- *Tea-breaks.* Do people need to leave their work stations to have a drink? In some activities it is desirable that they do, but could your people take the drink at their work?
- *Lunch-breaks.* Is a whole hour necessary, or desirable?
- *Time-keeping.* A 10-minute tea-break can easily drift into a 20- or 30-minute period once washing, popping out for some cigarettes, and discussing last night's TV have been got through.
- *Punctuality.* A 7.30 start should mean exactly that, not a 7.30 arrival and a start at 7.45; a 5 o'clock finish does not mean breaking off at quarter-to to start getting ready for the off.

If that sounds penny-pinching, think of the effect of letting things drift. Just by banishing tea-breaks and ensuring a punctual start and finish, you could employ one person less in every six or seven. That is not greed on your part, for it means greater efficiency for your firm which will enable it to beat off less disciplined competitors. In turn that implies more job security for your staff, which they might need reminding of.

A final few words on control, to do with keeping control of your stock. Remember the Forces' maxim, that nothing moves without a piece of paper: relying on memory and honesty are simply not enough.

9.4 SAFETY

Keep the working area clean and clear of obstructions and hazards; call in an outsider for a safety inspection, and shock yourself with the number of dangers that there are, and put things right straightaway. After all, you have no immunity against injury, and if you are off for a month, or lose an eye, or three fingers, who will run the business and keep your family? Even if you are insured, your income will be very low. And be careful when lifting: do not try proving to yourself, or to anyone else, how tough you are. Ask anyone with a hernia or slipped disc what it is like to live with. Display the statutory notices and read them (heavy going they may be, but they could save your life), and have some way of raising the alarm if you get hurt. Again, it is so obvious it should not need saying, but thousands every year ignore it and pay the price: observe the safety rules, work at a safe pace, use machine guards, never take risks, and wear the right protective gear.

You are legally obliged by the Health and Safety at Work Act to work safely and to ensure that your staff do the same, as well as to keep a record of any unsafe incidents. Consult the Factory Inspector, who is in the phone book under 'Health and Safety Executive'.

9.5 PURCHASING

This is the mirror-image of selling, and you will be fascinated to observe the techniques of persuasion that are used by the salespeople who call on you. As well as educating you in sales skills, they could of course rob you, so a healthy dash of scepticism is needed in dealing with them. Salespeople are eager to please, and without meaning to mislead can let you think that their product will do things that it cannot. Once more it seems so obvious, but so many people starting businesses buy pigs in pokes, and especially equipment they expect will do a particular job without really checking. Always, without exception, shop around. Usually the only reason for the seller to push for a fast decision is precisely to stop you from finding out just how common and cheap is the allegedly unique and expensive product. So get alternative quotes.

Get sales staff to criticise their competitors' products: like all of us, they are usually better at pointing out the shortcomings of others than of themselves. Then let them answer the criticisms of their own product. This applies ten times over if you are not familiar with the process, materials or technology involved. Here, you need specialist help before making any commitment, perhaps from one of the agencies listed in Section 13. Do not let yourself be pushed into buying more than you need or can afford. Any salesperson is happier with half a loaf than no bread, and if you stand firm they will either miraculously find a way of sending you a smaller order than the previously sacred minimum – as a special personal favour, of course – or fix up something with another customer so that you can buy a little from them.

If you have thought out properly in advance what you need the equipment or material to do, and have specified this to the salesperson, he or she can tell you whether or not the product meets your requirements. It will then be difficult to shift you from what is best for you to what is best for the seller – and remember, however plausible and fair-minded they may seem, that is exactly what they are paid for. In front of them, write down and date a note of the points that are important to you, and the promises made, and read them back. That should ensure that you get only reliable information. (If you ever sell to a really professional buyer, the odds are that the secretary will be sitting in the corner behind you. It is no accident that there is no typing while you are there – the secretary's job is taking shorthand notes of everything you say.) And don't forget that the law of contract applies to verbal agreements too, so do not say that you will buy without really meaning it, and never, ever, give someone an order to make them go away. Just tell them to go away – it is quicker and certainly cheaper.

9.6 NEGOTIATING WHEN BUYING

As a small business you may feel you have no buying power at all. Possibly that is true, but often it is not. Whatever your position, you can usually improve it. If they want you to order by phone, try to get them to send a salesperson. If actually having to visit, the salesperson will be keener to justify it by getting an order and opening a new account, and so may give away a discount or let you have a promotional offer that you do not really qualify for. You need to build up your case: they are nice people, their products are good, but their competitor is making a powerful pitch; and their goods are not exactly what you want . . . Leave it in the air, and let them try to think of how to persuade you. Keep on coming back with objections (and a smile) and keep showing interest, and sooner or later they will get round to thinking about reducing the price or increasing the value in some other way. How nice of them, that offer does really make the decision a lot easier, but you cannot agree to the conditions attached to it. Finally, they give in and you buy what you intended to buy all along but on much better terms.

If the firm deals from a trade counter you will find it difficult to use these tactics on the warehouse staff behind the counter. They are just there to fetch and carry, and the printed price-list is law as far as they are concerned. That is exactly the company's game – to make it look as if you are dealing with a brute machine rather than human beings open to persuasion. So refuse to play the game, but ask to see the manager about opening a new trade account. When you get face to face with that person, or with the rep they may send out to see if you are a genuine business, you can try negotiating discounts and credit exactly as suggested above. The more impersonal the contact, the more you are forced to accept their terms, so try to make it personal. If they are a constant supplier, keep the relationship going – send a Christmas card at least, and don't abuse the credit terms too much. If you cannot pay this month, let them know that it will help your cash flow greatly if they would allow you a couple of weeks' extra credit. Do not wait until you appear on the 'Stop' list.

9.7 QUALITY CONTROL

Even if it means delivery will be late, check quality before your product leaves your workshop. A few hours' lateness gets you less of a bad reputation than a delivery of faulty goods made on time. Consignments of goods delivered to you should be checked for completeness, freedom from damage, and quality, as soon as they are received. Any shortcomings or shortage should be notified by phone and confirmed by letter immediately. If you leave it until later, it may be too late for your claim to be verified as the carrier holds 'proof of delivery' documents for only a short time. You can then find yourself forced to pay for something you did not receive. If you let anyone take back goods that are damaged or faulty, do get them to sign for them, and to print their name. Otherwise some slip-up or change of staff by the supplier (and they do happen all the time) could mean you can't prove that you no longer have the goods, so you still have to pay.

You may hear mention of BS EN ISO 9000. That is a British, European and international standard covering quality management, and major buyers of goods and services are increasingly insisting that their suppliers should observe it. Details can be had from small firms agencies and from the British Standards Institution (www.bsi-global.com).

9.8 PRODUCT DESIGN

In many companies there is a constant tug-of-war between the selling side, who would love to have products personalised for each customer, and the production people, who can see the benefits of standardised manufacturing. In the very small firm this struggle goes on in the head of the owner, who can feel completely bemused by the choices presented. In the end he or she will recognise that the customers' needs come first, but no chance should be lost to standardise where possible. The benefits are obvious: simplicity, economy, lower stocks, less design time, and so on. Even where quite different end products are being made, it might be possible to standardise some components or sub-assemblies – but only within the limits of customer acceptability. It is worth checking with customers what they will accept: products are often wildly over-specified because the engineer thought that this was what was needed, whereas the customer would have been delighted with something less substantial or complex.

Although this section is to do with production matters, a few words should be said about the marketing aspect of design. The textbooks are full of classic stories about minor changes to specification, or just to appearance, that transformed the appeal of a product. It can work for your products, too. But the very best design-led marketing successes usually involve much more. They show that designers who address basic marketing principles are the big winners. Instead of titivating a product's cosmetic appeal they go right to the root of the customer's real needs. They deliver better *value*, which does not just mean cutting prices (see Section 2.9).

9.9 KEY JOBS TO DO

- Plan in detail how each job will go through the system.
- Set up controls to alert you to the state of play and make sure you and staff operate them.
- Set up a safety policy and a means of updating it and ensuring that all staff conform to it.
- Consult the Health and Safety Executive.

Section 10: Bookkeeping, financial housekeeping, VAT and tax

10.1 AIMS OF THIS SECTION

This section highlights some points on keeping simple but clear records and tries to demystify the dreaded VAT. It does not contain an attempt to train you in bookkeeping: it takes the view that as little time as possible should be spent on this chore consistent with accuracy, keeping within the law, and providing information for you to know where the business is going.

10.2 BOOKKEEPING

In the excitement of starting a business, many people forget the importance of the records that the State and others will expect them to keep. It is easy to get into trouble, and then try to rescue yourself, but better to set up a good administrative system from the start and operate it properly. So you will do yourself a considerable favour by getting this under way well in advance of actually starting to make and to sell. How to do it? If you try to do it yourself the traditional 'double entry' way, you may need a lot of training. It is unwise to set up your own system, however simple your business might be at first. Unfortunately, a do-it-yourself set of books has a nasty habit of being unable to cope with unforeseen complications. The professional productions take them into account. The sensible alternative is to use one of the simplified systems like Safeguard or Kalamazoo. They are not hard to master and the people who make them will always help out if you get stuck. Clear with your accountant which system you plan to use, and make sure that simpler records for you do not mean more work for him or her (and thus higher fees for you to pay). Or you could use one of the bookkeeping services that are often run from a person's home. That is not recommended as first choice – you should run your own accounts and know what is going on financially in the firm.

Absolutely the way not to do it is to do no bookkeeping until you have accumulated a carrier bag full of cheque-book stubs, bank statements, invoices, and so on, and then dump the lot on your accountant. A professional will sort it out for you, but at a price that will make your hair curl. To avoid this, systems can be developed of varying complexity. The simplest of all is one based on the four drawers of your desk, or four files or, indeed, four old shoeboxes. Two drawers are used for invoices that are unpaid – one for purchases, one for sales. When invoices are paid, they move across to the other two drawers. The point is that no invoices go astray, and by adding up the contents of the 'unpaid' drawers you see exactly what you owe and are owed. Your cheque book and paying-in book complete the picture by enabling you to work out how much is in the bank. The very simplest type of business can probably manage on this, but only if it never needs to get quick information on profits.

The next stage up is the simplified system already referred to. Thereafter, you might move up to a more sophisticated 'one-entry' system, where putting in one figure can complete more than one essential record. Then to a full double-entry system designed in conjunction with your accountant. On the other hand, many businesses start off with a computerised system. If and when you do use a computer for bookkeeping, take proper advice and remember that the system must be approved by Customs and Excise for VAT calculations before you install it. Try to avoid the temptation to go for anything less than a fully proven business system.

All bookkeeping needs to be done promptly – at least weekly, preferably daily. Receipts must be got and kept for every purchase, and bank statements should be carefully checked against cheque and paying-in books. And they have to be kept for seven years, to satisfy the tax authorities.

10.3 BANK ACCOUNTS

A very small sole trader or partnership can easily get business transactions mixed up with personal money. The simplest way of operating to avoid this is to have two bank accounts, each with its own cheque book. One is your personal account, or joint account with your spouse or partner, out of which you pay all the personal and home bills, and draw your pocket money. The other, the business or Number Two account, is kept to the business only. In addition to paying the business creditors and receiving the business income, it pays a wage (known to accountants as 'drawings') to your personal, or Number One, account. There is nothing to say you have to keep business and personal accounts at the same bank, although bank managers like to have both under their control.

10.4 VALUE ADDED TAX – VAT – IN OUTLINE

If you are ever tempted to fiddle your VAT, remember that in extreme cases HM Customs has the right to confiscate most of your records for investigation, and thus practically to close you down. Look up Customs and Excise in the phone book or visit their website and ask for their free leaflets and any advice on special VAT situations which may arise with your firm. A simplified explanation of the principles follows.

Products you sell can be taxed either at standard rate (17.5 per cent at the time of writing), or at zero rate (strictly speaking, 0 per cent, so not taxed at present but the mechanism is there if the government feels like imposing it), or exempt altogether. (There is another, special rate for fuel and power.) Let us say that you are registered for VAT and sell 10 widgets, which are standard-rated, at £10 each to XZ Ltd, and your invoice says: '10 Widgets at £10 = £100 + VAT = £117.50 payable'. The £17.50 tax is called an 'output', the name in VAT jargon for the tax on the goods you sell. Now for – you guessed it – 'inputs'. That is the tax on your purchases. For the sake of the illustration, you buy in unfinished blanks for widgets from Smith Stampings, and their invoice says '10 Widget blanks at £1 = £10 + £1.75 VAT = £11.75 payable'. That £1.75 is of course your 'input', the VAT on your purchase. So far, so good. At the end of the quarter, you send in a return to HM Customs and Excise, showing your total inputs and your total outputs. If you have charged out (say) £1,000 of output tax and have been invoiced for £800 of input tax, you send a cheque for the £200 difference. On the other hand, if you invoice for only £800 of output tax and are charged for £1,000 of tax on inputs, HM Customs and Excise will send you a cheque for £200.

In principle, it really is that simple, but you should remember that only VAT-registered bodies are allowed to show VAT on an invoice. That does not deter some tricksters who charge VAT even though unregistered. The resulting loss is carried by the poor mug who paid out the alleged VAT unless he can recover it through the courts.

10.5 REGISTERING FOR VAT

You are not compelled to register for VAT if you are working in a very small way. Equally, you can de-register if your sales fall below the limits. At the time of writing (2005) the limit for compulsory registration is a turnover of £60,000 in either the last 12 months or the next 30 days: it is raised from time to time in the Budget to allow for inflation.

While you do not have to register in your early days if you are very small, it can be worth doing. You are allowed to under a system called 'Voluntary Registration'. The main snag is that you must remain registered for at least two years. The motive for doing so is if you pay out a lot of VAT on equipment or stock that you buy before you have built up sales to the limit where you must register. It enables you to claim back the VAT on those early purchases as an input. Bear in mind that VAT on cars cannot be reclaimed, but vans are different. Before setting up, consult Customs and Excise and your accountant about when would be best to register.

Another aspect of that decision is how it affects your prices. If you sell to the public, it makes no odds whether your price is £117.50 with no VAT payable, or £100 + £17.50 VAT = £117.50. On the other hand, if you sell to businesses registered for VAT, and most are, there is a lot of difference. To a business customer an invoice for £100 + £17.50 VAT means that the goods cost £100: the £17.50 is merely part of a tax-collecting exercise, to be offset by his inputs at the end of the quarter.

There is a simplified scheme for firms with sales under £150,000 a year. In essence, you record the VAT you collect and pay out, subtract one from the other, and multiply the result by the Flat Rate percentage to arrive at the VAT you owe or are owed. Under this Flat Rate Scheme, businesses pay a rate related to the industry they are in – an IT consultant, for instance, pays 13 per cent and most manufacturers 8.5–10 per cent. There is a snag, in that a number of purchases do not qualify. However, in your first year of registration you get a reduction of 1 per cent in the rate.

10.6 INCOME TAX AND CORPORATION TAX

The Inland Revenue Inspectors of Taxes publish an excellent free leaflet called 'Thinking of working for yourself?' (PSE1). It outlines your position so well that there is no point in repeating it all here. Their website (www.inlandrevenue.gov.uk) is also helpful, but will often transfer you to the site for Business Link for detailed information.

10.7 NATIONAL INSURANCE

Although it started off more or less as a State insurance arrangement, NI has now become virtually another income tax. As a self-employed person (active partner or sole trader) you have to pay Class 2 contributions weekly, which are at a straightforward flat rate. On top of this you pay a

Class 4 contribution, which is earnings-related on profits (or fees and benefits if you are self-employed as a director) between certain limits (for the tax year starting April 2004, it is set at 8 per cent of profits between £4,745 and £31,720).

You can pay Class 2s by direct debit, either monthly or quarterly. Class 4s cannot be assessed until your results for the year are complete. Consequently, they are collected via the income tax system as a result of completing the self-assessment form. For both income tax and Class 4 NI, it is best to put some money aside every week so you can pay the bill when it arrives. Again, all the details are listed in PSE1 (see Section 10.6). If you have any difficulties, the Inland Revenue self-employed helpline (0845 3021458) is very good.

10.8 TAX RELIEFS

Most of the expenditure on items connected with business are allowable for tax relief. There may be some that you do not automatically think of, and again your accountant's advice is vital before you start in business or even start buying things for the firm. If you work from home you may be tempted to claim tax relief on part of the household expenses and it might be granted, but when you sell the house the Inland Revenue might, in return, claim capital gains tax on part of the proceeds (homes are normally exempt from CGT). Again, check with your accountant. A basic understanding of tax is important to a business owner but it is such a complex field that professional advice is essential before decisions are taken.

When you start in business on your own you may be able to claim back some of the tax you have paid in previous years. This does not apply if you trade as a limited company, but only if you are self-employed as a sole trader or partner. It all revolves around the idea of 'tax losses'. A tax loss need not be a real loss – indeed, highly profitable companies try to acquire them all the time. To take an example:

In the same tax year	
Net profit before tax	£5,000
Tax allowance	£15,000
Tax loss	£10,000

The £10,000 'loss' can be claimed against earlier taxed income to produce a refund of tax already paid. It can be seen that the company used as an example was in fact profitable – it made £5,000 – but it chose to invest some of its cash (and/or some loan – we are not told) in new equipment.

In return, the tax authorities will chip in with an offer to let the firm carry forward that £10,000 tax allowance into future years, or to repay tax paid on £10,000-worth of income in earlier years. This concession extends over the first four years of the new firm's life, and allows the back claim to refer to as much as the total of all the tax paid in the three years before setting up. If your firm might want to take advantage of this arrangement, careful timing of your formal start is advisable, which needs the expert help of your accountant.

Tax allowances usually arise because the business has bought a capital asset against which the tax regulations permit a 'writing-down allowance' each year, which can be changed in the Budget. If on machines and equipment it had been 40 per cent, the business quoted above might have spent £37,500 on machinery (40 per cent of £37,500 = £15,000 writing-down allowance). Allowances are also available against property, but at much lower rates. IT equipment and development expenses have been given especially favourable treatment in recent years. As the situation keeps changing, it is worth keeping up with it.

10.9 KEY JOBS TO DO

- ∎ Set up a VAT-approved bookkeeping system.
- ∎ Set up bank accounts.
- ∎ Understand VAT, NI and taxes in outline.
- ∎ Take professional advice.

Section 11: Employing people

11.1 AIMS OF THIS SECTION

Life would be simpler for many business owners if they could do everything themselves and manage without staff. In some businesses it is possible to do just that, but problems come when you want to expand. Better organisation and more mechanisation may help up to a point, but if you have any growth ambitions at all you usually find that you become an employer before very long. This section aims to point out the main traps and to help you to avoid them.

11.2 THE LAW: A BIG PROBLEM?

Most of the small business horror stories centre around employment law, ending on the refrain, 'you can't sack anyone these days'. Don't believe it. Certainly, you are not allowed to play ducks and drakes with employees' livelihoods in the way that our great-grandparents could. But the reasonable, decent employer has very little to fear from the law. The biggest problem is in minimising and solving the problems caused to employees, finding good staff in the first place, and finding the time to spend with them to ensure that they stay. To help, the Business Link website publishes full information describing obligations and rights, with links to ACAS (Advisory, Conciliation and Arbitration Service) to deal with the paperwork.

11.3 FINDING GOOD PEOPLE

The first job, as with any other management task, is to decide what you want done and how. In other words, define the job systematically, without any fixed ideas about who should do it. Think about what needs to be done now, of course, but also how it will evolve in the future. What special qualities are needed to do all this? You are now able to get a picture of the person; if a mature telephone manner is essential, a 17-year-old is unlikely to suit. If you might want them to run up and down ladders, some 60-year-olds might not have the energy and fitness. Equally, if the job is likely to change dramatically in three years' time, it could be worth taking on someone who is three years from retirement and recruit new people for the new job after two and a half years. Where and how do you find good people? In three main ways: putting the word out, advertising, or going to an employment agency. Each has its benefits and drawbacks. The author's preference – though it does not suit everyone – is for the ads that you place yourself. They cost money whether or not you find someone (agencies charge only for people recruited) but you control exactly what the ad says and how you are described; not all agency staff are so careful. Application forms are a must, to check on candidates' writing ability and presentation, to give you a written and signed record of the applicant's past achievements and to protect you from charges of discrimination.

One day you might be asked to prove that you selected a candidate on the basis of qualifications for the job, and that sex, colour and religious beliefs did not come into it. For that reason you do not destroy completed application forms for at least a couple of years.

11.4 THE INTERVIEW

Having received the completed application forms you are now ready to call people for interview. Although time will be short, you should try to hold more than one interview, and to have someone else present whose judgement you respect. Typically (depending on the job) you might ask seven people to first interviews and shortlist three for your final choice. Make allowances for interview nerves, try to put candidates at ease, but do not give more than an outline sketch of the job itself until after you have drawn out of the candidate what he or she is looking for, is good at, is bad at, and wants to avoid in a new job. If the job involves contact with children, undertake the necessary checks (your local Social Services department will advise). Take up references from previous employers if candidates give their permission: the only objection should be to approaching the current employer before a job offer has been made and accepted, subject to the references proving satisfactory. When taking up references, do it by telephone and get exact dates as far as possible. Why? There may be something that the employee wants to hide – and that, by definition, is what you want to know about. It is worth mentioning here that your employee nowadays has legal immunity from telling the truth about old criminal convictions, and you cannot fire him or her if you find out about it later. So if that is important to you, your checking needs to be very thorough before any job offer is made.

A step-by-step guide to the whole recruitment process is given in Appendix 4.

11.5 REFERENCES

As discussed in Section 11.4, a satisfactory reference from the current or last employer should be obtained. It should agree on the main facts and the exact period of employment, but the rest should be taken with caution. Spite, self-justification, rationalisation, all can play a part in how a reference is phrased. An unwise employer will give a good reference to an employee whom they want to see the back of. Unwise, because you could claim damages if you sustained a loss as a result. For example, someone who had been suspected of fiddling is given a reference for exemplary honesty. Let us say that there was not enough evidence to prosecute, but some was building up. He then joins you, and six months later you find that he has helped himself to £2,000. You would probably have a case against the former employer. For just that sort of reason, you in your turn would be wise not to give references. Of course, you want to help former employees, so you do not refuse a reference outright – that looks like a condemnation in itself – but you send a standard letter which confirms that Mr Smith worked for you from June 2002 to February 2005 and was employed as a driver, rising to warehouse supervisor, but going on to say that it is your company's practice never to comment on any employee's performance or reasons for leaving.

11.6 THE JOB OFFER AND ITS ACCEPTANCE

The offer should be made in a letter, with written acceptance by the successful candidate. Do not turn down the unsuccessful candidates until you have written confirmation that the job has been accepted. Incidentally, if an applicant accepts a job offer and then does not start, causing you the trouble of re-advertising, he or she could be liable to pay the costs (but you could have trouble getting them). When they join, tell the local Income

Tax office, who will give you the necessary forms and tax tables. If the person is under 18, then notify the local Careers Office.

11.7 GETTING WHO YOU WANT, AND MAKING SURE THEY STAY

Nothing is for ever, so always know what you will do if a key employee gives a week's notice just as you are off on three weeks' holiday. Blame yourself if you are unprepared. You could not have blamed the individual if he or she had died, yet the effect is the same. Equally, you should never get into the position where a key part of your business is out of your control and is understood by only one of your employees. If he or she is the only one who knows the way round parts of the business, not only can you not afford to lose that person but you are also open to fraud.

Remember, too, that it is easy to make staff disgruntled. Treat them badly, and you can be sure that any suffering that they experience will rebound tenfold on you. If you manage your people well, you do yourself, as well as them, a favour. The right way to treat employees is the way you would expect to be treated yourself: openly, honestly, equally with other employees, being told unpleasant news straightforwardly, being expected to contribute fully, and having effort recognised. Your employees will not have the grievances there are in so many larger firms: dealing with frightened superiors who dare not give decisions, seeing the bosses arriving at 9 o'clock (with no clocking-on) when they have clocked on at 7.30 am, seeing white-collar staff getting separate (and better) dining arrangements, and so on. Your staff will know that you work harder and longer than they do, in the same conditions, and that is what earns you the respect that few managers ever command in larger firms. You might not be able to pay them as much as a bigger firm – but you might have to. It is worth not being flamboyant in the type of car you get. An old Aston-Martin, or a new Ford, may not be overdoing things, but you tempt your employees to think how much they have contributed to a new Aston-Martin, Maserati or Porsche.

While you will want your employees to share in the success that they have helped to create, beware of bonus schemes. The annual Christmas bonus rapidly becomes thought of as a natural entitlement and loses motivating power, and bonuses based on output can cause more ill-feeling than almost anything else. Probably the best – or least bad – scheme is one based on value added. Your best bet is to seek specialist advice on its design and installation. Pension schemes and medical insurance schemes are worth looking at. Pensions are almost essential for good staff, and it should be a scheme which makes it easy for staff to transfer their accumulated rights on joining, and out of it on leaving. Pensions policy is under review, so firms large and small need to watch developments carefully.

Although people may be employed for 40 hours a week, they cannot work effectively for all of that time. Most firms think that they do well to get 30 hours' production from a week's work, and many get far less. See Sections 3.4 and 9.3.

11.8 CONTRACTS OF EMPLOYMENT

You are obliged by law to give a 'written statement' of the terms of the contract of employment within two months of the employee joining you. It applies only to employees working at least 16 hours a week. As you will know from Section 7 on law, the contract exists even if it is not written down. To keep the relationship with your employee clear and above board, the written statement should be given at the earliest stage of the employment – say, during the first week. The written statement has by law to contain the particulars listed below. But you should not try to write your own. It is full of pitfalls and needs advice from someone experienced in the field. The usual advisory agencies can help, as could a lecturer in industrial relations from your local college or business school. Your solicitor is technically capable of writing it, but may slip into legalese in its wording. The employee's reaction to a document not written in plain language may be to run straight to the trade union for advice and protection – not quite what you wanted to achieve.

The written statement of the terms of employment should show:

- names of the employer and employee;
- when the employment began;
- when the period of *continuous* employment began; for example, staff working for a firm that you took over would have this period operating from when they started work for the firm, not from the take-over;
- the date of expiry, if employment is for a fixed term;
- job title;
- how pay is calculated, the pay rate and the pay period (hourly, weekly, monthly);
- normal working hours and overtime requirements;
- holiday entitlements, holiday pay calculation, public holidays;
- sickness and injury absence rules;
- sick pay calculations;
- pension scheme details, if any, and whether or not the employment is contracted out of the State scheme;
- length of notice required and given;

- disciplinary rules;
- the person to whom the employee should apply if dissatisfied with a disciplinary ruling;
- the person to whom the employee can take a grievance connected with work.

The last two items, disciplinary and grievance procedures, may be shown in separate documents to which employees have access – the usual place is the staff noticeboard. The same goes for the firm's health and safety policy (yes, you should have one of those too).

Each of these papers needs proper and careful design by a specialist. The list above is shown so that you can brief your adviser properly, and thus use less of his or her time, which will be costing somebody money.

Not only do they deserve specialist attention, but they should also be written with an individual business – your business – in mind. Again, the advisers can help. Indeed, some of the advisory agencies have on their staff specialists who offer this service. As an alternative, a standard form can be bought from a commercial stationer, but this seems too impersonal for a firm that is trying to show its staff that they are valued. To the boss, the written statement may be an irritating routine matter, to be got out of the way as soon as possible. But to the staff it is an important document which confirms what the boss thinks of them, and speaking volumes about how they can expect to be treated. And they have to be given it by the time they have been with you for two months – just about the time when the jobs that they did not get, or declined, might become free again. If the headhunter phones your new young star at home one evening, the last thing you want is for them to start talking seriously about a possible move. So do not encourage it by giving the wrong sort of written statement.

11.9 EMPLOYMENT PROTECTION

Twelve months after the employee joins he or she qualifies for protection from dismissal without good reason. The period of immunity does not apply if you dismiss on grounds of race or sex, or because the employee becomes pregnant, or has to do with trade union activity, or because the employee has not disclosed a 'spent' criminal conviction and a number of other reasons. If you employ five people or fewer, a pregnant employee may not have the right to insist on reinstatement if it is not reasonably practicable for you to take her back following the birth. In larger firms she can insist, subject to certain conditions being met.

11.10 INDUSTRIAL TRIBUNALS

If an employee feels that he or she has been dismissed unfairly you could be hauled up before an Industrial Tribunal, where the onus will be on you to prove that you did dismiss fairly. The employer is guilty unless he or she can prove otherwise! But things are not as bad as they seem.

Before all this happens, the law demands that you make every effort to resolve matters in the workplace. Not to have done so will count against you. Let us now assume that your efforts have failed and the ex-employee has taken out an action against you.

An officer from ACAS will then try to sort things out between the two of you, and should succeed unless one of you is being really stubborn. If the matter is settled at that stage, so be it. If not, the ACAS officer will report to the Tribunal and it will not look too good if you come out of that looking stubborn and inflexible. You and the ex-employee will give evidence, which is at least one day out of the office (plus solicitors' fees for a day) and the Tribunal will usually give its decision there and then. The awards can be many thousands of pounds, so it is worth fighting if you have a good case. If your case is bad, bargain with the ex-employee through ACAS to try to get acceptance of a cash payment in full and final settlement of the claim. ACAS will record it in such a way that the claim is withdrawn. If either side ignores the ACAS arbitrator's recommendation and insists on pushing ahead to a full Tribunal hearing, which they lose, they risk having costs awarded against them.

11.11 FAIR DISMISSAL

To dismiss fairly you have to prove you acted reasonably, given all the circumstances, and that the reason for dismissal was admissible. Admissible reasons include redundancy, misconduct, incapacity for the work, some other major reason why you could not keep the employee on (such as strong personality conflict), or if by keeping him or her on you would break the law. The way you handled it also affects the Tribunal's view of whether or not you acted 'reasonably' (see Sections 11.12 and 11.13).

The ACAS website (www.acas.org.uk) gives comprehensive guidance on fair dismissals and the all-important procedures that accompany them.

11.12 DISCIPLINARY PROCEDURES

A rather forbidding title for a very necessary subject. You need to lay down these procedures and to stick to them in the interests of fairness, consistency, and being on the right side of the law. If someone misbehaves really badly you could sack him or her on the spot: in your disciplinary procedure you can list examples of behaviour which fall into this category. They might include drunkenness, horseplay, violence, theft, refusal to carry out lawful instructions, unjustified absence, wilful damage to company property, unauthorised removal of property from company premises, disobeying safety rules – and that is not a full list, and neither should yours attempt to be.

It should be made clear that it illustrates only the sort of offence involved, as there may be others which apply to your type of work. A printer, for instance, could reasonably sack on the spot someone who smoked in the paper store. As it happens, you would be ill-advised to sack instantly – far better to send the employee home, suspended on full pay (it is illegal not to pay) while you cool off and get to the facts of the case. After all, the person you catch putting an expensive meter into the boot of their car may have been told by their supervisor that it is OK to borrow it over the weekend to help the vicar to check on that worrying bulge in the church wall. Of course, serious misconduct is one thing, and minor matters are another. Someone who is repeatedly late with no good excuse can be even more of a problem than the one who takes two days 'sick' for a mid-week away football match. Similarly, there are other minor offences that you cannot let slide. If things get so bad that you have to dismiss, you should have built up a case and recorded it in writing. The first instance should attract a verbal warning which is noted on the employee's file. A written warning would be issued for the second, making it clear that a repetition could lead to dismissal. On the third offence he or she could be sacked, and the reasons put in writing with your solicitor's help. Of course you do not sack someone for three minor offences in five years. Perhaps you would put a time limit on the record and ignore them in this 'totting up' procedure if they were more than six months old.

11.13　GRIEVANCE PROCEDURE

So far we have looked at the trouble that misbehaving employees can cause you. But you, their boss, can be as big a problem to them, or more so, because they can rarely put you out of a job, while you have the power to do that to them. So fair dealing requires that they can question any decision that affects them. The mirror-image of the disciplinary procedure is the grievance procedure. If the employee feels that you have been harsh or unfair, he or she should have the right to complain formally. In large firms, these formal procedures can be very complex, involving unions, works councils, ACAS, and heaven knows who else. In very small companies the appeal is usually straight back to the boss. That can make it a bit ticklish: how does this person dare question your instructions? In the hurly-burly it is easy to react instinctively, but in the interests of good management it is worth hearing them out. You will not be the first boss to be saved by one of the staff from doing something which would have unintended, unjust side-effects, or from asking the impossible, or from giving contradictory orders; so listen. Most complaints stop there and are sorted out on the spot. If, however, your considered view is that a collision is inevitable, in the best interests of the business it would be as well to hold a formal grievance meeting at which notes would be taken of both sides' views. If things ever escalated, you would thank your lucky stars that evidence of such a meeting was available for your solicitor to build into your case.

If at all possible, have two tiers in your grievance procedure, the supervisor being the first, with you as the final arbiter. At least in the early days of your firm that is unlikely to be possible, but you can introduce it as you grow. In such a situation, the supervisor will need to be trained regarding this, as well as other managerial aspects of his or her responsibilities.

11.14 REDUNDANCY

If work falls off you can sack people by this route quite straightforwardly. As it is not a key element in starting your firm, the subject can be left there as far as this book is concerned. But take specialist advice well in advance if you think you may have to do it: an apparent redundancy can easily become an unfair dismissal if it is handled amateurishly. In any case, most employees are entitled to a redundancy payment, so a cost may be attached to the decision.

11.15 HEALTH AND SAFETY AT WORK ACT 1974

Very important: many small firms could be virtually closed down overnight if their working practices led to a serious accident. In some cases their staff, owners and/or directors could be imprisoned. While the law does not normally expect you to do much more than lead the horse to water, under HASAWA you are expected to get it to drink as well, or at least to have a very good try. In practice, you should have safe working methods, safety training, and powerful sanctions for unsafe working (see Section 11.12). It is not practicable to list all of the rules and regulations here as they are so numerous and there are special ones for many industries. The best plan is to consult the Factory Inspector before you set up and to get advice on every aspect of your proposed operation. It will include what official notices must by law be displayed in your type of workshop and advice on accident recording and reporting procedures. Do what you are told and record it on file.

11.16 CONTROL OF SUBSTANCES HAZARDOUS TO HEALTH (COSHH) REGULATIONS 1988

All employers should complete an assessment of health risks from all the hazardous substances in the workplace. Measures exist to control and record the risks, and any incidents and training that is called for. The Health and Safety Executive polices the regulations and will give advice.

11.17 KEY JOBS TO DO

- Create job and person specifications; check that they do not discriminate unlawfully.
- Recruit.
- Create written contracts of employment.
- Be aware of employees' rights.
- Create grievance and disciplinary procedures.
- Conform to HASAWA and COSHH regulations.

The key to your successful business.

Could you employ and motivate a team of people to make and deliver quality pizzas, made with fresh ingredients to order on time, every time?

Domino's Pizza is looking for tenacious, business focused individuals whose personal energy knows no bounds.

With over 40 years in the pizza delivery business, Domino's will deliver a tried and tested business system. This includes intensive training and excellent support to help make your business part of the UK's number one pizza delivery company.

Up for it? Get in touch with the Domino's Franchise Department.

Tel: 01908 580657

For more information, visit: www.dominos.uk.com/franchise

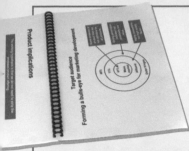

This is the business plan...

that I worked day and night on... got a solicitor to sort the contracts, got an accountant to go through everything from VAT to cashflow, made sure that the bank is going to stay on my side...

Here is the office plan...

with everything we need to run the show smoothly. Got the experts to spec me up the best PC for the task, got the email, got broadband, got the website, got the storage. All planned to cope with next year's growth...

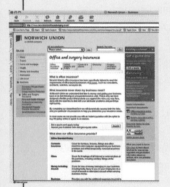

But what about the insurance plan?

What was the best way to make sure I've got the right insurance? Should I buy it online? Will I have everything covered? There was so much to think about – what level of liability and professional indemnity do I need? How do I protect my business equipment? I had to get it right.

So I quickly pulled one more contact out of the book. The insurance broker that someone recommended. And he covered the issues, one by one. The equipment, the premises, everything my business needed. And who did he recommend? Norwich Union. Well, if you're looking for the right solution, you might as well choose the market leaders.

And then he reminded me that it only takes a bit of bad luck and all that planning would be for nothing. So just cover yourself. It's not hard.

To cut a long story short. (And here is the line that sums it all up.)

Taking care of risks while you take care of business.

Talk to your broker about Norwich Union business insurance – or go to www.norwichunion.com for more information.

Norwich Union Insurance Limited. Registered in England Number 99122.
Registered Office: 8 Surrey Street, Norwich, NR1 3NG. A member of the Aviva Group.
Authorised and regulated by the Financial Services Authority.

NORWICH UNION
an **AVIVA** company

Section 12: Insurance

12.1 AIMS OF THIS SECTION

Insurance is something everyone can do without until disaster strikes. You can never insure against absolutely every possibility, and even if you could it would be ridiculously costly. The trick is to be carefully selective and to match costs to needs, updating your idea of what constitutes 'needs' as time goes on. Always enquire what reduction in premiums is available in return for accepting the first part of the risk.

12.2 A SUGGESTED APPROACH

The new firm needs only two categories of insurance:

■ the ones that the law requires (statutory);
■ insurance against catastrophe.

Only when you have made some money is it worth looking at other ways of spending it, whether on insurance or otherwise.

12.3 STATUTORY INSURANCES

These include cover for employer's liability, motor vehicle, lifting tackle and pressure vessels. Some professional organisations insist on their members taking out professional liability policies, which is the next best thing to a legal requirement if you are not permitted to practise unless you conform with their requirements. Other industries have had their own insurance arrangements confirmed by the law, like the travel agents' ABTA insurance, to protect customers' money in cases of insolvency. If you are unclear about any special requirements for your type of firm, talk to the trade associations and to a good commercial insurance broker. Remember that if you do not actually have any employees it could still be worth having cover for employer's liability in case of injury to a part-time helper, spouse, friend, schoolchild, or anyone else who might help out at some time.

12.4 CATASTROPHE INSURANCES

These are policies that keep you or your family going even in the face of disaster. They include fire, flood, theft, death, disability, sickness, injury, loss of a partner's contribution, public liability, product liability (especially if you deal with the USA and likely to come to the UK, courtesy of the EU, in due course), and many more. The main thing is to buy what you can afford, while not falling below quite a high bare minimum.

In the early days, try to buy the cheapest variation of what you need – life insurance is the main area in which you can buy, and pay for, extras when all you really need is something basic but effective. Instead of a with-profits life policy (the most expensive kind, which also pays its sellers the highest commission) you need a term policy – say, £500,000 cover for five or ten years. The amount should be calculated to clear up your debts in the event of your death, pay off the mortgage and provide a capital sum for the family; the period of cover should last for as long as you expect to be building your business. Partners should each be insured properly, to relieve the survivor of the responsibility to maintain two families. After a few years you can review the position and possibly take up other kinds of policies. According to your family and business circumstances there will be other forms of cover to consider.

12.5 INSURANCE PACKAGES

Most insurance companies offer standard policies for small firms which lump together the main types of cover you need. The contents or the extent of the cover under each heading may be negotiable. Thus you might be able to get reductions if some parts are cut out.

12.6 INSURANCE COMPANIES AND THEIR POLICIES

If you insure for one thing and expect to be covered for another, you have only yourself to blame if the insurer will not pay up on your claim. So do not assume, but read the policy and understand it (which may be easier said than done). And always insure tangible property for full replacement cost, and insure everything. If you insure for half the value of your property, the insurer will probably pay only half of a claim. Especially important is the need to tell your insurer of changes to your circumstances – like using the family car for deliveries. (Have an accident when you are not covered and you could lose your licence as well.) Or using the house, garage or shed for your business. That is far from being a complete list. In matters as important as these it may be worth not just sending off a letter but asking for an acknowledgement and pressing until you get one.

12.7 INSURANCE BROKERS, AGENTS AND CONSULTANTS

They may all look the same, but they are vastly different. 'Agents', 'consultants', or anyone but *registered brokers* are in business to sell insurances, pure and simple. The registered insurance broker, however, is required by professional rules, backed by the law, to act on behalf of you, the client. They are your representative chasing the best deal for you from insurance companies. Although there are arguments for conducting some types of life insurance direct with the so-called 'non-tariff companies' (those that do not pay commission to brokers) the wide-ranging insurance needs of the small firm virtually dictate the use of a broker. Not all brokers are the same. You need one who specialises in insurance for industry and commerce rather than one whose main interest lies elsewhere. Get the benefit of their professional advice – lay your cards on the table, and let them tell you what they can do. Try this with a couple more, and settle for the one who seems to have your interests most at heart, perhaps helped by taking up references with satisfied customers. If there are any, they should be only too glad to give their names. They get extra points if they insist on clearing it with the customers first.

12.8 KEY JOBS TO DO

- Decide on your insurance needs.
- Select supplier(s).

Section 13: Sources of help

13.1 AIMS OF THIS SECTION

Nearly everyone needs a shoulder to cry on at some time, and a friend, sister, brother-in-law or other relation can be invaluable in this respect. The owner of a bigger business could also be a useful ally, as they can bring new ways of looking at things – they have seen it all before. But the technical problems of running a firm also cause problems. Many people starting businesses make elementary errors precisely because they are in unfamiliar territory. Yet there are many agencies, mainly paid out of local or national taxation, to help you spot pitfalls and sharpen up your ideas as well as to give technical help and advice. Some of the best are very good, yet do little advertising, so this section tries to describe what they do and where to find them, as well as how to use them. The main national organisations' addresses are shown in Section 17. One characteristic of human beings is our extraordinary generosity to people who ask for advice or help. Your fellow human will help, but usually only if asked.

13.2 SELECTING A CONSULTANT OR ADVISER

Ask around among business contacts to see who they use, and who they would not touch at any price. Take a look at all the bodies available in your area, meet the people and see who looks right for you. Then ask for the names of a couple of people that they have helped in the early stages of business whom you could telephone for a chat to see exactly how their users find they can help. (Be careful not to make it sound too much like taking up a reference.) Their attitude, and the 'referees' that they have supplied, should point you to the one source that you can rely on and use in depth. He or she will not necessarily be the most flattering of the people you meet, but will be interested in the project, quick on the uptake, have useful knowledge of a broad range of businesses, have management experience in the private sector, and above all will not try to impress you with his or her own importance or have a black-and-white attitude to everything.

13.3 USING AN ADVISER

No adviser can run your business for you: beware the one who tries to. All advice should be listened to, but you take the decisions and the responsibility, so no advice should be taken undiluted if you do not believe it is right and don't understand clearly why it is recommended. Any worthwhile adviser will not seek to dominate, but will work with you to help you reach the best decisions. It is therefore important for you to give them room, so do not dominate them, either. As the best of these people are usually very busy, they tend to deal verbally with the sort of general enquiry you will make at the outset, rather than writing a report to you.

Keep a notepad at the ready and jot down the points that the adviser makes, and the names and phone numbers they will give you. Ask what their specialities are and what back-up there is on weak areas, and how deeply involved they get with their clients. Some agencies offer little more than one or two general interviews at the start of your enterprise, some will act virtually as guide, philosopher and friend, helping you to found your business and orchestrate its development. All the time you need to encourage an atmosphere of openness and trust. Your secrets will usually be kept but, more importantly, advisers cannot do their job if you hold back vital information. If you hedge or do not do what you have agreed to, they will lose interest and spend scarce time on other, more rewarding, clients.

13.4 PRIVATE SECTOR ADVISERS

Your accountant and solicitor have been mentioned elsewhere as advisers to be used for their great strengths in their own specialist fields. Brief them fully, and ask what they can do for you. Your bank's manager or small-business specialist, too, can be useful. Bank managers have seen more business failures and successes than most, and the better type will have wise words for you. There are the consultancy groups who will work for anyone, large or small, who pays their fee. Unfortunately, they can be a bit costly with fees that can run to over a thousand pounds per day. Because this type of expertise is so crucially important to small firms, various public sector bodies have set up subsidised consultancies to make it available more affordably. Finally, there are the independent business consultants, some of whom are absolutely excellent, and cost considerably less than their larger counterparts. Equally, there are also people who insinuate themselves into businesses on the pretext of helping them to solve pressing problems, and proceed systematically to defraud. Many of them are clever enough to do it so as to get away with it. That does not mean that independent consultants should be dismissed out of hand, but that at least three satisfactory references should be obtained. The cost of using a consultant could be offset by grants introduced by the Department of Trade and Industry's 'Enterprise Initiative'.

13.5 PUBLIC SECTOR ORGANISATIONS

These fall into two divisions: nationally organised, and locally organised. Local organisations are usually based on city or county councils, district councils, colleges and universities, development corporations, chambers of commerce, Business Links and local enterprise agencies. To locate them all you need to do is phone around, not forgetting your public library, and make up a list. National organisations include the Welsh Development Agency and Scottish Enterprise (both of which now operate locally, mainly through TECs or LECs). If your product is related to agriculture DEFRA (Department of Food and Rural Affairs) or ADAS (Agricultural Development and Advisory Service) may help with advice, support or funding. Some people use these advisers as sounding-boards for their ideas, and for a periodic check-up on progress as a form of preventive medicine for their firm.

13.6 BUSINESS LINK

This nationwide chain of private-sector run partnerships offers an impressively comprehensive website (www.businesslink.gov.uk) with advice and support for smaller firms. They also employ local advisers and run courses, making it their business to know everything a small business person needs to know. New starters tend to make extensive use of them. Their central telephone number is in Section 17.

13.7 GEOGRAPHICALLY BASED HELP

Scotland, Wales and Northern Ireland have their own equivalents of Business Link. There is, of course, nothing to stop someone based in those parts from looking at the Business Link website, but not all of its information applies to the UK as a whole.

The main organisations concerned are:

■ Scotland: Business Gateway.
■ Northern Scotland: Highlands and Islands Enterprise.
■ Wales: Business Eye in Wales.
■ Northern Ireland: Invest Northern Ireland.

Contact details are in Section 17.

13.8 SOME YOU MIGHT NOT HAVE THOUGHT OF

If you are in your teens or twenties, the Prince's Trust and Livewire may be able to help with grants, loans and advice.

Trading Standards Departments, which used to be known as Weights and Measures, and the Health and Safety Executive (formerly Factory Inspectorate) can be a great help to any small firm. Like most enforcement agencies, they prefer to set you on the right road rather than let you go wrong and then prosecute you. If you depend on tourist traffic, the regional Tourist Boards could help. Local chambers of commerce and small firms' clubs offer informal advice. Universities are sometimes stuck for projects for business students, and could do research work for you free of charge. (They increasingly offer access to their resources for a fee.) Suppliers, customers and even competitors can be helpful, too. If you are under 18 or planning to employ a young person, Connexions will advise on legal issues, training, pay and so forth. Their website appears in Appendix 5.

Some firms can benefit from being seen to be involved in community work. If yours is among them, Business in the Community (www.bitc. org.uk) could help.

13.9 KEY JOBS TO DO

■ Investigate possible sources of help.
■ Select a chartered accountant and a solicitor.

earning

not
yearning

Live in the lap of luxury

Owning a Kall Kwik franchise won't always be plain sailing, however with effort and commitment the rewards can be significant. Average Centre sales are among the highest in the sector. Top Centres achieve sales well in excess of £1 million.

With substantial net profits available, a Kall Kwik franchise can deliver the wealth to fulfil your personal ambitions. To find out how you can start living the dream

call **0500 872060** or visit our web site www.kallkwik.co.uk

unique opportunities for *unique* individuals

kallkwik®
business design + print

Section 14: ICT and the new firm

14.1 AIMS OF THIS SECTION

ICT (Information and Communications Technology) can enhance a business owner's personal productivity hugely, or it can take up a lot of time to no real effect. As with any other equipment, you need a clear idea of what you want to do and why, before considering which hardware and software to acquire. You also need some idea of the main pitfalls so as to increase the chances of your installation being successful.

People who have a good grasp of these issues may wish just to skim this section. It is written mainly for those who are not at all clear about what is available and what it can do.

14.2 WHAT YOU DON'T NEED TO KNOW OR LEARN

You do not need to understand anything about electronics or programming. You do not need to learn any of the programming languages.

14.3 WHEN TO CONSIDER GETTING A COMPUTER

If your operation is straightforward, simple, is unlikely to grow, and does not involve much complexity, it is likely that a computer will be more trouble than it is worth. A mobile phone may be all the ICT equipment you need.

Firms which display complexity, in the sense meant here, are likely to benefit from a more extensive system; they will have one or more of the following characteristics:

- many customers or suppliers;
- many orders;
- many quotations, most or all of which use standard elements;
- large number of items in stock requiring frequent reordering;
- much or frequent financial analysis;
- large number of calculations, especially if they involve formulae;
- many agents or employees;
- complicated records;
- lots of drafting and revision of documents;
- frequent need to present numerical information in the form of charts;
- many personalised letters, quotations or other documents.

There can be other, specialised, reasons why a computer can help, which the individual entrepreneur will know of as part of his or her knowledge of their industry. Alternatively, you may have a compelling reason to have frequent access to the internet – to run web pages of your own or to send and receive e-mails.

In general, a firm which displays any of the characteristics listed above ought to be looking at an IT system. If a system is required to deal with a special need, it is worth thinking of getting it to do other routines of which it is capable, such as the payroll, for instance, even though the workforce may not be big enough to justify it on its own.

Nobody is compelled to have a computer. Many simple small firms are run using traditional systems such as card-indexes and books. However, they can also make possible a wide range of tasks, including very sophisticated analyses of where enquiries and orders come from, so as to sharpen your marketing drive. Most businesses will find ICT useful, if not essential. The biggest problems you may face are likely to be not whether to employ ICT, but the specification of the system to match needs of which you may not yet be fully aware.

14.4 HOW ICT CAN HELP

In theory it is possible to get a programmer to write a program which will get the computer to do exactly what you might want – to reproduce your manual methods. Regrettably, the cost would be astronomical. Therefore you have to think in terms not of getting exactly what you want, but of getting as close as you can within the limitations of the off-the-shelf software. Software exists for all kinds of jobs: there are literally hundreds of payroll programs, for instance, which will calculate each employee's wages, NI, tax and pension contributions and even work out exactly how many notes and coins of which denominations you have to draw from the bank to make up the pay-packets.

In addition to the special-purpose programs (such as payroll) there are the four main workhorses which most firms can put to work in some way. They are databases, spreadsheets, word processors and communications.

14.5 DATABASES

A database is a clever version of a card-index. It can carry the sort of information you would put on to record cards. If we take as an example a set of customer records, the obvious information for them to carry is name, address, telephone, dates of visits, what ordered, value and dates of purchases, names and positions of contacts and so on. What sets the database apart from the card-index is the facility instantaneously to:

■ Sort the records into any order you like: they will already be in alphabetical order by customer names, perhaps, but you can change that to descending order by value of purchases last year if you want to (and then back again).
■ Perform calculations, such as adding up the value of sales to all customers in one county last year.
■ Perform conditional operations, such as finding the value of sales to customers who have not bought product X and have more than three branches of which one is in Staffordshire.

Setting up a database requires a great investment of time and effort. It takes time to learn how to set it up; it takes time to enter the information; and it takes time to learn how to extract the information you want.

Critical factors in selecting a database include its overall capacity – whether it fits in your machine, and whether it is big enough to take your records, now and in the future; its ease of use; and the speed with which it performs the routines you will use.

What is described here is a 'relational' database, in which the different kinds of information on each record can be related to one another. To be avoided by the serious business user is the simpler sort which is incapable of relational work.

14.6 SPREADSHEETS

A spreadsheet is like two vast sheets of squared paper overlaying one another and reacting together. On the top sheet you can write words and numbers, which are normally visible on the computer screen. You can place the computer's screen over any part of the spreadsheet that you want to view at any particular time. On the lower sheet you can write formulae which act on the figures on the top sheet. If you want to look at the formulae, you can. A simple example of how it can be used is to give quotations. A landscape gardener is often asked to give a price for laying slabs, so he programmes his spreadsheet to do the calculations automatically. He puts in the number of square metres to be covered on this job, and the computer looks up the price of hardcore, aggregate, sand, surface materials and labour which the owner has entered previously (and can change at will), works out how much of each is required, multiplies them out and totals them up, then adds the VAT to give the answer. Someone who knew what he or she was doing, perhaps after a few months of playing with spreadsheets, would set up the entire example above in under an hour, including headings and the introductory words necessary. Having done so, he or she would never have to do such sums themselves again.

While all spreadsheets look pretty big at first glance, it is important to check that their dimensions are right for what you have in mind. For example, a program which allows 100 columns across sounds very large. But a firm which wants to keep track of its targets and achievements week by week will need at least 107 columns: one for the headings down the left-hand side, then one for each of the weekly targets plus an annual total (53) and the same for the outcomes (another 53). To make the report really useful, you might want another 53 for the differences and doubling it all over again to show the cumulative position. As an alternative it could run the two sets of figures and their labels in 54 columns by putting one set above the other, instead of side-by-side. But there are so many spreadsheets to choose from that this sort of compromise is rarely necessary.

14.7 WORD PROCESSORS

A 'dedicated' word processor is a typewriter which allows you to see what you have typed before printing, save it to disk, and change it if need be. A word processor is also a program run on a computer which enables the computer to do the same, making it more versatile. Many include spell-checkers (though some occasionally challenge non-American English). To the amateur typist they are a godsend – this writer would not be without one – for he can eliminate his mistakes so easily, hack documents around until they look right, move chunks of text from one place to another, experiment with layout and so on. Another thing it can do is to link up with spreadsheets and databases to bring in information from them. An example might be a personalised mailshot aimed at getting customers to buy 20 per cent more than they did last year. The customer's address would be taken off the database to head up the word processor letter, the buyer's name would likewise be lifted into the word processor for the greeting, and last year's purchases would also be switched across. If you want to be really clever you can perform some calculations on a spreadsheet to see how much bonus the customer would earn, and pop that into the letter too. The more powerful word processors will even do the sums themselves. This sort of switching-about of information between different programs is vastly easier if the three are bought as a 'suite' in which they are designed to talk to one another. However, compromise may be necessary if this is important to you. Not every element in the suite may deliver the full specification you require.

A further argument in favour of suites is that they may allow you to break off in the middle of one job to do another without a lot of rigmarole. If an urgent customer query comes up in the middle of some word processing it can be tedious to have to save the incomplete document, go into database, come out again and reload. If you are using Microsoft's Windows® (see Section 14.9) this will be possible anyway.

The factor which most people find important in selecting a word processor is whether it will do all the jobs they want it to, and only then how easy it is to use. They reason that you can always learn difficult routines, but you can never extend the program's power.

14.8 SELECTING YOUR SYSTEM

You find out which program suits your operation best by:

- carefully specifying exactly what you want the program to do;
- comparing the specifications of each program in your price and capacity range with what you are looking for;
- reading the reviews in magazines to see what problems the experts have unearthed, and how they compare with other programs of the same type;
- only then going to see what it looks like on the screen in the dealer's showroom;
- taking as much time as you need to explore the demonstration before deciding.

Contrary to most people's understanding, the software is the thing you really spend time and trouble to find out about. Hardware is a lot less important, in the sense that there are really only two big decisions to make. The first is to choose between an Apple Macintosh (said by many to be the best there is, but not very popular) and systems based on IBM's PC standards (which account for over 90 per cent of installations). The second issue is the speed and capacity of the hardware – it is worth buying the biggest and fastest you can afford. After that, there is not a lot to choose between the machines (except price, reliability and the all-important matters of the speed, availability and rigour of support services).

The hardware to pick is really up to you. Perhaps the most important factor is dealer back-up. If your local dealer is likely to be around for a time and knows the business well, it is almost worth specifying the brand that he or she stocks. Then when (not if) things go wrong you have someone local to pull you out of the mire.

Your printer is worth a little thought. Most of the printers bought today fall into two categories: ink-jet and laser.

Laser printers can give a black-and-white image like that of printed text and pictures. Even the cheapest can cost around £300, but some also double as photocopiers. An ink-jet printer works by firing tiny spots of black or coloured ink at the paper. They are cheap to buy (£80 upwards) and very portable. Both are near-silent.

One area to enquire closely about is the cost of consumables – ink cartridges for a an ink-jet, toner for a laser – and of routine servicing.

14.9 COMPUTER PROBLEMS AND OTHER CONSIDERATIONS

Some of the worst problems users have with computers are self-inflicted, when they fail to back up the work they have done. Suddenly you can find that the machine will do nothing that you tell it to. That is because some freak event in the electricity supply can cause the machine to freeze up, refusing to respond to any commands. The only thing to do is switch off, then on again. Simple enough, but you lose everything you have not recorded, which is not funny at the end of five or six hours' work. The way to reduce the risk of a freeze, incidentally, is to spend £30 or so on a device that smooths out the accidental 'spikes' in the mains supply. That does not eliminate the need for frequent backing-up while working on a task; it merely reduces the number of times the system freezes.

You will be presented with a choice of disk-drive size. Most people believe that this is the area in which it is worth pushing the boat out. The cost of memory is now so low, and continues to fall, that it is worth getting the largest hard disk you can afford. You will almost certainly find that eventually you will use it all.

Windows, the Microsoft system, is now almost universal. When you switch on, all your programs are shown for you to work on, and switching from one to another is simplicity itself.

If you never use a disk from someone else, nor e-mail, nor the internet, and only ever use software bought in its original box, you will not need a virus checker. In other words, almost everyone does need one. A 'firewall', usually sold as part of a virus-protection package, will help to deflect e-mail from possibly dubious sources.

An inescapable expense is a maintenance contract. They usually cost annually about 10 per cent of the equipment's value, which is not cheap. But having your business out of action while the engineer gives priority to his contract customers incurs a cost, too.

Don't believe that a modem will operate at its declared speed. Rarely do they run much above half that speed because of the 'noise' on the telephone line. The only way to overcome that is to have an ISDN line installed, which is expensive, but worthwhile for many firms. That will enable all your online applications to run faster, as well as ensuring a really effective broadband connection.

14.10 COMMUNICATIONS

Many people already use their computers to send e-mail (electronic mail) to each other. You type your message, edit it if necessary, and send it via the telephone lines to another computer. It goes instantaneously and at low cost. It can reach someone wherever they are in the world, at any time of day. Computers already send and receive faxes. It is simple to compose your fax on-screen and send it off electronically, without having to print a hard copy. Clips of video can be sent as attachments to e-mails.

The next development will be to bring to the mass market the ability to act as telephones and video-image transmitters and receivers, that is as video-phone terminals. Already they are used widely for conferencing, whereby a number of people can discuss a topic and see each other's contributions to the debate, and for playing CDs and DVDs.

Your choice of ISP (internet service provider) is important. There are so many, and the market is constantly changing, so the best advice is to read the business computing press, and particularly its ISP reviews.

14.11 KEY JOBS TO DO

- Decide on your strategy for record keeping, communications and information processing and determine whether it requires a computer.
- Specify and select your system.
- Select your supplier(s).

Section 15: Your business plan

15.1 AIMS OF THIS SECTION

A great deal of this book is given over to the idea of planning ahead to create the future you want. In many places it advocates getting those plans down on paper, partly so that you can see what you think and criticise it objectively; partly so that you have a record of where you are trying to go, to make it easy to judge how well you are doing and provide early warning of unscheduled departures from the route; and partly to ensure that all the pieces fit together (that you are not planning to sell more than you can make, for example). Much of that sort of planning is often left written in longhand, and some of it may be comprehensible to its writer alone. This section aims to help you to take that information, add to it further facts that you are expected to supply, and present the whole thing in a form that ought to satisfy a complete stranger, sitting in an office, who may know next to nothing about your sort of firm. Increasingly, small firms are expected to do that: and if they do not they can miss out on quite a lot of the help that is available.

15.2 WHO WANTS YOUR PLAN AND WHY?

The new business will find more and more that it is asked to submit a business plan to support its application for loans, grants or even just a lease on a building. Those who make such requests are not busybodies. Even if they were, it matters little, for if they have something that you need it makes sense to go at least part of the way to meet them. The plan written for the owner's personal use is rarely suitable, for it uses unexplained jargon and abbreviations and takes a great deal of knowledge for granted.

The reasons why such people will call for a business plan fall under several headings. Among other things it is expected to:

■ demonstrate that the applicant has a coherent plan;
■ show that the applicant can read, write, do sums and understands at least something of what running a business entails;
■ illustrate how the business will establish itself and show that its chances of survival and success are good;
■ show how risky areas are to be made safe;
■ communicate that good use will be made of the reader's resources;
■ impress and reassure.

Nobody wants to provide money or premises to someone who seems likely to go broke and cause them a lot of trouble. Everyone wants to see vibrantly healthy firms in their patch. A well-formed and well-presented business plan can get potential helpers on your side.

15.3 WHAT GOES INTO A BUSINESS PLAN?

The plans of a large firm, or a smaller one that is involved in particularly turbulent markets, may comprise very many pages and sections. The new, small firm rarely has to go to those lengths. Indeed, there is a lot of merit in keeping it very simple: plans stretching to hundreds, or even dozens, of pages quickly lose the reader. In one sense you are engaged here in salesmanship, so don't drone on about how much you know, but instead give the reader what he or she is looking for.

The purpose of the plan is to answer the key questions that everyone will ask: who, what, why, when, where and how? To help readers to get their answers it makes sense to divide the plan up into sections which tell:

■ the background to the project;
■ what your aims are;
■ relevant information about the market, production and finance;
■ what you will do if things don't go according to plan;

. . . and answer the 'who, what, why' etc questions under each heading.

The project's background: up to two pages
In general terms, what is happening in the industry you plan to enter (market size, competition, structures, prices etc)?

What is the opportunity?
How do you plan to exploit it?
Is it a 'flash in the pan'?
What are the qualifications of each participant?
Effects of outside factors (commodity shortages, social/demographic/technological change, public attitudes, legal controls etc).

Aims of the project: one page
What is your long-term aim for the business?
What markers will it pass at what times on the way there?

The market: up to two pages
How is the market structured: users, distributors, trade margins and discounts, competitors?
Do any special financing conventions apply?
What seasonal or trade fluctuations are typical in the trade?
How do you fit in: why should they buy from you?
How does your pricing compare with competitors'?
How will you sell your goods; who will do that work, over what area, and by what method?
What is your sales forecast for each of the next five years?
How big a market share does this represent (the smaller the better, or it might look over-optimistic)?
What is your sales forecast for each month of the first year?
What promotional support do you propose and at what cost?
How will the product be packaged and presented?
Where will you get the people, how will they be trained and controlled?

Production: up to two pages
What production processes will be conducted in-house and which outside, and why?
What knowledge do you have of these matters and how will you cover any shortcomings?
What premises will you get and at what cost?
How will you know product costs, and what are they?
How many productive hours per person per week are you assuming, and for how many weeks a year?
Which process represents a bottleneck, and how will you deal with any limitations it imposes?
How readily available is essential labour, and at what cost?
What training is needed, how will it be provided and at what cost?
How will you control production?
How will you control quality?
How will continuity of supply of components be assured?

How will component stocks be controlled?
(NB: The last two questions are only for firms which are critically dependent on particular components or suppliers, or where stocks of components represent a major part of their financial requirements.)

Finance: four pages or so (there are several tables)
How profitable will the firm be?
(Answered by a *profit-and-loss projection.*)
What finance will be needed when, and for what purposes?
(This question is best dealt with by providing a *capital budget,* showing how much is needed for each of the main capital items; and a *cash-flow forecast,* showing temporary shortfalls and surpluses of working capital.)
Where will the money come from?
(This is the *funding budget,* showing who contributes how much and in what form.)
What security is offered to lenders?
Opening and closing *balance-sheet projections* can be shown for the start and finish of each trading year. They answer the question: how much better off does the firm expect to be as time moves on?
What strengths and weaknesses are displayed in these figures, and how will weaknesses be dealt with?
What is the projected break-even point for each year, and how far above it does the firm expect to trade?
(This shows how much leeway there is for accidents and emergencies.)

Administration
What financial records will be kept, how and by whom? What is the firm's ICT strategy?

Control
What financial controls will be exercised and by whom?

People
Who will be required, how available are they and at what cost?

Clearly, most people who wish to write this sort of business plan will need help, especially with the financial projections. It is always a good idea to have somebody to help: it greatly increases the chance of removing embarrassing errors. Watch out for the lazy adviser who puts it all on computer and projects your monthly sales as exactly one-twelfth of your forecast for the year. It sticks out like a sore thumb to your reader, who is tempted to conclude that it is all as slapdash as that. Remember – bank managers and others have seen a lot of these plans and can most readily spot insincerity. They are also very keen on the idea that you should understand the plan. A response to questions – and there will always be questions – that suggests you don't understand what the figures mean will not go down well. That might explain why some readers are in two minds about plans prepared by prestige accountants. On the one hand they know that a professional job has been done; on the other they may suspect that some well-paid person may be trying to put one over them. All in all they probably feel happiest with something you have prepared but which has been checked by an accountant (who may well have helped with the number-crunching).

It is also worth subjecting the plan to critical scrutiny at the draft stage from someone who is used to writing or judging these documents. There is plenty of help on hand from the small-business agencies, both by way of preparation and constructive criticism.

When it is in its final draft, have it checked for its use of English: misspellings and inappropriate usage detract from the appearance of professionalism that you doubtless wish to push across. Your PC's spell-checker does only a small part of this job.

15.4 PRESENTATION

Appearances ought not to matter as much as they do, perhaps. But it is an inescapable fact that those reading your plan will be influenced by what it looks like: the cover, the layout, the quality of paper and the standard of typing. For those reasons it is worth having it professionally word-processed and printed on a laser printer. If the person who does that work cannot supply a cover of the sort you want, your local commercial stationer can. While you are at it, it will not cost much more to have several copies printed.

15.5 AFTERLIFE

Once the main plan has achieved its initial objective – of attracting a loan, for example – it ought not to be filed away. It represents your template for the firm and you need to be sure that you will spot any deviations from the plan before they begin to have serious implications. For instance, if sales are 20 per cent higher than the plan, you need to do some quick thinking about your working capital requirements. If you are not constantly comparing the plan with the outcome, you could miss such vital links and put the firm's very existence at risk.

So, keep it handy, check progress against it regularly and revise it as often as you need to.

15.6 KEY JOBS TO DO

- ▪ Create a written plan, taking appropriate advice.
- ▪ Use the plan to monitor progress.
- ▪ Revise the plan when actual performance differs from it significantly.

Can You Hit the Right Note?

♫Music ♫Singing ♫Movement

Run your own business offering pre-school music and singing classes

Are you looking for a new career opportunity?

Do you enjoy working with young children?

Can you sing?

If your answer is 'YES' to these questions then a JO JINGLES FRANCHISE may be of interest to you. Professional music or teaching qualifications are not essential but an interest in business, children, music and education is.

The Classes

Jo Jingles is the UK's leading provider of music and singing classes for pre-school age children. Our classes are fun, educational, structured and interactive and we have more than 15,000 children currently attending on a weekly basis.

The Franchise Opportunity

Founded in 1991, Jo Jingles has now been established as a successful national franchise for 10 years. We have more than 80 franchisees currently operating throughout the UK and in Ireland and we aim to expand further.

The Jo Jingles franchise offers:

- Flexible working hours to suit family life
- Low start-up costs from £6,000 - £8,000 + Vat (depending on size of territory)
- Comprehensive training & class programmes provided
- Full promotional support
- Full Members of the British & Irish Franchise Associations

For further information contact JO JINGLES LIMITED on
Tel: 0044 (0) 1494 719360
headoffice@jojingles.co.uk
or visit
www.jojingles.com

JO JINGLES

THE MUSIC & MOVEMENT EXPERIENCE

Section 16: After a successful launch. . . developing your firm

16.1 AIMS OF THIS SECTION

Once your firm is established, new opportunities will constantly present themselves. How can you decide which to take? What will the implications be? This section takes a look at these questions, but can offer only a generalised overview. Limited though that may be, it could still be useful in helping to predict some of the main issues and difficulties.

16.2 THE MAIN ISSUES

The first question that arises is: do you actually want the firm to grow? While it might make you rich, do you want the hassle and the risk involved? Think carefully before assuming that you have no alternative. If you are inundated with work, could you cut down demand by putting up your prices for new customers? Doing so would turn you into a specialist in high-price, high-quality work, dealing only with the rich who want perfection and are prepared to pay for it, or the desperate. Your earnings could soar without the need to become any busier or expand the firm. However, your marketing may need to change to deal effectively with that elusive specialised market segment.

If you decide to go ahead and grow, recognise that growing a firm is a different job from founding it. At a strategic level, there are several matters you need to consider:

- your expansion strategy and how you will actually go about it;
- the nature of your new job and what skills it calls for;
- the culture to be encouraged within the firm;
- how to develop yourself as a manager and acquire the new skills needed to operate differently;
- consultants and how to use them – good ones can have wonderful effects;
- your mission statement – you need one, and it mustn't be waffle.

16.3 YOUR EXPANSION STRATEGY

Another early decision is how you propose to undertake the expansion. Broadly, two ways are open: to do it all in-house by taking on staff or to send all the work out of house to subcontractors. The former keeps things under your control, but may mean taking on more space and will mean more time spent managing the extra people. The latter looks easier – you just brief the contractor's salesperson and let them get on with things. However, it often leads to problems involving questions of confidentiality, deadlines, quality, cost and a host of other issues.

The answer may lie in doing it by stages. You could start by subcontracting areas of work that are not special or unique to your company – something that almost anyone could do. Matters of critical importance to your performance in the eyes of customers could be completed in-house. In this way, you would keep control of the things that really matter, and in the more trivial areas exchange the risk of things going wrong for the blessing of dropping the burden of day-to-day responsibility.

However, you may find it difficult to decide what to delegate, feeling that *everything* you do is important to your customers. In this case, applying the Pareto principle (the 80/20 rule mentioned in Section 1) might help you to make the distinction. Alternatively, you could hire a consultant. Expensive as they may be, consultants are likely to be very valuable. Some thoughts on consultants appear in Section 16.7.

16.4 YOUR NEW JOB

In the early stages of the firm's existence, you probably did everything yourself. As the firm grows, it is likely that you will become used to giving work to other people to do, yet you have kept a firm hold on the reins.

Now, you may be at the stage where, even with this extra support, there are just not enough hours in the day and things are beginning to go wrong. This is the stage that most entrepreneurs find most difficult to manage.

At this point, there is a further transition that you must make or your growth is doomed – a move to a structure through which you can delegate work.

Once this is made, you will find yourself not actually doing any of the jobs that you used to do. Instead, you will rely on others to get them done, and your task will become one of overseeing the whole process, leading, troubleshooting, inspiring and – when necessary – supporting the people who do the real work. Let's look at those stages in a little more detail and explore what they mean for you.

Stage 1: foundation

- *Staff or contractors:* few or none.
- *Other people's tasks:* minimal and menial, entirely under your direction.
- *Your tasks:* everything that involves importance and responsibility.
- *Your knowledge of other people's tasks:* total.
- *Your focus:* getting the work in, getting the jobs out, collecting payment.
- *Structure:* wheel-shaped, with you as the hub and everyone else looking to you.

Stage 2: development

- *Staff or contractors:* 5 to 50 (approximately).
- *Other people's tasks:* specialised, but still under your direction, either directly or via a supervisor.
- *Your tasks:* still carrying overall responsibility and requiring others to do things your way.
- *Your knowledge of other people's tasks:* variable – limited in some cases to a general view, total in others.
- *Your focus:* getting the work in, getting the jobs out, getting payment, staff management.
- *Structure:* a pyramid, with you firmly at the top.

Stage 3: delegation

- *Staff or contractors:* from around 50 to thousands.
- *Other people's tasks:* specialised, delivering their small part of the big jigsaw.
- *Your tasks:* still carrying overall responsibility but unable to exercise direct leadership of the workforce. Now operating entirely through intermediary managers or supervisors.

- *Your knowledge of other people's tasks:* highly variable – low in relation to mundane details, but higher in the case of the challenges facing your subordinate managers.
- *Your focus:* the business environment, key customer and supplier relationships, company culture, managing and developing your managers.
- *Structure:* the traditional organisation chart or, in some cases, a soft systems diagram (there's no space here to go into what that is, but if you know the jargon you'll recognise it; if you don't, it's not important).

In terms of this discussion, stage 3 is the most important as it represents the outline of your new role. It is obviously very different from stages 1 and 2, so the skills and qualities you developed in those stages alone are not enough to enable you to make a success of this new job.

16.5 COMPANY CULTURE

This matter was mentioned under 'your focus' in the description of stage 3 in Section 16.4. Unlike all the other issues listed (except for 'managing and developing your managers'), it is not dealt with elsewhere in this book. So what is it and why is it important?

There have been many studies of culture in many sorts of organisations. Since this is not an academic book, they are not reviewed here (causing a sigh of relief from many readers, no doubt). However, in this brief summary it is clear to see that the culture of your firm is a key influence on job satisfaction felt by staff, on their motivation and on your ability to retain them. (As time goes by you are likely to concern yourself increasingly with retaining good people.) So it is important. But what is it?

This is not the easiest question to answer. The best definition I've come across is still pretty vague: 'It's the way we go about things here; how we treat the customers, the suppliers and each other and the sort of atmosphere that creates' (there are other definitions, usually involving terms like 'behavioural norms', but they all boil down to something close to this). Whilst many social scientists would scorn such a statement, I think there is a lot in it. It draws attention to the issue of atmosphere – is there a lot of shouting at and hectoring of people and a sense of excess stress, or are things done quietly and smoothly with gentleness and consideration for feelings? Do people feel that their managers respect them and treat them as important partners in the enterprise, or do they sneer and bully, inspiring fear and a sense of worthlessness in their staff? Are customers there to be taken advantage of, or for their needs to be served? Should suppliers be treated with respect or be cheated and bullied at every opportunity? This isn't a comprehensive list, but it serves to show the sorts of specific issues that fall under the general heading of 'culture'.

Culture is of enormous importance because it represents the framework within which your managers operate. Staff will take their cue from the manager's behaviour, so the whole organisation can become affected by the action of an individual. When you are no longer in hourly touch with most of the firm's staff, almost anything could be going on without you realising it. You will get to know, of course, but usually too late. Notification will come eventually when you see that all the key people in one department have resigned or you receive a notice from an Industrial Tribunal. The best approach is to head off any trouble by setting a strong lead and making it clear to managers what is 'the way we go about things here', reinforcing the message by personal example and during coaching sessions.

16.6 DEVELOPING YOURSELF AS A MANAGER

Managing a firm is a complex business, as you will by now have realised. Expansion imposes a whole new set of demands on you and requires new expertise and a broader understanding in a number of areas. None of it comes quickly or easily, as learning is a process of change and humans are, fundamentally, slow to change. The means available are obvious: reading books, attending courses, where you will also have the benefit of discussing with others the challenges you face. Some full-time short courses may be useful, but most businesspeople find part-time to be the only learning mode they can consider. The traditional way of taking part-time courses – twice a week, 7.00–9.00 pm – works for so few people that new methods have sprung up. The Open University's business school has led the way in so-called 'distance learning', allowing students to learn at their own pace in their own time. Many instructional CDs are available. The internet delivers all kinds of learning, but as with anything in this medium, one has to be satisfied about the integrity of the source before signing up.

One thing is certain: if you are not prepared to put in the extra work needed for self-development, your expansion is at greater risk and may flourish less than it could do.

16.7 YOUR FIRM AND CONSULTANTS

Yes, we all know the objections to consultants. They're the ones who borrow your watch to tell you the time, then keep the watch. Now we've got that out of the way, let's look at why they stay in business and how they deliver satisfaction to their customers – people like you. Their survival is down to three factors: however unique you may feel your firm to be, a good consultant has seen several similar examples before and will be equipped with analytical techniques to enhance understanding; they are up to date with everything in their field to a higher level of competence than yours, so they save your precious time; and, however bright you are, you may be too close to your own situation to see it clearly – a *good* consultant (not all are good) will help you to take a short cut to effective operation.

How do you tell a 'good' consultant? Not easily, for some charlatans are very plausible. Common sense will tell you to ask for several examples of past work and permission to contact those clients. The obvious expedient of going to one of the big firms may not be your best plan. Few of them have experience of working for small firms and so do not understand the pressures on you and some may work to a formula designed as much to minimise the risk of successful lawsuits as to help the client.

However resistant you may be to using consultants – and I hope that the above has weakened your resolve not to – you will be forced to use them for certain activities. If you float your firm on the stock market, for example, you just can't do without a merchant bank and a stockbroker, as well as others. There is sometimes a fine line between, on the one hand, justified confidence in one's own powers and, on the other, arrogance – even the most self-confident entrepreneur can come to realise that an occasional touch of humility can save him (it usually is a man) from committing an extraordinary folly.

16.8 YOUR MISSION STATEMENT

Usually an expansion is market-led. A new opportunity appears and you have to decide whether or not to pursue it. You must not chase everything that comes up or your operation will become totally confused. Decide what it is about your firm that makes it unique, what you ideally want it to offer its customers and express that in a 'mission statement'. You may think that mission statements are all waffle and hot air, but ask yourself why corporations employing some of the brainiest people in the business world have them. The answer is that it helps them decide what they are there to do (and thus not do), what the firm is for (and thus not for), and this makes it easy for them to decide where to concentrate their efforts.

Let's take an example. A publisher of business books might have a mission statement that goes like this:

> We aim to be one of the three most popular publishers throughout the British Commonwealth for practical instruction texts on people's professional lives

to those with technical or managerial responsibilities in organisations in all sectors of business.

Yes, it does read like gobbledegook at first. But let's take it apart and look at the pieces, one by one:

We aim to be one of the three most popular. . .

This gives them a clear target to aim at and, once they've arrived, to maintain.

. . . throughout the British Commonwealth. . .

This ensures that they work in those parts of the world where UK English is the main language. It also makes sure that they do not stray off to pursue opportunities in, for example, the United States (this is not to say that work in the United States would be bad for them; it's just what their board has decided for the time being). It doesn't forbid the sale to other publishers of the right to translate titles for non-UK-English-speaking countries, but does make sure that employees don't actively chase these opportunities. Again, this may or may not be a good strategy, but it is the one the board selected.

. . . for practical instruction. . .

This makes sure that the company concentrates on practical readers and stays away from others – academic readers, for example.

. . . texts. . .

This keeps the company's attention on textual material, which can be distributed in printed or electronic form, and so moves attention away from audio and video publications.

. . . on people's professional lives. . .

This keeps the focus on work-related matters and eliminates the temptation to publish, for example, cookery books for amateurs, leisure-travel guides or any other apparently lucrative opportunities that may arise.

. . . to those with technical or managerial responsibilities. . .

This clearly defines the target audience, which will give this publisher a distinct profile among them.

. . . in organisations in all sectors of business.

This ensures that the company offers something for managers and technicians in *all* sectors – public, private, government, public authority, charitable and so forth.

The mission statement is occasionally redefined, as the perceptions of the organisation's managers change. In the above example, the managers might want to reword it to allow them to go for the audiovisual market, enabling the company to produce and distribute training films, for instance. Alternatively, they may wish to make changes to the self-imposed limits to their geographical boundaries, or indeed any other specification made in the statement. The point is that the mission statement unifies the efforts of everyone in the entire organisation, making them all 'point in the same direction'. The option of not having one would involve everyone pushing in the direction that seems best to them, resulting in a rag-bag of activities and a complete lack of identity in the eyes of potential customers.

There is tremendous potential for the practical use of a mission statement in the marketing function. The mission statement does two things: it screens all the ideas that come up, rejecting those in conflict with it; also, by being used in this way, it places itself under constant review. From time to time, the process of review will lead to the mission statement being changed. In no way does this invalidate it – indeed, it strengthens the case for its existence.

Once you have drafted the mission statement, get others to comment on it. Encourage constructive criticism. This may not be easy to come by if you have always exercised strong leadership and control, but persevere. You don't want something people pay lip service to, you need something that they believe sums up what the firm is really there to do and validates the efforts they put in. Once the statement is agreed, publish it. Distribute copies to everyone's workstations. Constantly review the statement in the light of changes in the business environment, opportunities that come up and comments from colleagues and, when you agree that it needs revision, make the changes, yet afterwards continue the constant process of review.

16.9 KEY JOBS TO DO

- Decide if expansion really is for you.
- Decide the strategy for carrying it out.
- Understand the nature of your new job.
- Decide on what culture you should encourage within the firm.
- Create a programme for developing yourself as a manager.
- Select a strategy for using consultants.
- Prepare, agree and communicate a mission statement.

Success. Luxury. Freedom.

We can't guarantee an easy ride. Setting up a business – even one with such a valuable support network behind it – will always present challenges.

You know that. That's partly what attracts you. The rewards do too:

The freedom of running your own business. The flexibility to expand at your own pace, make your own decisions. The independence to dictate your own destiny.

The opportunity to excel.

And, of course, the potential for serious financial success.

AlphaGraphics stores perform at over double the average turnover for the quick-print franchise market.

Serious about franchising? So are we.

To find out more, please call free on 0800 257 424 or visit our website at www.alphagraphics.co.uk

alphaGraphics ®

miracles in print

Franchising The Little Gym

Enjoy a Fun and rewarding Career We will make it Happen Together

As you strive to give **children** the best **foundation** to build a lifetime of success, The Little Gym is here to help you along the way. Our professionally developed, non-competitive curriculum has been designed to **build motor skills** whilst having fun, and simultaneously fosters emotional, intellectual and social skills. For over 30 years, parents have trusted The Little Gym in helping their children build the skills and confidence that benefit all aspects of their lives. Today, The Little Gym is the **world leader** in children's motor skill development. **Already 300 franchisees** around the world are living their **dream** whilst leveraging their entrepreneurial capabilities. They are striving for excellence and enjoying building strong customer relationships. This is your opportunity to join them! Today, besides their success, they share a common **passion: working with kids** in a professional and fun environment. Our **ongoing owner support programme** includes curriculum and business training, materials and manuals, business consulting, advertising and marketing. Do you wish to run your own company and live your dream? We could be your partner. Just contact us.

The Little Gym UK
44 Highview Avenue, Edgware, Middlesex • HA8 9UA
Tel: 0208 958 7373 • Fax: 0208 357 8860
Mobile: 07977 462263
Web: www.thelittlegym.com
Email: bevregan@thelittlegym.co.uk

Building skills for life

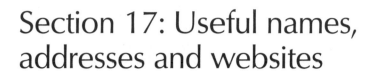

Section 17: Useful names, addresses and websites

Advisory, Conciliation and
Arbitration Service (ACAS)
27 Wilton Street
London SW1X 7AZ
Tel: 020 7210 3000
Website: www.acas.org.uk

Agricultural Development
Advisory Service (ADAS)
Tel: 0845 766 0085
Website: www.adas.co.uk

BBC World Service
PO Box 76
Bush House
Strand
London WC2B 4PU
Tel: 020 7240 3456
Website: www.bbc.co.uk

British Franchise Association
Franchise Chambers
75a Bell Street
Henley-on-Thames
Oxfordshire RG9 2BD
Tel: 01491 578049
Website: british-franchise.org

British Insurance and Investment
Brokers Association
BIIBA House
14 Bevis Marks
London EC3N 7NT
Tel: 020 7623 9043
Website: www.biba.org.uk

British Overseas Trade Board
1 Victoria Street
London SW1H 0ET
Tel: 020 7215 7877

Building Research Establishment
Bucknalls Lane
Garston
Watford WD25 9XX
Tel: 01923 664000
Fax: 01923 664010
E-mail: enquiries@bre.co.uk
Website: www.bre.co.uk
and
Kelvin Road
East Kilbride
Glasgow G75 0RZ
E-mail: eastkilbride@bre.co.uk

Business Eye in Wales
Tel: 0845 796 9798
Website: www.businesseye.org.uk

Business Gateway (Scotland only)
Tel: 0845 609 6611
Website: www.bgateway.com

Business in the Community
137 Shepherden Walk
London N1 7RQ
Tel: 0870 600 2482
Website: www.bitc.org.uk

Business Link
Tel: 0845 600 9000
Website: www.businesslink.gov.uk

Central Office of Information
Hercules Road
London SE1 7DU
Tel: 020 7928 2345
Website: www.coi.gov.uk

Chartered Institute of Marketing
Moor Hall
Cookham
Maidenhead SL6 9QH
Tel: 016285 427500
Website: www.cim.co.uk

Chartered Institute of Patent Agents
95 Chancery Lane
London WC2 1DT
Tel: 020 7405 9450
Website: www.cipa.org.uk

Companies Registration Offices:

Companies House
Crown Way
Maindy
Cardiff CF4 3UZ
Tel: 01222 388588
Website: www.companieshouse.
gov.uk

Companies House
55 City Road
London EC1Y 1BB
Tel: 020 7253 9393
Website: www.companieshouse.
gov.uk

102 George Street
Edinburgh EH2 3DJ
Tel: 0131 225 5774
Website: www.companieshouse.
gov.uk

IDB House
64 Chichester Street
Belfast BT1 4JX
Tel: 01232 234488

Country Land and Business
Association
16 Belgrave Square
London SWIX 8PQ
Tel: 020 7235 0511
Website: www.cla.org.uk

Crafts Council
44a Pentonville Road
London N1 9BY
Tel: 020 7278 7700
Website: www.craftscouncil.org.uk

DTI Publications Orderline
Tel: 0870 150 2500
Fax: 0870 150 2333
Website: www.dti.gov.uk

Design Council
34 Bow Street
London WC2E 7DL
Tel: 020 7420 5200
Website: www.designcouncil.
org.uk

EIU Research
Tel: 020 7830 1007
Website: www.EIU.com

Export Credits Guarantee
Department
Tel: 020 7512 7887
Website: www.ecgd.gov.uk

Federation of Small Businesses
Sir Frank Whittle Way
Blackpool Business Park
Blackpool FY4 2FE
Tel: 01253 33600
Website: www.fsb.org.uk

The Forum of Private Business
Ruskin Chambers
Drury Lane
Knutsford
Cheshire
Tel: 01565 634467
Website: www.fpb.co.uk

Greater London Enterprise
28 Park Street
London SE1 9EQ
Tel: 020 7403 0300
Website: www.gle.co.uk

Highlands and Islands Enterprise
Bridge House
Bank Street
Inverness IV1 1QR
Tel: 01463 234171
Website: www.hie.co.uk

Hotel & Catering International
Management Association
Trinity Court
34 West Street
Sutton SM1 1SH
Tel: 020 8661 4904

Institute of Directors
116 Pall Mall
London SW1Y 5ED
Tel: 020 7839 1233
Website: www.iod.com

Institute of Patentees and Inventors
PO Box 301
Kingston-upon-Thames KT2 7WT
Tel: 020 8541 4197
Website: www.invent.org.uk

Institute of Trade Mark Attorneys
Canterbury House
4th Floor
2–6 Sydenham Road
Croydon CR0 9XE
Tel: 020 8686 2052
Website: www.itma.org.uk

Invest Northern Ireland
44–58 May Street
Belfast BT1 4NN
Tel: 028 9023 9090
Website: www.investni.com

LiveWire
Hawthorn House
Forth Banks
Newcastle upon Tyne NE1 3SG
Tel: 0845 757 3252
Website: www.shell-livewire.org

Manufacturers' Agents' Association
of Great Britain and Ireland
Incorporated (MAA)
Unit 16, Thrales End
Harpenden AL5 3NS
Tel: 01582 767618
Website: www.themaa.co.uk

MINTEL
Tel: 020 7606 5932
Website: www.mintel.com

MOPS (Mail Order Protection
Scheme)
see The National Newspapers' Mail
Order Protection Scheme Ltd

National Farmers' Union
Agriculture House
164 Shaftesbury Avenue
London WC2 8HL
Tel: 020 7331 7200
Website: www.nfu.co.uk

The National Newspapers' Mail
Order Protection Scheme Ltd
18a King Street
Maidenhead SL6 1EF
Tel: 01628 641930
Website: www.mops.org.uk

Office of the Deputy Prime
Minister
26 Whitehall
London SW1A 2WH
Website: www.odpm.gov.uk
(for planning permission)

The Patent Office
Concept House
Cardiff Road
Newport NP1 8QQ
Tel: 0845 9500 505
Website: www.patent.gov.uk

Prince's Trust
18 Park Square East
London NW1 4LH
Tel: 020 7543 1234
Website: www.princes-trust.org.uk

Production Engineering Research
Association
Melton Mowbray
Leicestershire LE13 0PB
Tel: 01664 501501
Website: www.pera.com

Scottish Enterprise
5 Atlantic Quay
150 Broomielaw
Glasgow G2 8LU
Tel: 0845 607 8787 (outside
Scotland: 0141 607 8787)
Website: www.scottish-
enterprise.com

Small Business Bureau Ltd
Curzon House
Church Road
Windlesham
Surrey GU20 6BH
Tel: 01276 452010
Website: www.smallbusiness
bureau.org.uk

The Stationery Office
PO Box 29
Norwich NR3 1GN
Tel: 0870 600 5522
Website: www.tso.co.uk

Trade Marks Enquiry Unit
Tel: 0845 500 505
Website: www.patent.gov.uk

UK Trade and Investment Enquiry
Service
Kingsgate House
66–74 Victoria Street
London SW1E 6SW
Tel: 020 745 8000
Website: www.uktradeinvest.
gov.uk

Venture Capital Report
Website: www.vcr1978.com

Welsh Development Agency
Plas Glyndŵr
Kingsway
Cardiff CF10 3AH
Tel: 01443 845500
Website: www.wda.co.uk

ADVERTISERS' CONTACT DETAILS

Ablett & Stebbing
Caparo House
101–103 Baker Street
London W1U 6FQ
Tel: 020 7935 7720
Website: www.absteb.co.uk

AlphaGraphics
Thornburgh Road
Eastfield
Scarborough
North Yorkshire YO11 3UY
Tel: 0800 257 424
Website: www.alphagraphics.
co.uk

@UK PLC
5 Jupiter House
Calleva Road
Aldermaston
Reading
Berkshire RG7 8NN
Tel: 0800 486 6000
Website: www.ukplc.net

Benjys
33 Cornhill
London EC3V 3ND
Tel: 0845 330 0126
Website: www.benjys-
sandwiches.com

Boult Wade Tennant
Verulam Gardens
70 Gray's Inn Road
London WC1X 9BT
Tel: 020 7430 7500
Website: www.boult.com

Business for Breakfast
31 Eccles Street
Eccles
Manchester M30 0NG
Tel: 08717 814314
Website: www.bforb.co.uk

Business Inc
1–2 Universal House
Wentworth Street
London E1 7SA
Tel: 0800 376 0641
Website: www.business-inc.co.uk

Business Post
Express House
Wolseley Drive
Heartlands
Birmingham B8 2SQ
Tel: 0121 335 1010
Website: www.businesspost.biz

The Camping and Caravanning
Club
Greenfields House
Westwood Way
Coventry CV1 8JH
Tel: 08701 287240
Website:
www.campingandcaravanning
club.co.uk/franchise

Chem-Dry (UK)
Belprin Road
Beverley
East Yorkshire HU17 0LP
Tel: 01482 888195
Website: www.chemdry.co.uk

CompactLaw Ltd
Sun House
10 Western Road
Tring
Hertfordshire HP23 4BB
Tel: 0845 166 8711
Website: www.employers
pack.co.uk/index.html

Consult GEE
100 Avenue Road
London NW3 3PG
Tel: 0800 376 1763
Website: www.consultgee.
essential-hr.co.uk

Domino's UK & Ireland Plc
Lasborough Road
Kingston
Milton Keynes
Buckinghamshire MK10 0AB
Tel: 01908 580657
Website: www.dominos.uk.com/
franchising

Duport Associates
Southfield House
2 Southfield Road
Westbury on Trym
Bristol BS9 3BH
Tel: 0117 330 8910
Website: www.duport.co.uk

Dyno
Zockoll House
143 Maple Road
Surbiton
Surrey KT6 4BJ
Tel: 0800 316 4604
Website: www.dyno.com

Eric Potter Clarkson
Park View House
58 The Ropewalk
Nottingham
Nottinghamshire NG1 5DD
Tel: 0115 955 2211
Website: www.eric-potter.com

Hire Intelligence
1 Goldhawk Estate
2a Brackenbury Road
London W6 OBA
Tel: 0845 600 7272
Website: www.hire-
intelligence.co.uk

HSBC
Level 31
8 Canada Square
London E14 5HQ
Tel: 0800 032 1322
Website: www.hsbc.co.uk/startup

Institute for Entrepreneurship
School of Management
Building 25, Level 3
Highfield
Southampton SO17 1BJ
Tel: 02380 598960
Website: www.ife.soton.ac.uk/
programmes-and-courses

Internet Business Pages Ltd
21 Armstrong House
First Avenue
The Finningley Estate
Hayfield Lane
Doncaster DN9 3GA
Tel: 01302 623111
Website: www.118freerate.com

Jo Jingles
Myrtle House
Penn Street Village
Nr Amersham
Buckinghamshire HP7 0PX
Tel: 01494 719360
Website: www.jojingles.com

Jordans Ltd
21 St Thomas Street
Bristol BS1 6JS
Tel: 0117 923 0600
Website: www.jordans.co.uk

Kall Kwik Printing Ltd
Artemis
Odyssey Business Park
West End Road
South Ruislip
Middlesex HA4 6QF
Tel: 0500 872060
Website: www.kallkwik.co.uk

Law Society Commercial Services
7th Floor
Fox Court
14 Gray's Inn Road
London WC1X 8HN
Tel: 020 7405 9075
Website: www.lfyb.lawsociety.
org.uk

The Little Gym UK
44 Highview Avenue
Edgware
Middlesex HA8 9UA
Tel: 020 8958 7373
Website: www.thelittlegym.com

Morethan (Royal & SunAlliance)
Park Side
Chart Way
Horsham
West Sussex RH12 1XA
Tel: 0800 107 8391
Website: morethanbusiness.co.uk

Morris & Co
Ashton House
Chadwick Street
Moreton
Wirral
Merseyside CH46 7TE
Tel: 0151 678 7979
Website: www.moco.co.uk

National Business Register Plc
Somerset House
40–49 Price Street
Birmingham B4 7LZ
Tel: 0870 700 8787
Website: www.anewbusiness.co.uk

Norwich Union
4th Floor
51–56 Fenchurch Street
London EC3M 3LA
Tel: 020 7817 6105
Website: www.norwichunion.com

The Office Express Group
Unit 2 Chantry Industrial Estate
Kingsbury Road
Curdworth
Sutton Coldfield B76 9EE
Tel: 0870 902 0202

Oxford Brookes University
Business School
The Enterprise Centre
Wheatley Campus
Oxford OX33 1HX
Tel: 01865 484534
Website: www.business.
brookes.ac.uk/enterprise

Page White & Farrer
54 Doughty Street
London WC1N 2LS
Tel: 020 7831 7929
Website: www.pagewhite.com

Pirtek UK Ltd
35 Acton Park Estate
The Vale
Acton
London W3 7QE
Tel: 020 8749 8444
Website: www.pirtek.co.uk

PlumbLocal
Local Group Services
Melville House
High Street
Dunmow
Essex CM6 1AF
Tel: 0808 000 0000
Website: www.plumblocal.co.uk

Prontaprint Ltd
Artemis
Odyssey Business Park
West End Road
South Ruislip
Middlesex HA4 6QF
Tel: 0845 762 6748
Website: www.prontaprint.com

Red Magnet
Parkshot House
5 Kew Road
Richmond
Surrey TW9 2PR
Tel: 0845 257147
Website: www.redmagnet.co.uk

Reddie & Grose
16 Theobalds Road
London WC1X 8PL
Tel: 020 7242 0901
Website: www.reddie.co.uk

Sage (UK) Ltd
North Park
Newcastle Upon Tyne NE13 9AA
Tel: 0800 447777
Website: www.sage.co.uk

Sales 101
32 Crespigny Road
London NW4 3DR
Tel: 020 8203 2448
Website: www.sales101.co.uk

Specsavers Optical Superstore
The West Lancashire Technical
Management Centre
Moss Lane View
Skelmersdale
Lancashire WN8 9TN
Tel: 01695 554200

Sunbelt Business Advisors
UK/IRE PLC
11 Henrietta Street
Covent Garden
London WC2E 8PY
Tel: 020 7836 4900
Website: www.sunbeltnetwork.
com/uk

Wildbore & Gibbons
Wildbore House
361 Liverpool Road
London N1 1NL
Tel: 020 7607 7312
Website: www.wildbore.co.uk

Workspace Group Plc
Magenta House
85 Whitechapel Road
London E1 1DU
Tel: 020 7377 1154
Website: www.workspacegroup.
co.uk

love retail?

Retail Joint Venture Partners

Are you passionate about retail? If you are, we'd like to hear from you. We're looking for exceptional individuals with extensive retail management experience to join us in locations across the UK and Ireland. This represents a substantial business opportunity with one of the world's most successful optical groups. For more information call Chris Howarth on 01695 554 200.

Should you have gone to Specsavers?

Appendix 1: Budgeting exercise – Yule Fuel Company

John Smith had worked for many years in a large sawmill. Being brought up to dislike waste, and being a bit of an amateur engineer, he had been experimenting with a machine for converting sawmill woodchips and sawdust into logs of fuel. Disposing of it was a problem for the mill, who could get rid of it only by selling it cheaply to horse and pet owners as a litter material. While it made some money for them, it was a nuisance to deal with the many visitors.

An imminent change in working methods at the mill meant that John's job would cease to exist in six months' time. The manager was sad to have to tell him, for John had been a good worker, but he could offer no alternative employment.

Once he and his wife had recovered from the shock they started to consider the alternatives. His wife had a good job, so he did not really need to earn a lot. John's neighbour was the first to suggest that he should start up on his own. The logs were coming out well now from the machine he had developed; and many of the people whom he knew owned wood-burning stoves and were complaining that firewood was getting more expensive.

John researched the market carefully and concluded that he could go ahead. People reported favourably on how the fuel burned, they liked his price, and all the garages and shops he approached said that they would stock it. The mill was happy to let him take all of their waste at £8 per tonne. He would not need it all at first, but reckoned that he could still turn a penny by selling some to the pet owners whose supply would dry up. That would be a bonus, though; his main concern was the logs, and he sat down to prepare a financial plan.

The facts he had established were:

Material costs	Dust: £8 per tonne (1,000 kg) paid on collection
	Bags: £1 per 25 kg bag, cash on delivery
Rent	£5,000 pa, paid January, April, July, October
Rates	£1,000 pa, paid April and October
Wages	£1,000 per month
Transport	£200 per month
Electricity	£300 per quarter, paid March, June, September, December
Post and phone	£100 per quarter, paid March, June, September and December
Insurance	£400 pa, paid in January
Packages	25 kg bags, selling for £5
Customers pay	Half pay cash on delivery, half pay two months after delivery
Output	500 bags per month (6,000 pa)
Orders	500 bags per month January to March, 300 April to September, 800 October to December (5,700 pa)

The equipment John has assembled is worth about £2,000 and will last some five years. So he allows for depreciation at the rate of £2,000 ÷ 5 = £400 pa.

YULE FUEL COMPANY

Product cost per bag

Materials $\dfrac{25 \text{ kg}}{1{,}000 \text{ kg}} \times £8$	=	£0.20
Packaging	=	£1.00
Total cost		£1.20
Selling price	=	£5.00
Value added	=	£3.80

So the first arithmetic John does suggests that materials costing him £1.20 can be sold for £5, leaving him with £3.80 per bag to pay the costs of the business and to give him a wage. (To keep the example simple, I have omitted VAT.) Now he wants to know whether the quantity he expects to sell will actually meet his costs and earn him a living. He draws up a profit-and-loss budget, as shown on page 218.

So it looks as if the business should pay John's modest wage, but make no profit in its first year. He might expect it to make more in the second year, because 300 bags from the stocks he builds up this summer will be available to be sold after Christmas: this year he could sell only the 500 bags that he can make each month, despite having orders for more. But it is still a slim margin of safety, as it gives him only £12,000 of wages, out of which interest and tax may have to be paid. So he may need to rethink the proposal rather radically, or even abandon it in its present form.

YULE FUEL COMPANY

Profit-and-loss budget year ended . . .

	£	£
Sales 5,700 bags @ £5		28,500
Materials: Bags	4,560	
Dust	1,140	5,700
Value added		22,800
Overheads		
Rent and rates	6,000	
Wages	12,000	
Transport	2,400	
Electricity	1,200	
Post and phone	400	
Insurance	400	
Depreciation	400	22,800
Profit before interest and tax		0

He decides to persevere with the arithmetic at least. The next part of the plan is to produce the cash-flow budget (shown on page 219). Remember that he will keep on making 500 bags a month throughout the year, although he will not be selling them all during the summer.

The last line of the cash-flow budget, in effect, forecasts the bank balance. It makes sorry reading. The debt mounts until it gets to nearly £8,000 in October and then reduces. On the whole, we might conclude that this is not too bright an idea. It sounded fine at first, making nearly £4 profit per bag; the equipment is all bought and paid for; and the redundancy cheque will more than cover the firm's financial needs. But as John himself now sees, a little more analysis shows up the flaws; this is no place to invest his redundancy money.

He might now look at how the plan can be changed. The main problems it suffers from are its seasonal nature and inflexible output, so that stocks have to be built up during the summer while little is sold; and the high overheads in relation to turnover. You do not need to work out the break-even point to see that it is a fragile proposition. The idea that nothing might be left over out of nearly £30,000, if all the other forecast figures come true, allows little room for error. A building society would be far safer.

On the other hand, the building society would only pay interest on the loan, whereas the business does plan to pay John a very basic wage. So

Table A1.1 Cash-flow budget for Yule Fuel Company

YULE FUEL COMPANY

Cash-flow budget for year ended . . .

	Jan	Feb	Mar	Apr	May	Jun	Jul	Aug	Sept	Oct	Nov	Dec
Production: bags	500	500	500	500	500	500	500	500	500	500	500	500
Sales: bags	500	500	500	300	300	300	300	300	300	800	800	800
Invoiced sales	2,500	2,500	2,500	1,500	1,500	1,500	1,500	1,500	1,500	4,000	4,000	4,000
Receipts: Cash	1,250	1,250	1,250	750	750	750	750	750	750	2,000	2,000	2,000
Debtors			1,250	1,250	1,250	750	750	750	750	750	750	2,000
(a) Total receipts	1,250	1,250	2,500	2,000	2,000	1,500	1,500	1,500	1,500	2,750	2,750	4,000
Payments: Rent	1,250			1,250			1,250			1,250		
Rates				500						500		
Wages	1,000	1,000	1,000	1,000	1,000	1,000	1,000	1,000	1,000	1,000	1,000	1,000
Transport	200	200	200	200	200	200	200	200	200	200	200	200
Electricity			300			300			300			300
Post, phone			100			100			100			100
Insurance	400											
Materials	600	600	600	600	600	600	600	600	600	600	600	600
(b) Total payments	3,450	1,800	2,200	3,550	1,800	2,200	3,050	1,800	2,200	3,550	1,800	2,200
(a)–(b) Cash flow	−2,200	−550	300	−1,550	200	−700	−1,550	−300	−700	−800	950	1,800
Cumulative cash flow	−2,200	−2,750	−2,450	−4,000	−3,800	−4,500	−6,050	−6,350	−7,050	−7,850	−6,900	−5,100

what do we conclude? Well, everyone's circumstances and attitudes are different. Some people would run a mile from a proposition like this; others would find it acceptable. Insofar as one person can make an objective judgement, my opinion is that the risks of self-employment need to be better rewarded than this. If John can possibly get a job and put his money in a safer place he would be well advised to do so.

Now, if he could raise prices by £1 – or £1.99 – a bag, the picture would be transformed. Provided, of course, that the volume does not fall much. You might like to work out what price level would give the income that would satisfy your personal income and profit requirements. If you were doing this in real life you would then try to reassess the size of the market at the new price. Who knows, far from shrinking, it might grow!

Appendix 2: Help for small businesses

The following organisations are some of those which offer help of various sorts for small firms. If you are in any doubt as to how to get in touch with them, your local Business Link should be able to tell you. Their contact details appear in Section 17.

Banks. Most banks publish free booklets on many aspects of starting and running a business, give away forms on which to do financial planning, and run newsletters.

British Overseas Trade Board. This government body, within the Department of Trade and Industry, gives leaflets, help and advice on exporting.

Chambers of commerce. Joining the local chamber can be a good way of making business contacts, as well as giving you access to a library and information service, help with exporting, and a voice in representations to public authorities.

Chambers of trade. Quite separate from the chamber of commerce, which usually serves industry and commerce, the chamber of trade does similar work for retailers and wholesalers.

Co-operative Development Agencies. These organisations give help and advice to people wishing to set up a co-operative venture.

County courts. They give away a booklet on making claims for payment of debts of up to £5,000, and what to do if such a claim is made against you.

Customs and Excise VAT offices. Their staff offer advice on all aspects of VAT and dispense free booklets (visit www.hmce.gov.uk).

Department of Employment. Advice and information on setting up and running a small firm, and useful free booklets.

Department of Trade and Industry. This government department is the main source of grants for industry. Its regional offices can advise on every facet of their help (visit www.dti.gov.uk).

Development agencies (for Scotland, Wales and Northern Ireland). These are government bodies that can offer a wide range of advice, help, premises and funds for business.

Enterprise agencies. These partnerships between the public and private sectors aim to offer advice, help and other facilities to encourage new and existing businesses.

Highlands and Islands Enterprise. This northern Scottish organisation supports, helps and promotes small businesses in its area.

Industrial Training Boards. Although many have been abolished or changed in nature in the last few years, some offer excellent publications to help new and small firms in their particular industry.

Inland Revenue Inspectors of Taxes. Leaflets and advice are given on the tax position of businesses, which can be most useful to new starters (visit www.inlandrevenue.gov.uk).

Jobcentres. Not only are they a source of recruitment, but Jobcentres also carry a stock of leaflets and Department of Employment publications, many of which are essential reading for an employer.

Local authorities. They can usually provide information on any industrial aid which may be available locally. In addition, as one of the most influential enforcement bodies acting on small firms, they can advise you on how to avoid trouble. The main contacts are the planning department, health inspectors, fire department, building inspectors and trading standards offices.

Newspaper Publishers Association. This body lays down the rules governing, among other things, mail order advertising in most newspapers and magazines. Anyone planning to sell by this method should contact them well in advance of trying to advertise.

Patent Office. The Patent Office offers an informative set of leaflets on its concerns.

Royal Mail. The Royal Mail gives considerable concessions to volume users of its services in general, and especially to first-time users of direct mail selling. Postal sales representatives at Head Post Offices provide the details.

Tourist Boards. Organised on a regional basis, the Tourist Boards offer management advice, publicity and grants for tourism-based enterprises. These do not have to be just hotels: they are concerned to help most firms having some tourism aspect to their operations. They also publish some useful guides to running different sorts of tourism businesses.

Training and Enterprise Councils (TECs). These bodies offer courses for new starters, together with living allowances, all paid for by the government. It also gives the Enterprise Allowance for unemployed new starters and the Young Workers Scheme subsidy for employing a young person, and funds the Youth Training Scheme.

Build your future with a market leader ·····⋮⋮

In the competitive world of express delivery, Business Post is an acknowledged leader. Operate a franchise depot with Business Post and you'll have access to the widest range of express services available in the UK market today.

You'll have good people management skills, be passionate about customer care and want to grow your business through a structured and dynamic sales programme.

Bring those attributes, and a minimum investment of £100,000, and we'll provide the rest, including an established territory with income from day one.

Excellent field support, world class systems and in depth training will ensure you achieve your goals.

To learn more of what Business Post could offer you call **08452 30 30 10**. Or log on to www.businesspost.biz/franchising.

Businesspost
Worldwide Express *Parcels & Mail*

Business Post Ltd, Express House, Wolseley Drive, Birmingham B8 2SQ www.businesspost.biz

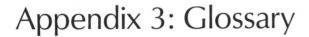

Appendix 3: Glossary

ACAS. Advisory, Conciliation and Arbitration Service.

accounts. Periodic, at least annual, reports usually consisting of *profit-and-loss* account and *balance sheet.*

accounting period. Period of time to which a set of accounts refers.

accrual. Allowance in accounts for costs and benefits accrued but not yet realised.

agent. See *sales agent.*

AIDA. The sequence of a sales presentation: Attention, Interest, Desire, Action.

amortisation. Writing off an initial cost over a period of time; see also *depreciation.*

APR. Annual Percentage Rate, ie the true rate of interest.

artwork. Finished design ready for photography, eg for making printing plates.

assets. Property having measurable value.

    current. Debtors plus stock and cash.

    fixed. Plant, equipment, vehicles and buildings.

    liquid. In cash, or easily convertible to cash.

    net. Total assets less liabilities.

    net current. Current assets less current liabilities; also known as working capital.

audit. Independent check and comment on financial records.

authorised capital. The amount of capital which a company is permitted to issue and in what form.

bad debt. Debt that is not recovered.

balance sheet. Statement at a moment in time showing sources and disposition of funds.

bankruptcy. Statutory confiscation of personal assets to settle debts, and prohibition from trading.

base rate. The basic rate of interest above which banks will lend.

bill of exchange. Document unconditionally arranging a future payment.

bill of lading (B/L). Receipt from a ship's master for goods loaded on board.

black (or grey) economy. The informal part of the economy, usually evading taxation.

bleed. Printing that extends over the entire page and is not surrounded by a 'frame'.

block. A photographically prepared special item for use in *letterpress* printing.

book value. Value of an asset shown in the books, ie after deducting allowances for depreciation; often different from resale value or replacement cost.

BRAD. British Rate and Data: a monthly publication listing advertising media.

break-even. The level of activity at which a firm's profit equals its costs.

broker. A go-between.

budget. A forecast expressed in figures, eg a sales budget, an overheads budget, a cash-flow budget.

capital. Total resources invested or available for investment.

capital gain. Rise in the value of an asset.

capital goods. Same as fixed assets.

Careers Office. Local authority office charged with finding jobs for young people.

case. The package protecting goods from damage in transit.

cash. Money in readily accessible form, eg in a current account or in banknotes.

cash book. Daily record of cash payments and cash received.

cash flow. The movement of cash into and out of the business as income is received and debts are settled.

Certificate of Lawful Use Development. See *Existing Use Certificate*.

channel. Channel of distribution, eg wholesaler – retailer – consumer.

charge. A legally registered right to the proceeds of the disposal of an asset in return for an unpaid debt.

civil law. The system of law relating to private rights, developed by judicial decisions rather than Parliament.

clearing banks. Banks of the type familiar to the general public.

closing stock. Stock held at the end of an accounting period.

collateral. Security pledged against borrowing.

condition. Matters in a *contract*, breach of which entitles the offended party to a refund plus damages.

consignment note. Same as *delivery note*.

consignment stock. Stock placed with a distributor and not charged for until sold.

consumer. The end user of a product or service.

consumer goods. Products of the type supplied to the public.

consumer research. Research aimed at identifying the needs, wants and preferences of, and influences on, consumers.

contingency. An item often found in *budgets* – a safety margin.

contract. Binding agreement on two or more parties.

control. Process of identifying and correcting deviations from plan.

cooperative. A business constitution in which the employees own the business: there are many varieties.

copy. Written material for publication.

copy date. The latest date by which a publication can receive material for inclusion.

copyright. Legal protection from copyists automatically applying to any original work, and often signified by a © (date, name).

corporation tax. Tax on the profits of companies.

COSHH. Control of Substances Hazardous to Health (regulations).

cost of sales. The cost of goods sold, as shown in *profit-and-loss* calculations.

credit. Arrangement for deferring the payment of debts; *also* positive figures in accounts.

credit control. Ensuring that payments due are, as far as possible, received on time.

credit sale. Sale on instalments where ownership passes before payment is complete.

creditor. A person to whom money is owed.

current. Due within one year (in accounting).

debenture. A document recording a charge over the *assets* of a company in return for a loan.

debit. Subtract; *also* negative figures in accounts.

debtor. A person who owes one money.

delivery note. A list of goods delivered on one occasion, usually arriving with the goods themselves.

depreciation. An amount, usually a percentage, by which the using-up of *fixed assets* is expressed as a cost.

direct mail. Sending sales material direct to *consumers*.

direct response. Selling via advertising which solicits orders and payment direct to the advertiser.

direct selling. Selling direct to the *consumer* outside the normal trade channels.

disciplinary procedure. A defined procedure for dealing with offences by employees.

display. A small advertisement within its own frame.

distress. Legally, to 'levy a distress' is to confiscate goods to enforce payment.

distress purchase. A purchase that has to be made under pressure, usually of time, eg replacement car windscreen.

dividend. Payment to shareholders from a company.

draft. An interim attempt which can be improved upon, eg draft plans; *also* banker's draft: a bank's instructions to pay money from its funds.

E & O E. 'Errors and omissions excepted'; a let-out, sometimes found on invoices.

EFT. Electronic Funds Transfer.

EFTPOS. Electronic Funds Transfer at Point of Sale. A system whereby shops can instantly transfer payment from the customer's bank account to their own.

employer's liability insurance. A class of insurance which employers are required to have by law.

endorse. To sign on the back of a cheque, bill etc to transfer its ownership.

equity. That part of a company's funds raised by the sale of shares.

Existing Use Certificate. Written acknowledgement from local authority that a particular use of a building or site is sanctified by the passage of time.

facing matter. Material facing editorial content in a publication.

factor. Wholesaler; *also* one who buys a firm's debts to give it an inflow of cash and obtains settlement of those debts himself.

financial year. Year covered by an annual set of business accounts, not necessarily January to December.

fixed assets. See *assets, fixed.*

fixed capital. Long-term debt, usually shareholders' funds plus long-term loans.

fixed costs. Those costs which do not vary with the level of activity within certain limits, eg rent, rates etc.

franchise. The right to sell a franchisor's products and services.

free issue. A system whereby materials are bought by a firm and issued at no charge to a subcontractor to do work on them.

FRI. Full repairing and insuring (lease).

gearing. Relationship between borrowings and owners' funds in a business (high borrowing and little equity is 'highly geared').

going concern. Assumption that the business is a continuing operation, not about to be liquidated.

goodwill. Difference between the 'going concern' valuation of a business and its book value; a monetary expression of its earning potential over and above its break-up value.

grievance procedure. Defined procedure enabling employees to have employment grievances dealt with.
gross. Full price or total figure before any subtractions are made; *also* serious, as in 'gross misconduct'.

HASAWA. Health and Safety at Work Act.
hire purchase. Payment by instalments where ownership transfers only after payment is complete.

ifc/irc. Inside front cover/inside rear cover.
indemnity. Undertaking to recompense.
inflation accounting. System of accounting which attempts to deal with the effect on financial performance of the changing value of money.
input. Purchase on which VAT is calculated.
insolvency. Inability to pay bills through immediate shortage of cash (could possibly be cleared by realising assets).
inventory. Stock; *also* a list.
invoice. A 'bill' in everyday language.
issued capital. The amount of money raised by a company by the sale of its shares.

joint and several. Together and individual; usually of guarantees etc which can be made by a number of people who are collectively and separately responsible.

letterhead. Writing paper printed with a business name and address.
letterpress. A printing method using pre-formed letters.
LGS. The government Loan Guarantee Scheme.
liability. Money owed; obligation.
limited company. A legal 'person', separate from its owners, whose liability for its debts is limited to the issued share capital.
lineage. Advertising which is sold by the line, as in typical classified advertisements.
liquid. Having enough cash to meet obligations.
liquidation. Sale of assets and collection of monies owed, to pay off debtors.
liquidity. Ability to meet demands for payment of debts; *also* extent to which a company's assets are in the form of cash or can quickly become cash.
lithography/litho. A method of printing which uses photographically created printing plates.
loan capital. That part of a company's capital raised through loans as opposed to equity and retained profits.

mail order. A method of shopping by post from catalogues.

margin. The profit margin on which a company works. A distributor usually adds a proportion to cost, or expects a percentage of his selling price.

market. A defined public, actually or potentially consumers of goods or a service, or a group of goods or services, eg the leisure market, the baked bean market, the French market.

marketing. The approach to business that starts from the customer's needs and seeks to profit by satisfying them; *also* research, design, distribution, promotion and pricing activities towards that end.

market research. Investigation of the characteristics of a presumed market.

mark-up. The profit that a distributor or shop adds to the cost of an item. Often erroneously used for profit margins in general.

media. Plural of 'medium', frequently used to mean carriers of advertising and information, such as television, radio, newspapers, magazines etc.

Memorandum and Articles of Association. The constitution and rules of a company.

merchant banks. Risk investment bodies.

MOPS. Mail Order Protection Scheme.

mortgage. A form of charge, usually over land and premises, but sometimes over chattels, in return for a loan.

net. After subtraction of discounts or wastage; *also* 'payment net' – no discounts given for payment.

net assets. See *assets, net*.

net current assets. See *assets, net current*.

net worth. Total assets less all liabilities.

news release. Same as *press release*.

NPA. Newspaper Publishers Association.

off the page. Same as *direct response*.

opening stock. Stock held at the beginning of an accounting period.

operating profit. Gross profit less overheads; excludes cost of finance, tax etc.

operating statement. Document showing gross sales, cost of sales, gross profit, *overheads* and net profit before tax and interest.

outer. The outer transit case holding, say, a dozen packs of a product.

output. Sales on which VAT is calculated.

overdraft. A loan on current account which may fluctuate with day-to-day transactions up to a defined limit, and may be recalled at a moment's notice.

overheads. General costs which cannot be accurately attributed to individual products, eg rent, telephone, insurance etc.

overtrading. Having difficulty with liquidity due to a level of sales greater than the capital base can support.

P&L. Profit and loss. Calculation of profit over a past period of time; or in *budget*, expected in the future.

Pareto Principle. 80 per cent of activity produces 20 per cent of results, and vice versa.

partnership. Business constitution in which each partner is personally responsible for the entire liabilities and obligations of the business.

party plan. A method of selling to parties of people at the home of one of them.

passing off. Pretence that goods were made by other than their true manufacturer.

patent. An expensive but powerful legal protection for an original technological invention.

PAYE. Pay As You Earn; usually deduction of income tax and National Insurance made by the employer from employee's gross pay.

plant. Equipment, machines.

plc. Public limited company.

pos/pop. Point of sale/point of purchase; the place where sale or purchase occurs.

preferential creditor. Creditor with a right to be paid before unsecured creditors; includes the government, employees etc.

presentation. An explanatory and persuasive address to an audience, usually involving visual aids.

press release. A news story, written by or on behalf of its subject, and circulated to the news media in the hope of publication.

profit and loss. See *P&L*.

profit margin. See *margin*.

pro-forma. Documents sent in advance of transaction, eg a pro-forma invoice is one which will be paid before goods are despatched, or will alert a customer (particularly overseas) to the full cost of the consignment; *also* a standard document or letter fulfilling statutory requirements, eg the statement of terms and conditions to employees.

proof. An example of printing for checking and approval before the main print run is started.

PR/public relations. Activity designed to influence public opinion favourably.

QA. Quality assurance.

quality circles. A system whereby all employees contribute to management consideration of quality affairs and problem-solving.

QC. Quality control.

R&D. Research and development.

rate card. Price-list for advertising.

receiver. Person appointed by a court to take control of and protect the assets of a company which is unable to meet its obligations.

redundancy. The disappearance of a job causing dismissal or transfer of an employee; *also* intentional over-specification to reduce risk of failure.

registered design. An original design protected by registration; this gives better security than copyright.

registered office. The office of a company registered with the Registrar of Companies. Often it is the office of a professional adviser to the firm.

registered trade mark. A trade name or mark protected by registration.

registration number. The number allocated on registration of a company by the Registrar of Companies.

reservation of title. Retention of ownership of goods until (usually) they have been paid for.

retained profits. Profits that have not been distributed to shareholders as *dividends.*

revaluation. Valuing existing assets on present-day criteria.

Romalpa. A legal case affecting rights to *reservation of title.*

rop. Run of paper (in advertising); placed where it suits the publisher.

sales agent. A person who obtains orders in return for payment of commission.

sales promotion. Activity which motivates desired purchasing patterns.

scc. Single-column centimetre (in advertising).

Schedule D. Income tax regime for the self-employed.

Schedule E. Income tax regime for employed people.

segment. A defined portion of a *market.*

segmentation. The process of dividing a market into notional portions.

self-employed. Working on own account while supplying tools and equipment, and for hours which are self-determined.

semi-display. Advertising which rules off one advertisement from its neighbours in a column.

settlement discount. Discount for paying debt within a time limit.

share capital. Funds invested in a *limited company* in return for shares.

small claims procedure. Informal procedure for recovering debts of up to £5,000 via county courts.

sole trader. A self-employed person trading on his own responsibility. See also, *self-employed.*

solvent. Having enough cash to pay bills.

sor/sale or return. Arrangement whereby distributor pays only for stock that he sells.

SSP/Statutory Sick Pay. Employer pays sick employee and reclaims from government.

statement. A summary of transactions on an account.

statute. Act of Parliament.

stay. Delay.

stock. Raw materials, work in progress, and finished goods.

structure plan. Local authority plan delineating town and country planning policies.

suspension. Requiring an employee not to report to work, but without dismissal; normally, suspension on full pay.

SWOT. An analysis of a company's internal Strengths and Weaknesses, and external Opportunities and Threats.

tangible asset. Asset that can be touched, eg machine, but not goodwill.

tender. A fixed-price offer to sell or buy, typically used by public authorities' purchasing departments.

term loan. A loan repayable over a fixed period of time.

terms and conditions. Conditions under which commitments are accepted.

title. Ownership; see *reservation of title*.

tort. A civil wrong; see *civil law*.

trade description. Description of goods or services; by law, it must be true.

Trading Standards Department. Local authority department responsible for enforcement of much consumer-protection legislation.

tribunal. Industrial Tribunal appointed to hear cases of misconduct in employment matters alleged by current or former employees.

Truck Acts. Acts of Parliament mainly requiring wages to be paid in cash.

unsecured creditor. One with no security for his debt other than a promise to pay.

value. A perception based on a combination of price and expected or actual performance.

value added. The difference between the cost of materials and their sales value in processed form.

variable costs. Costs which vary with the level of activity, eg materials consumed.

VAT. Value Added Tax; a sales tax.

visual aid. Graphic or other tangible aid to explanation.

Wages Council. Statutory body which sets minimum wages for employees in a low-paid industry.

warranty. A term in a *contract*, breach of which entitles the aggrieved person to a refund.

Willings Press Guide. A directory of publications.

winding-up. Closing down a business, selling assets, settling debts, and distributing any residue among its owners.

working capital. Funds used to finance day-to-day dealings; formally defined as *net current assets* (current assets less current liabilities).

work in progress. Part-finished goods in the production process.

writing-down allowance. Same as *depreciation.*

written statement. Written confirmation of the terms of an employment contract.

Appendix 4: Recruiting staff

Taking people on looks straightforward, but there are hidden pitfalls set for the unwary. Doing the things I propose will not eliminate risk altogether, but will certainly reduce it. If risk elimination is important to you, get a specialist in employment law involved: either a consultant or perhaps a lecturer from your local college will have more of a practical grasp of the realities than a solicitor. The problem with the pure lawyer's approach is that too often, in properly seeking to defend you from all dangers, it erects a panoply of paper in strict legalese that may frighten off desirable recruits.

Here I break the process down into its elements and comment on each one. It is important not only to commit all this to paper but also to *preserve it for a couple of years after the recruitment process is complete*. If you were ever accused of any form of prejudiced behaviour this file would be a key element in your defence.

THE JOB SPECIFICATION

This is where you define the purpose of the job, to whom the person is to report and what duties are expected. There is no point in skipping it as it is reproduced when you complete the written statement of the contract of employment. You need to define:

- the purpose of the job;
- to whom the person is to report;
- each duty expected of him or her (and finally, 'any other duty reasonably required by the management').

When doing this it is *vitally important* to clear your mind of any specific person or type of person who might fit the bill. For the purposes of illustration, let us say you are recruiting a secretary and personal assistant; we shall carry this example through every element of the process. Just because every secretary you have ever met has been female, do not carry in your mind a picture of a female secretary. Do not picture them as able-bodied, from any particular ethnic group or, indeed, as male. Keep your mind completely open. Best to banish all mental images and just state the requirements of the job.

THE PERSON SPECIFICATION

Here you say what minimum capabilities the person must have to discharge the duties of the job specification, listed as 'essential', as well as any extras that might be desirable. For example, familiarity with all aspects of the latest release of Microsoft Word might be 'essential', whilst the ability to use Excel and PowerPoint would be 'desirable'. Once again, you banish mental images of individuals.

The specification needs to list:

- physical and mental capabilities required;
- any formal qualifications;
- experience necessary (duration and type);
- disqualifications from the job (make sure they are of the type permitted).

Spend plenty of time and effort on this and the preceding stage. If your final selection is made on grounds not covered by one of the descriptions you risk it being seen as discriminatory.

THE ADVERTISEMENT

This covers not just ads you might place in the local press but also e-mails, letters, telephone calls, discussions with recruitment agencies, conversations with individuals – in fact, any form of communication about the vacancy whatsoever.

It is essential that these communications are shorn of any and all aspects that could be interpreted as discrimination against some protected group. That such apparent discrimination may be unconscious and unintentional is no defence, so examine everything you say before opening your mouth. Indeed, to be on the safe side, you may want to use the job and person descriptions virtually as scripts when speaking about the job. Written ads are less tricky, as you have a chance to mull over what you are planning to say before finally publishing it.

Clearly, the ad needs not only to avoid the potential for causing trouble, but also to present the firm in a good light. Look at the ways in which businesses, large and small, present themselves in recruitment ads. The smaller ones may seem less attractive to potential employees, offering fewer perks and perhaps worse premises, but they can make up for it. You will find them describing themselves as 'fast-growing', 'informal', 'offering opportunity' and so on, phrases calculated not only to make them sound attractive, but to pull in replies from exactly the sort of can-do people they want to recruit, rather than those more interested in security and the safety of routine.

Before sitting down to write the ad, define its objectives. They are (I imagine) to pull in at least 10 replies from people qualified to do the job – 10, because not everyone who enquires actually bothers to complete the forms, or to turn up for interview. This demands that the ad is legible, so do not skimp on size or use fancy colours; especially, do not reverse the print out of a dark background, which almost guarantees illegibility.

APPLICATIONS

Each applicant should complete and sign an application form. Sample formats can be found in specialist books on recruitment, and you can ask for application forms for jobs you see advertised. Using those templates, create the form that suits you best. When sending forms out to candidates, be sure to enclose the job and person descriptions and state clearly the deadline for return of forms and the date and place of interviews. Make sure you specify your policy on asking for references: it is fairest to everyone if you contact referees other than current employers immediately, but hold off until the job has been offered and accepted before approaching the current employer. Candidates ought to be given the chance to ask you to postpone all approaches to referees until offer and acceptance: if necessary, you can explore the reasons at interview.

Shortlisting applications

It is best if more than one person undertakes this activity, and the interviewing, to reduce charges of personal prejudice. If you want to be safe, the sole criteria you may use are those of the two descriptions, of job and person. Record clearly why you turned down the rejects and write to them straight away.

Those selected need to be invited to attend the interview and given directions to find its venue.

SETTING UP INTERVIEWS

In advance of the day you need to:

- decide how many interviews there will be;
- decide times;
- decide format;
- make bookings;
- invite candidates, offering to refund travel expenses;
- prepare materials;
- brief interviewers.

We shall now look briefly at each of these in turn.

How many interviews

For almost all jobs, two is desirable. That may sound excessive, but experience has taught me that the outstanding candidate of the first meeting often turns into a mediocrity on the second, whilst the earlier also-ran later proves to have hidden depths.

Times

Are conventional office hours really best, or might you attract more attendance by holding interviews early in the evening or before work in the morning? For most jobs, allow 30–45 minutes for meeting each candidate (though see 'format' below) plus a further 15 minutes for consideration, discussion and writing up your thoughts afterwards. Thus candidates need to come in at hourly intervals.

Format

Someone needs to greet candidates, to deal with their expenses claim if a refund is offered, to offer them refreshment and the use of the lavatory and to let interviewers know that the next candidate has arrived.

The usual format is for the interviewers to describe the programme and duration of the interview, then take the candidate through their application as it relates to the job and person descriptions. Interviewers make notes of replies. Candidates should be given every encouragement to show how they meet the demands of the person description, and interviewers should note the efforts they make and the responses made. When all aspects of the person description have been exhausted the candidate is invited to put any questions they might have. The interview concludes with a promise to be in touch by a particular time (best practice is the same day) with the decision.

For many jobs, the usual face-to-face interview is supplemented by an 'activity centre'. That involves candidates being presented with simulations of situations that might occur in real life and dealing with them as best they can. It can reveal a great deal about people's capability to do the job.

Our hypothetical secretary/PA will be expected to do a number of things. Fast, accurate typing will be among them. He or she should be given a tape of dictation that incorporates difficult and ambiguous usages (standard tests are available). That demonstrates spelling ability. Likewise, some copy-typing should be given which has all sorts of crossings-out, scruffy amendments and shifts of sentences from one paragraph to another, to test comprehension and ability to sort out meaning from chaos. Another exercise might be to compose a letter accepting a dummy proposal for a meeting, to check on spelling, grammar, ability to select the right sort of language for a particular application and general skill with English. A time limit is given for each task.

He or she will have to deal effectively with people on the telephone. A call can be made from an extension for the candidate to deal with. In the interests of demonstrable fairness the person testing the response should work from a script used for all candidates. Interviewers really worried about potential accusations of unfairness will tape this, having told the candidate beforehand.

None of these tests is designed to present difficulty above the level with which the jobholder might be dealing for 70 per cent of the time. Their purpose is not sadistic but to allow good candidates to demonstrate their abilities.

Another exercise is an 'in-tray' that simulates the kinds of enquiries the candidate would have to deal with in real life. It would comprise a bundle of perhaps 10 to 15 sheets of paper, each carrying a different message of the kind that might come in routinely. One could be a telephone message, another an e-mail, another a letter, or a message from someone who looked in while the boss was out, and so on. Each message contains a clue as to its urgency and importance and thus ought to alert the candidate to the type of action to be taken. The boss can be assumed to be asleep in New York on a known telephone number and thus available, but only in dire emergency. He or she will telephone in at 3 pm UK time. The candidate's task is to rank the messages in importance and urgency and write on each what he or she would do about each of them. The options are, clearly, to wake the boss, ring once the boss has woken up, wait until he or she telephones at 3 pm, pass on to someone else to deal with or for the candidate's own action. Exercises of this sort do not take much time or trouble to set up, but can reveal extraordinary things about candidates' thought-processes that might never emerge from an interview. They need only the lightest supervision to ensure that friends are not consulted by text or telephone, and the candidate can leave after completion. Alternatively, one candidate can be doing the exercises while another is being interviewed.

Make bookings

If interviews are to be held on the firm's premises rooms need to be reserved, which may cause inconvenience to operations. If suitable rooms do not exist at the office, a hotel is an obvious alternative. Be sure that it has adequate car parking and inspect the actual rooms you would use before reserving them. Venue staff will need briefing about what to do when candidates approach the reception desk.

Invite candidates

You might already have cleared candidates' availability before fixing dates and times, but either way it is wise to confirm the date, time and venue, in writing, with clear directions and a contact telephone number for use on the day. You may choose to refund out-of-pocket travel expenses altogether for junior staff, or over £10, for example, for more senior appointments.

Prepare materials

Any 'activity centre' materials will need designing and copying before the day, with one folder holding a complete set per applicant, labelled with the name of the candidate.

Interviewers will need a timetable showing interviewees' names and the times that they have been invited for, with copies of each application form and any references supplied.

Each interviewer will also need a record sheet for each candidate showing the elements of the person description with space for notes to be made of applicants' responses.

Brief interviewers

Part of any demonstration of the fairness of the process is that interviewers were working to the same unprejudiced brief. Moreover, to look like the kind of organised outfit that would attract a good candidate, they need to fix who does what during the interviews. They must therefore get together and agree procedure.

HOLDING INTERVIEWS

Having set the process up with such care, you ought to find that the actual interviews proceed smoothly. Again, both interviewers need to be alert to the language and terminology they use, avoiding references to traps from common English usage such as 'Christian name', 'manning the phones', 'blacklists', 'going pale' and so on. Set aside any feelings you may have about the effects that the discrimination industry has had on vocabulary and just recognise that there is no point in causing offence and attracting trouble. Remember that one of the many definitions of improper discrimination is that the person concerned feels discriminated against – no matter whether that feeling is based on reasonable grounds or whether there was intent to offend. Never ask a woman if she is pregnant nor what her plans may be for having a family, nor whether she has adequate arrangements for caring for her children. Apart from the issue of pregnancy, the same list of prohibitions attaches to men. Nevertheless, if you are told that a candidate has young children you might be concerned about his or her likely reliability. Thus, in a separate part of the interview, you might enquire about his or her timekeeping and absence record, providing you ask the same of all candidates. The point is that asking a woman about the family could be construed as a matter of sex discrimination, whereas asking about attendance relates specifically to ability to do the job and is thus sex-neutral.

Having asked if the candidate has any further questions, your final move of the interview is to tell him or her what happens next and ensure that, if you have offered to, his or her expenses are paid.

The interviewers finalise their separate notes of the interview, then prepare for the next candidate. As yet there is no discussion or decision.

MAKING THE DECISION

Once all interviews have been completed and the results from any activities have been evaluated (in writing), the interviewers consolidate their findings. Each can summarise their own ranking of candidates by transferring their point-by-point evaluations of candidates' performance against each element of the person description to a blank form used as a summary sheet. Now, at last, they are able to discuss their results. Despite the previous lack of discussion it is unusual for there to be much dissent and a decision is usually reached quite quickly. This is an effect to beware of, for it must not inhibit a comparison of the full evaluations of each candidate made by the interviewers. Again, the discussion is minuted.

MAKING THE OFFER

The lead interviewer should telephone the candidate immediately and ask if he or she is still interested in the job. If so, the offer is made, subject to satisfactory references if they are still outstanding. Candidates may wish to take a few hours to think or to talk with family, which should be allowed. The interviewer may want to ask if there are any further points the candidate might like to ask about and to offer a home or mobile telephone number for any queries that arise. After all, this is someone you want to employ, so you will want to make it easy for him or her to clear up any last minute wavering.

It is important to spell out the expected timescale of the events that follow. It might take a fortnight for references to arrive and thus be some time before the candidate receives the unconditional offer in writing: candidates who are job-hunting need to know this, and you need to know if your chosen applicant has any other irons in the fire. After all the work you have done it would be vexing to leave a three-week silence only to find that, in the meantime, your recruit has accepted another job.

TAKING UP REFERENCES

You may wish to do this by telephone as well as in writing, explaining to the referees that it helps to have written confirmation of their views. The reason for this is that many people speak more freely than they write, so the telephone conversation may reveal more than the subsequent letter.

When writing to referees enclose an SAE for their reply, marked 'private and confidential'.

CONFIRMING THE OFFER

If references are in any way unsatisfactory you are entitled to an explanation from the candidate. This is a ticklish area as there is an unspoken assumption that references are confidential between the company and the referee, so tactful handling may be needed if you are to preserve that confidence. A referee might reasonably feel upset if, after trying to alert you to problems they had with a former employee, that employee sued them for slander or libel.

Once you are happy you should telephone the candidate to tell them, with written confirmation the same day. The letter should spell out the terms of the offer and enclose two copies of the written statement of the contract of employment, one for the recruit to keep, the other for them to sign and return. They are now in a position to put in their resignation from their present job, if any, and you can agree the date of their start with you.

INDUCTION

Before the recruit can play a full part in the firm they will need to be introduced to it and to the job. Before they join you have the chance to plan this induction, which may well begin before their first day at work.

Before the recruit joins you can assemble information about the firm that they will need to know and let them have copies. Since the person has not yet begun work it may be best to confine what you send out to what is already in the public domain or of little interest to competitors. Emphasise that such reading-in is purely optional at this stage.

On the first day on the premises, the first thing to do is to go through any necessary statutory briefings and to issue any special equipment. The briefing will comprise at least a review of Health and Safety policy, fire escape arrangements, personnel procedures and grievance and disciplinary procedures. Depending on your business the law may lay other requirements on you. The recruit also needs to meet each member of staff for at least 15 minutes to be given an explanation of what they do. Little of this will stick, which does not matter as its main purpose is social. It serves to help the recruit to get to know everyone, and vice versa. You may also need to have done some thinking about the processes that the recruit will be involved in and to draw up diagrams and manuals to explain them. This may sound excessive, but it is not. Your recruit will be keen to prove himself or herself and will not want to keep on asking other people about processes and procedures. If it is all, or mostly, recorded in an easily understood form the person will feel supported and also that they are making less of a nuisance of themselves.

Depending on the duties of the recruit you may want to prepare a workstation for them in advance or to let them specify it up to a predetermined budget. The latter would confer a sense of ownership of part of their job early on in their career with you. However, you might want to retain a veto over their choices in case they select some ghastly colour scheme to 'cheer the place up'.

For at least the first couple of weeks you, or the person they report to formally, must be constantly available to the recruit. That is not solely to give the recruit comfort, but to recognise that they might have applied for other jobs, one of which may turn into an offer. The last thing you want is for your new staff member to announce that he or she doesn't like it here and is leaving.

Appendix 5: Some useful websites

Some of these sites also appear under 'names, addresses and websites'. They are split out separately here for ease of use by people with existing web connections. The list isn't meant to be comprehensive, but it does contain some of those most useful to a small firm. A couple of evenings spent surfing websites that seem of most interest should expose quite a few that are worth bookmarking, as well as yielding some information of more immediate interest.

Advisory, Conciliation and Arbitration Service	www.acas.org.uk
Agricultural Development and Advisory Service	www.adas.co.uk
British Employment Law	www.emplaw.co.uk
British Franchise Association	www.british-franchise.org
British Standards Institution	www.bsi-global.com
British Tourist Authority	www.visitbritain.com
Business Eye in Wales	www.businesseye.org.uk
Business Gateway	www.bgateway.com
Business in the Community	www.bitc.org.uk
Business Link	www.businesslink.gov.uk
Central Office of Information	www.coi.gov.uk
Companies House	www.companieshouse.gov.uk
Confederation of British Industry	www.cbi.org.uk
Connexions	www.connexions.gov.uk
Customs and Excise	www.hmce.gov.uk
Data Protection Registrar	www.informationcommissioner.gov.uk

Department for Education and Skills	www.dfes.gov.uk
Department of Trade and Industry	www.dti.gov.uk
EIU Research	www.EIU.com
European Information Centres	www.euro-info.org.uk
Export Credits Guarantee Department	www.ecgd.gov.uk
Government e-business Envoy	www.e-envoy.gov.uk
Government search site	www.direct.gov.uk
Highlands and Islands Enterprise	www.hie.co.uk
Inland Revenue	www.inlandrevenue.gov.uk
Invest Northern Ireland	www.investni.com
LiveWire	www.shell-livewire.org
Mail Order Protection Scheme (MOPS)	www.mops.org.uk
Manufacturers' Agents' Association	www.themaa.co.uk
MINTEL Research	www.mintel.com
National Federation of Enterprise Agencies	www.nfea.com
Office of National Statistics	www.statistics.gov.uk
Patent and Trade Marks Office	www.patent.gov.uk
Prince's Trust	www.princes-trust.org.uk
Sales agents	www.sales-agents.com
Scottish Enterprise	www.scottish-enterprise.com
Stationery Office	www.tso.co.uk
Welsh Development Agency	www.wda.co.uk

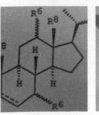

ABLETT & STEBBING

Providing patent, design and trademark protection around the world.

Ablett & Stebbing
Caparo House
101-103 Baker Street
London W1U 6FQ
Tel: +44 (0) 207 935 7720
Fax: +44 (0) 207 935 7790
www.absteb.co.uk

Innovative ideas frequently form one of the core assets of a business. Typically, they are based around one or more of, for example, inventions, trade marks, designs or know how. All too often, such assets are left unprotected or unrecognised, which in the long term leaves the business both weak and vulnerable to conflict with similar assets of another business.

As patent and trade mark attorneys, we specialise in advising exclusively on those areas of the law relating to these assets and in identifying and obtaining appropriate intellectual property rights for them. In addition, it is our aim to provide a service of the highest quality at a reasonable cost.

We believe that we are able to offer this through careful selection, training and supervision of our staff, together with the development and investment in uniquely efficient office systems.

As a result, since the founders of the firm started in business in 1988, we have progressively expanded to now represent a diverse range of clients from all parts of the world, varying from small enterprises, Universities, and major companies in Europe, Japan and the United States of America.

Our Clients include:
Aberdeen University
Alcoa (CSI) Europe Limited
Alza Corporation
C R Bard Inc
Manolo Blahnik
Marks Barfield Architects
Pentax Corporation
Rhino Linings USA Inc
USB Warburg
W S Atkins Limited
Wyeth

A one-stop shop for setting up and growing your company

@UK PLC® has revolutionised the process of setting up a company and getting it trading. You can now get a company formed today, and have it trading online the same day for less than £35. Over 60,000 businesses have taken advantage of @UK PLC® services and the number joining is increasing by thousands every month.

@UK PLC® was set up to allow small companies to compete with large businesses on a level playing field, because you access sophisticated computer systems online for a fraction of the price of stand-alone software. It has invested heavily in making it as quick and easy as possible to set up your company and get it trading.

Traditionally you had to go through an accountant or solicitor to get your company formed. This process cost hundreds of pounds and could take weeks. @UK PLC® forms your company the same working day, with your chosen name for only £24.99 – a staggering improvement in speed and cost...

At the same time as forming your company you can set up a free trading website (the SiteGenerator EasyAndFree) – so you can get going selling your goods and services online within minutes. Select a good name for your website and check immediately that it is available. .co.uk domains cost just £2.50 p.a.

"247Ink" www.247ink.co.uk started off as a small Northumberland company. It is now the largest online seller of inkjet cartridges based in the UK with a turnover measured in millions, its many trading websites all hosted by @UK PLC®.

@UK PLC® is also partnered with Sage PLC, the largest provider of accounting software to small and medium sized businesses, so if the accountancy package you select is Sage Line 50 (v11.0), life is even easier, with the potential to avoid all retyping of information when you account for your online trading. Visit **www.ukplc.net** today and see how easy it is to begin your own successful company.

Join the @UK PLC® community and start building your business.

   **www.ukplc.net**   Tel: 0870 486 6000

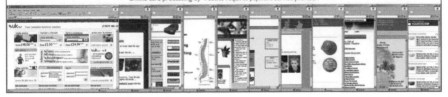

INTERNET BUSINESS PAGES
REALISE YOUR POTENTIAL & SECURE YOUR FUTURE

Despite the fact that the Internet has been an integral part of our lives for almost ten years, there have been few business opportunities available to the everyday investor.

What opportunities have existed have usually required either massive investment in expensive and highly technical equipment or have required the investor to learn web design skills.

All that has changed with the arrival of Internet Business Pages. The company, based at the new Robin Hood International Airport in Doncaster, own and market an innovative Internet based business directory that already has more than two million companies listed.

Having spent over two years in development and testing the sales process the company is now totally confident of having found both the correct site and sales formulae. Direct sales supported by telephone-canvassed appointments have been found to be the most cost effective and efficient means of soliciting new clients.

Confidences have been further boosted from an array of compliments from site users all over the UK. It is always pleasing to be regarded by the public as being just as good as, if not better than established players in the marketplace.

It is the company's goal to become the market leader in the field of web based directory enquiries within the next three years.

IT or sales skills are not essential as every IBP franchisee can rely on an exceptional training and support package. An IBP franchise can be run as a "hands-on" operation that can easily be developed into a business employing several additional sales personnel.

With a first year earning potential of over £100K an IBP franchise is only limited by the level of commitment our franchisees make. To help secure that commitment IBP are offering an automatic share issue to all successful franchisees after a brief qualifying period.

To find out how IBP will achieve this allow you to realise your true potential, and secure your future call **01302 623111** or **07841 424027** today, and ask for a full prospectus.

INITIAL INVESTMENT: £15-35K

iBP
Internet Business Pages
where your business comes first

the commercial directories of Great Britain

Today, there are more than five million businesses in the UK. Most are to be found in one or more classified telephone directories.

These publications are successful because people using a directory have already made the decision to buy. Businesses acknowledge this fact and accept the cost associated with a prominent advertising presence.

Now there is an alternative...

the 118 free rate service

Over 75% of the UK population now has direct access to the Internet whilst the price of print continues to rise, making paper directories progressively less cost effective as an advertising medium.

All our 120 regional directories are now active, covering 100%, of the UK mainland and Northern Ireland. Each is stocked with contact information on more than 2 million businesses.

Display advertising within the 118 free rate service is available exclusively through our franchisees. In each of those areas the role of the Franchisee demands management and communication skills coupled with drive and ambition. Previous computer or IT experience is not necessary.

If you are looking for a franchise that offers:

* an exclusive territory
* a unique and highly effective proven concept
* a highly profitable sales ratio
* a clear advantage over all competitors
* a service that all businesses need
* a full and easy to understand training programme
* a first class support system
* the potential to earn YOU £100K within the first year
* repeat monthly income within 90 days
* extensive ongoing regional and national marketing
* a database of 2 million business customers
* an opportunity to realise your potential

Then look no further and be part of our success

For your free information and brochure call

01302 623111

Investment of £15-35K required

www.118freerate.com

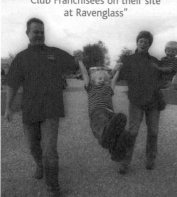

Finding the right space for your business may not be as painless as you imagine, especially if it's the first time you've embarked on such a project. Workspace Group plc is the leading provider of flexible business accommodation to small and medium sized enterprises in London and the South East. Through talking to new customers about their experiences of finding premises Workspace Group were told that it would have been very helpful to have a guide to take people through the process.

In producing such a book, 'The beginners' guide to finding the right business space', Workspace Group identified some key pointers. Knowing which type of property you need (e.g. office space/workshop) is only the beginning – you also need to consider the location, transport links and then ask yourself questions about what standard of facilities you need.

Before you start your search, you should consider your business' financial model, decide on your growth plans and the amount of money you want to spend on your move. This will give you guidance on the services you want the landlord to include in the package, those you wish to pay for and length of the lease term that suits you best. Also calculate your budget, including one off costs for items such as furniture and IT equipment, as well as ongoing costs like rates and service charges.

There are many ways to find potentially appropriate units – through commercial agents, online searches, local newspapers, and even from walking the streets. Then comes the viewing stage. There are questions to be asked that go outside of the obvious, such as can you control the room's climate and, is the building well maintained and water tight?

Once you've found the property that meets all your criteria check out the landlord before you agree to take the space. It is also important to be clear on what the monthly payment covers and what services the landlord is contractually obliged to give.

Before signing the first offer that you are presented with, try to negotiate – you may be able to achieve a rent free period, for example.

To obtain your copy of the 'The beginners' guide to finding the right business space', email **info@workspacegroup.co.uk**

Index of advertisers

Index

ALSO AVAILABLE FROM KOGAN PAGE IN
THE SUNDAY TIMES BUSINESS ENTERPRISE SERIES